No Undocumented
Child Left Behind

CITIZENSHIP AND MIGRATION IN THE AMERICAS
General Editor: Ediberto Román

Tierra y Libertad:
Land, Liberty, and Latino Housing
Steven W. Bender

No Undocumented Child Left Behind:
Plyler v. Doe *and the Education of Undocumented Schoolchildren*
Michael A. Olivas

No Undocumented Child Left Behind

Plyler v. Doe *and the Education of Undocumented Schoolchildren*

Michael A. Olivas

NEW YORK UNIVERSITY PRESS
New York and London

NEW YORK UNIVERSITY PRESS
New York and London
www.nyupress.org

References to Internet websites (URLs) were accurate at the time of writing. Neither the author nor New York University Press is responsible for URLs that may have expired or changed since the manuscript was prepared.

Library of Congress Cataloging-in-Publication Data

Olivas, Michael A.
No undocumented child left behind : Plyler v. Doe and
the education of undocumented schoolchildren / Michael A. Olivas.
p. cm.
Includes bibliographical references and index.
ISBN 978–0–8147–6244–8 (cl : alk. paper)
ISBN 978–0–8147–6245–5 (ebook)
ISBN 978–0–8147–6246–2 (ebook)
1. Children of illegal aliens—Education—Law and legislation—
United States. I. Title.
KF4217.I46O45   2011
344.73'0791—dc23   2011028194

New York University Press books are printed on acid-free paper, and their binding materials are chosen for strength and durability. We strive to use environmentally responsible suppliers and materials to the greatest extent possible in publishing our books.

Manufactured in the United States of America

For Hon. James DeAnda and Hon. Irma Rangel

Contents

Acknowledgments

As with so many things in life, book writing is a collaborative art. It is also among the most frightening enterprises a person can undertake, both because it is sheer hard work and because it is so revealing a project. Having read many books over the years, I can tell when an author is surefooted, nuanced, and confident. The obverse is also true, as tentativeness, timidity, and fear can just as easily be read between the lines. Even after more than a dozen books and many more pieces in print, I still find this whole exercise terrifying. The writing has become more accessible to me, a skill that is learned through repetition. But this is my first full-length immigration book project, and I have carried its seeds for a long time; especially in so contentious and complex a field as immigration policy in the United States, I wanted to get it just right. Despite the centrality of *Plyler* in public life and educational practice, this is the first full-length, single-authored book to appear on the topic. In the several years I have spent on various pieces of this project, I came to understand better why this was so.

Just as I learn from my students each time I teach, even after so many Fall semesters, I see this case and its spores in many of the current debates over how we constitute ourselves. It is this constitutive feature that originally drew me to the study of immigration law and this case, and that has sustained my interest over the years. But as I reread my notes and work over the years, as well as the many acknowledgments I have penned over time, I also realized that I have had the great fortune of working with many people who have schooled me on this subject. I begin with two persons whom I never had met, although we were so well met: two of the children who were among the various "Does" in *Plyler v. Doe*. These two persons, now adult, appeared on a panel in which I was participating, on an anniversary of the case. The panel included the lead Mexican American Legal Defense and Educational Fund lawyer in the case, Peter Roos, as well as school officials and the plaintiffs. They were grown, of course, with their own children and life trajectories, and they had been schoolchildren in Tyler, Texas, in the late 1970's, when the case began. They had come to know the significance of the case but laughingly recalled that they were disappointed when a temporary restraining order was issued against the schools, allowing them to return but ruining the school holiday they had received when Tyler Independent School District banned them from attendance because their parents could not pay the tuition. While they are the only original plaintiffs I have met, I have stayed in touch with many others over the years who have benefited from the courageous actions of their families, and many others who currently learn in our schools and colleges because of later litigation and legislation.

I dedicate this book to two friends and mentors who helped me in too many ways to acknowledge, in the hope that doing so will repay a small part of the debt I owe them: the late Judge James DeAnda and the late Representative Irma Rangel. They both served and led with distinction and displayed personal and professional courage in their trailblazing lives. The arc of their lives was remarkable and distinctive, and both taught me how to lean into the wind. In no small measure, I am a better scholar and advocate and person due to their examples. Although both led long and full lives, both passed too quickly.

I acknowledge the many legislators, staffers, and other public advocates who have worked tirelessly to pass laws and to litigate these matters: Representative Rick Noriega, the late Representative Marco Firebaugh, Peter Roos, Ambassador Vilma Martinez, Nina Perales, David Hinojosa, Nicolas Espiritu, Cynthia Valenzuela, James Ferg-Cadima, Peter Zamora, and many other MALDEF lawyers. Academic colleagues such as Professors Kevin R. Johnson, Hiroshi Motomura, Rosemary Salomone, Victor Romero, Marie Theresa Hernandez, Peter H. Schuck, David A. Martin, Harold H. Koh, Stephen Legomsky, Douglas Ford, Nestor Rodriguez, Francine Lipman, the late Joseph Vail, the late Keith Aoki, and many others have taught, encouraged, and prodded me over the years, even though we have not always agreed. Speaking of not agreeing, I would even like to acknowledge Professor Kris Kobach, against whom I have litigated and debated. I do not like his views, and I like his professional activities even less; if he did not exist, I would have to invent him as a foil. However, his extreme views, completely antithetical to my own, have caused me to sharpen my own pencil and to ask myself, "What would he do?" I hope that he has a Damascus horse-fall and conversion someday and comes over to the side of the angels.

I have employed or worked with almost too many research assistants and law students to keep track of them, but each in his or her own way has been a joy: Kristen Miller, Celina Moreno, Jacob Monty (now University of Houston

Trustee Monty), the late Nancy Snyder-Nepo, the late Celia Figueroa, Alejandro Perez, Deterrean Gamble, Lisa Luis (now Immigration Judge Luis), Lorie Hutensky, Helena Monahan, Luis F. Arandia, Jr., and Kristen Werner. The most recent in this long line of collaborators has been Caren DeLuccio, to whom I owe the largest debt. I have interacted with too many community organizers and others over the years to recall them all, but Barbara Richards, Rafael Magallan, Michael W. Klein, Dr. Inez Cardozo-Freeman, Iris Gomez, and Linda Christofilis come immediately to mind for their particular assistance. Behind every scholar, if he or she is lucky, is a research librarian. In one of the most fortunate circumstances of my professional career, behind me is Lauren E. Schroeder, assistant librarian of the UHLC O'Quinn Law Library. In the several years in which I have worked with her, there has been no task too daunting, no reference too obscure, and no snipe too hard to hunt. Other librarians who have assisted me include Chenglin Liu, Roberto Trujillo, Heather Phillips, Steven Mandeville-Gamble, and Polly Armstrong. Dr. Augustina H. Reyes and Deborah Jones contributed greatly, as they have done in all my work. And I thank my editor and enabler, Deborah Gershenowitz, the senior editor for history and law at New York University Press, whose support and prodding brought this project to completion. Thanks also go to the others in the NYU Press village: Gabrielle Begue, Despina Papazoglou Gimbel, and Andrew Katz. It was Professor Ediberto Roman who resuscitated this project when it hit a wall; I am delighted to have the book launched in the NYU immigration series (Citizenship and Migration in the Americas), which he edits. Inasmuch as we have never agreed on much, God knows, I absolve all these collaborators and even my foils. They have all made this a better book, whether or not they knew it.

As this book was going to press, following August 1, 2011, there was fresh hope and new despair, in the usual one-step-forward-one-back saga of *Plyler* over the years. In the same week, Illinois and California governors signed into law symbolic financial assistance legislation that allowed private funds to be collected for and distributed to undocumented students. However, while both states have long allowed in-state resident tuition for eligible undocumented students, neither allows these students to be eligible for their state financial assistance grant programs. Connecticut enacted a residency statute in Summer 2011. Also, good news came in the form of a June 2011 Senate hearing on the DREAM Act in the Senate Judiciary Committee's Subcommittee on Immigration, Refugees and Border Security, although it was the lifting of the debt ceiling, accomplished in early August, that drew all the oxygen in Congress, with no further action scheduled on the DREAM Act. Counterbalancing these positive or symbolically-positive events were the rescinding of the Wisconsin resident tuition law on June 26, 2011, after it took effect two years earlier, and a ballot initiative in Maryland that blocked that State's tuition bill from even taking effect, after it was signed into law in 2011. That election will play out the fate of the resident tuition provision. (See Table 1, p. 67, for the details.) Worse, states continued to enact restrictionist statutes, trying to preempt federal authority in this area. Thus, Georgia and Alabama passed such comprehensive anti-immigrant legislation, including provisions in the latter that threaten to require schools to register children for immigration status. On August 2, 2011, the Department of Justice filed suit against the state of Alabama to enjoin the implementation of H.B. 56, set to take effect September 1, 2011; DOJ also stepped in to sue Arizona for its draconian legislation, as have other groups. Reports from New York, New Mexico, and other states revealed additional efforts to require additional registration or requirements for public elementary and secondary enrollment, likely emboldened by the 2011 United States Supreme Court decision upholding portions of the Arizona law S.B. 1070, allowing states to enact strict employment verification statutes. While the Court did not have the issue of the other S.B. 1070 civil rights and other anti-Mexican restrictions in front of it, it did remand just such a decision in the Hazleton, Pennsylvania case to the lower court, which had struck them down. That Court might well again strike these down, and it is these provisions that would cause even more harm to the larger community, especially as Arizona public officials are required by its terms to report persons they believe to be undocumented, a tax sure to fall only upon those who look as if they are Mexican, whatever that will turn out to be, or who speak with an accent. Civil rights groups have sued to overturn nativist laws in Arizona, Alabama, Utah, Indiana, and Georgia. These events all happened in the otherwise slow months of Summer 2011, virtually assuring developments concerning *Plyler* in the years to come.

I have been laboring in this vineyard for many years, and my earlier writing covers nearly thirty years. In a synoptic, if not exact, sense, I have drawn in varying degrees from all of these works, as I have reread and reworked many of them over the years, adding nuance, updating cases, correcting errors, changing my mind, arguing with myself and others. This is my first full-length book project on immigration law, so like the film director Quentin Tarantino, whose work I greatly admire, I have drawn many of these pieces from my life and the observed lives of others. These are the credits that would roll at the end of a Tarantino film, maybe with a Van Morrison song as the score. I hold copyright or permission for all of them and list them here: *State Residency Requirements: Postsecondary Authorization and Regulation*, 13 College Law Digest 157 (1983); *Postsecondary Residency Requirements: Empowering Statutes, Governing Types, and Exemptions*, 16 College Law Digest, 268 (1986); Doe v. Plyler *and Postsecondary Admissions: Undocumented Adults and "Enduring Disability,"* 15 Journal of Law and Education 19 (1986); *Administering Intentions: Law, Theory, and Practice in Postsecondary Residency Requirements*, 59 Journal of Higher Education 263 (1988); *Preempting Preemption: Foreign Affairs, State Rights, and Alienage Classifications*, 35 Virginia Journal of International Law 217 (1994); *Storytelling Out of School: Undocumented College Residency, Race, and Reaction*, 22 Hastings Constitutional Law Quarterly 1019 (1995); *IIRIRA, the DREAM Act, and Undocumented College Student Residency*, 30 Journal of College and University Law 435 (2004); *The Story of* Plyler v. Doe, *the Education of Undocumented Children, and the Polity*, in *Immigration Stories* 197 (David A. Martin and Peter H. Schuck, eds., Foundation 2005); *Immigration-Related State and Local Ordinances: Preemption, Prejudice, and the Proper Role for Enforcement*, University of Chicago Law Forum 27 (2007); *Lawmakers Gone Wild? College Residency and the Response to Professor Kobach*, 61 SMU Law Review 99 (2008); *What the War on Terrorism Has Meant for US Colleges and Universities*, in *Doctoral Education and the Faculty of the Future* 249 (R. Ehrenberg and Charlotte V. Kuh, eds., Cornell University Press 2009); *Undocumented College Students, Taxation, and Financial Aid: A Technical Note*, 32 Review of Higher Education 407 (2009); *The Political Economy of the DREAM Act and the Legislative Process*, 55 Wayne Law Review 1757 (2010); *Immigrant Children—Hiding in Plain Sight in the Margins of the Urban Infrastructure*, in *Research on Schools, Neighborhoods, and Communities* 159 (William F. Tate, IV, ed., Rowman and Littlefield, 2011).

Why *Plyler* Matters

Que triste es un a dios
Mas triste que un a dios
No hay nada en esta vida
Es inmenso el dolor que
En my se horizino al
Desir a dios. Que triste
Es un a dios. A dios

[How sad a goodbye is
There is nothing more sad in this life than a goodbye
The pain that originates in me is immense saying goodbye
How sad is a goodbye
A goodbye]
                    —written by an unaccompanied minor in detention[1]

In the spring of 2008, I watched with fascination as the Republican candidates for their party's presidential nomination argued over immigration policy, especially a topic that I had been involved in for many years—whether the undocumented should be allowed to attend college and receive resident tuition. This small topic was one that I had come to consider my own, I and about six others in the United States. The next day, my phone exploded, and I was off to the races. Of course, the economy, the wars in Iraq and Afghanistan, trade policy, and other, less significant issues soon reasserted their primacy, so I had the topic to myself again, not even with the full fifteen minutes accorded me by the late Andy Warhol. But it reassured me that the mandala would turn and that the issue would be part of the likely debate that would ensue during comprehensive immigration reform.

In 1982, the United States Supreme Court held that undocumented schoolchildren could attend public schools without regard to their immigration status. Justice William Brennan's holding in the *Plyler v. Doe* majority is amberlike, with several elements subsumed into its analysis. He held that the children's illegal status was important but not determinative. Not only would many of the children remain in the country, but there were provisions in the law that would make such legalization likely. Of course, he could not have foreseen the large-scale legalization that was to occur within five years of the case, through the 1986 Immigration Reform and Control Act (IRCA), but there had historically been such provisions, through various means, and immigration status was, at the least, not immutable. He also refuted the more obvious objections that Texas had raised about the cost and efficacy of having such children in school, characterizing these efforts as "ludicrously ineffectual," a critique that surely is more apt today when the size of the illegal immigration stream is even more pronounced. If anything, subsequent federal efforts at curbing unauthorized immigration have failed spectacularly, not because the efforts were half-hearted, as they surely have not been. Indeed, these efforts have widened to address the substantial role of employers in this complex transaction. Prior to IRCA in 1986 and to other legislation directed at employer sanctions and employment-related restrictions, virtually all the onus of illegality had fallen on employees and undocumented workers, not on the corporations, companies, and individuals that actively recruited, hired, and exploited workers. Further, in several key cases, these populations were placed outside the traditional protections of civil rights jurisprudence and safety laws, rendering them more vulnerable and employers less accountable.[2]

Justice Brennan's equal protection analysis left virtually no role for state, county, or local efforts to deal with these issues outside the law, writ large, or to go after the children who were without immigration status, brought by their parents to the United States. Even without invoking the broad contours of the preemption doctrine, he reasoned that equal protection can deny the states and other jurisdictions the authority to differentiate between those citizens and noncitizens with permission to reside in the country and those who had no such permission (which he actually styled "inchoate permission"). In doing so, he acknowledged the unevenness of federal policy that tacitly encouraged foreign workers to come, even if there were no formal means to do so. This formulation strengthened the hand of the federal government to differentiate but clearly limited the role of subfederal governments to do so. It is this turn of events that has played out so surprisingly in the decades since *Plyler* and is the focus of my book.

Paradoxically, in the early 21st century, there has been a rise in the country's anti-immigrant sentiment, especially in the growing enactment of state and local ordinances, some of which are playing themselves out in courts and legislatures. At the same time, as noted by immigration scholars as different in their views as Peter Schuck and Hiroshi Motomura, there have been widespread efforts to incorporate these children and undocumented families into the larger community, not just in progressive enclaves but also in surprising mainstream and heartland areas. When Nebraska or Kansas passes a statute to allow the undocumented to establish residency in state colleges, something is afoot. When conservative U.S. Senator Orrin Hatch of Utah cosponsors a major piece of legislation to provide legalization for undocumented college students, all political calculations and assumptions have to be reexamined. These efforts may be the result of wider acceptance by citizen families, as they have seen undocumented children play and study with their own, as they live near them, and as they employ them, or it may just be the evident sense that immigrant communities bring a great deal to the polity and that efforts to integrate them are better than are building chimerical walls and undertaking Canute-like efforts to stem the tide. It may even be a sense that the United States needs new entrants lest we become aging societies like Italy and Japan, demographically imbalanced without replenishment of children and workers.

But as I pored over the many treatments of this case, I saw its kaleidoscopic nature and came to appreciate anew its significance. I hold no special insight into the nation's polity, but I have witnessed this particular case over these years, living in Houston, where part of the case originated, where I have met many of the actors on both sides of the case, and where I have seen widespread acceptance of the children into civic life, especially after the IRCA legalization of 1986, when so many of these families found themselves eligible for U.S. citizenship. I have also seen the hot breath of nativists and restrictionists, a number of whom I believe to be anti-Mexican, especially at the far end of the spectrum, where racial violence, vigilantism, and xenophobia reside. In between, there are many variegations of opinion, as it should be in a large family or in a democracy. As the oldest child of ten, I have seen the former, and as a U.S. birthright citizen, I am fully aware of the gift and accident of my nationality, conferred on me through no effort of my own.

I believe in my heart that there is a large portion of the U.S. community that bears no ill will toward immigrants, even in an attenuated fashion, and that accepts that immigration is in the nation's interests, provided it is done in a lawful manner. I have heard many of my audiences say over the years, "My grandparents came over from Italy [or Poland or insert country here], and they waited their turn and were legally admitted. All these Mexicans [or

Central Americans or insert country here] could and should do the same."
While it is unlikely that their families ever actually suffered restrictions, and
even with specific racial restrictions or other restrictions that worked against
specific groups such as the Chinese in the 1880s, Jews in World War II, or
Haitians under current practices, many of these regimes have been abolished
or shamed in the cycles of our national immigration and refugee history.

At the same time, I also have seen a coarsening of the public discourse,
especially the rise of nativist hate speech and organized racial violence,
enabled and spread by restrictionist demagoguery, the Internet, cable television, and other media. While there are those who encourage these developments as means of allowing the citizenry to blow off steam, to alleviate their
dissatisfaction with increased levels of immigration or with perceptions of
failure to assimilate, the counterevidence is strong and lurid: the undocumented are forced deeper into the shadows as they are hunted down, harmed,
or deported—in the contexts of employment, civic life, and the larger social
community.

This situation has real consequences. Recent episodes of racial thug-
gery, such as "beaner hunting" or roving gangs that attack Latinos as outlaw "others" or as "illegals," have shown the degree to which the discourse
truly matters, as it devolves into justifications for Anglos to "take back" their
rightful land and domain. Luis Ramirez, a Mexican immigrant and father
of two, was beaten to death in Shenandoah, Pennsylvania, in a 2008 hate
crime. Ecuadorian legal resident Marcelo Lucero was stabbed to death by
Patchogue, New York, high school students who racially taunted him as an
illegal "beaner," mistaking him both for being undocumented and for being
an undocumented Mexican. In March 2004, a group of Mexican American
citizens were violently assaulted, detained, and threatened with death by
Arizona ranchers acting as vigilantes. In September 2007, the Otero County,
New Mexico, sheriff and a number of deputies conducted a series of immigration raids against the Latino residents of Chaparral, New Mexico, including warrantless invasions of private homes, stops of pedestrians and driv-
ers without probable cause, and the filing of false charges against Latino
residents of Chaparral. The contradictory depiction of Latinos, as alternately
shiftless and lazy and also too eager to work and to steal jobs, has directly
and indirectly led to the rise of restrictionist laws and practices, especially
as the United States economy has worsened.[3] Scapegoating foreigners has a
long and inglorious history in the United States, a national and paradoxi-
cal trait that competes regularly with the country's more benign self-pride as
welcoming all the huddled masses.

It is with these conflicting developments in mind that I undertook this project, to better situate *Plyler v. Doe*, the case that brought about such change in the nation and its schools. While I do not have the last word on this landmark case, I have endeavored to bring it forth to the many who do not know it.

2

The Story of *Plyler v. Doe*

The Education of Undocumented Children and the Polity

"That's me," says Laura Alvarez, flipping through the pages of the *Alcalde*, her yearbook from John Tyler High School class of '87. She points to a photograph of a slender young woman with a thick cascade of dark brown hair, pensive in her cap and gown. "I really liked school."

The children of *Plyler* are now approaching middle age—"fixin' to be 40," as Alvarez described herself last spring. A surprising number—including all her six siblings—remained in the Tyler area, working and raising families. Two years ago, Alvarez married Juan Reyna, a high school classmate who had also migrated to Tyler illegally from Mexico as a child. They're now the parents of a baby boy, Juan Jr. Juan Sr. is a musician whose band plays at Mexican dances throughout East Texas and sometimes travels as far as Kansas.

Although she liked school, what was supposed to happen afterward for undocumented children like her was a little vague. In 1986, Congress passed the Immigration Reform and Control Act, providing for increased border security and sanctions on employers of illegal immigrants. It also created an amnesty program that eventually led to the legalization of about 3 million undocumented immigrants. Among them were Alvarez and other *Plyler* plaintiffs. But legalization—and a green card—was still down the line when Alvarez graduated from high school. She never thought about college. She worked as a teacher's aide with the Tyler Independent School District for 10 years, in charge of Spanish-speaking students. She usually juggled a part-time job and occasional class at Tyler Junior College, thinking she would become a teacher. Discouraged by the low pay, she found a job with the Smith County district attorney, where she worked in victims services until a few months before Juan Jr. was born.

Alvarez had never heard of *Plyler v. Doe*, much less her own role in it, until 1994, when she was contacted by a *Los Angeles Times* reporter. Her parents, who divorced during the case, didn't raise their children to "get into the adult business," she recalls.[1]

It is hard to know how Supreme Court decisions will come to be regarded, but one thing is certain: none of them exists in a vacuum. Getting a case to federal or state court in the first place is a lightning strike, and very few make it all the way through the chute to the Supreme Court. Fewer still are genuinely memorable, even within the specialty area in which the case is situated. *Plyler v. Doe* always stood for its resolution of the immediate issue in dispute: whether the State of Texas could enact laws denying undocumented children free access to its own public schools. But it also dealt with a larger, transcendent principle: how this society will treat its immigrant children. Thus, for the larger polity, *Plyler* has become an important case for key themes, such as how we treat children fairly, how we guard our borders, how we constitute ourselves, and who gets to make these crucial decisions. To a large extent, *Plyler* may also be the apex of the Court's treatment of the undocumented, a concept that never truly existed until the 20th century.[2]

In this chapter, I consider first how the issue developed and was treated on the ground, in school districts in Texas. Second, once the case quickened, it took on unusual procedural dimensions that warrant discussion. After the various strands of the cases were consolidated, its actual litigation strategy required case management, with complex backstage maneuvers essential to gaining traction for the parties. Because the decision itself is one with "epochal significance" for the undocumented population generally, in Peter Schuck's evocative characterization,[3] I then dissect the case and examine the extensive commentary it prompted. Finally, as a postscript, I examine the path *Plyler*'s teachings followed, both in related Supreme Court cases on similar issues and in allied settings, such as debates over federal legislation that would have mimicked the Texas law struck down in *Plyler* and in postsecondary education residency litigation and legislation. Understanding *Plyler*'s provenance ultimately sheds light on how important legal cases become recurring fugues, with themes that build and influence subsequent decisions and sometimes the polity at large.

On the Ground in Texas:
Undocumented School Attendance and the Legislative Reaction

In 1975, the State of Texas enacted section 21.031 of the Texas Education Code, allowing its public school districts (called Independent School Districts, or ISDs, in Texas) to charge tuition to undocumented children.[4] The legislature held no hearings on the matter, and no published record explains the origin of this revision to the school code. Discussions with legislators from that time have suggested that it was inserted into a larger, more routine education bill, simply at the request of some border-area superintendents who mentioned the issue to their representatives.[5] The statute, in pertinent part, read,

(a) All children who are citizens of the United States or legally admitted aliens and who are over the age of five years and under the age of 21 years on the first day of September of any scholastic year shall be entitled to the benefits of the Available School Fund for that year.

(b) Every child in this state who is a citizen of the United States or a legally admitted alien and who is over the age of five years and not over the age of 21 years on the first day of September of the year in which admission is sought shall be permitted to attend the public free schools of the district in which he resides or in which his parent, guardian, or the person having lawful control of him resides at the time he applies for admission.

(c) The board of trustees of any public free school district of this state shall admit into the public free schools of the district free of tuition all persons who are either citizens of the United States or legally admitted aliens and who are over five and not over 21 years of age at the beginning of the scholastic year if such person or his parent, guardian or person having lawful control resides within the school district.[6]

Not all ISDs in the state chose to charge tuition, although they were entitled under the statute to do so. In a 1980 random survey prepared by Houston's Gulf Coast Legal Foundation once litigation commenced, six of the ISDs polled with more than ten thousand students reported that their districts would admit undocumented students without charge, six would charge tuition, eleven would exclude them entirely, and the rest did not respond or did not know how they would respond to such an occurrence.[7] For ISDs with enrollments under ten thousand students, seven said they would not charge tuition, five would charge tuition, three would exclude entirely, and sixteen did not know or did not respond. The state's largest district, Houston ISD (with over two hundred thousand students), and a smaller one, Tyler (with approximately sixteen thousand students) would allow them to enroll but required parents or guardians to pay one thousand dollars annually for each child. In addition, several of the school districts nearest the border reported they excluded these children from enrolling, whether or not tuition were paid, such as Ysleta ISD (near El Paso and across the border from Ciudad Juárez) and Brownsville ISD (across the border from Matamoros), as did the state's second-largest district, Dallas ISD, many hundreds of miles from the border.

The Litigation and the Principal Players
Prologue

The first case to challenge section 21.031 was *Hernandez v. Houston Independent School District*, filed in spring 1977 in state court by a local Houston attorney, Peter Williamson. The district court and the court of civil appeals rejected his due process and equal protection arguments against the statute.[8] In November 1977, the appeals court held that such legislation was reasonable: "The determination to share [the state's] bounty, in this instance tuition-free education, may take into account the character of the relationship between the alien and this country."[9]

MALDEF's Role

Although observers of thirty-plus years ago recall some localized resistance across the state to the practice of charging the families tuition for what was generally referred to as "free public schools," the issue appears to have come onto the national radar in the late 1970s, prompted by a September 26, 1977, letter from Joaquin G. Avila, director of the San Antonio office of the Mexican American Legal Defense and Educational Fund (MALDEF). It was addressed to MALDEF's national director for education litigation, Peter Roos, located at the organization's national headquarters in San Francisco, California. Avila wrote,

This statute was made effective on August 29, 1977. Basically, this statute seeks to regulate the number of students who move in with relatives to attend another school district. As the amended statute now provides

(Section 21.031(a)), a student who lives apart from his parent, guardian, or other person having lawful control of him under an order of a court, must demonstrate that his presence in the school district was not based primarily on his or her desire to attend a particular school district. In other words, if a case of hardship can be established, a student will be able to attend the school district. Otherwise, the relatives will have to secure a court order of guardianship. This requirement will impose a hardship on those families who cannot afford an attorney to process a guardianship. So far we have not received any complaints, only a request by Pete Tijerina, our first general counsel to launch a lawsuit.

What are your feelings on the constitutionality of such a provision. What would we have to show to demonstrate a disparate impact. Please advise at your earliest convenience.[10]

This letter contains the spores of the *Plyler* case (without referencing the *Hernandez* litigation that was under way in the state courts in Houston at the same time), even though Avila does not appear to have appreciated the full dimensions of the matter that had been flagged by MALDEF board member (and one of the organization's founders in the mid-1960s) Pete Tijerina. To Avila, the issue kicked up to San Francisco was whether the revised Texas statute improperly affected the residency of undocumented students, by requiring the parents or formal legal guardians to reside in the district. This was a related issue but one far less essential to the algebra of undocumented school attendance than was the tuition issue presented eventually in *Plyler*, especially for school districts in the interior, away from the border. Indeed, a year after *Plyler* ruled in favor of the school children, the exact issue Avila noted in his letter reached the Supreme Court in *Martinez v. Bynum*,[11] in which it was resolved in favor of the school districts involved. By that time, however, the more fundamental and important threshold issue had been settled; all else was detail.

But this was not clear in 1977, when Peter Roos began to sniff out the full extent of the practice in Texas and other states. He looked especially at the southwestern and western states, where most undocumented families resided, where undocumented Mexican immigration was most pronounced (as opposed to undocumented immigration from other countries and other hemispheres), and where MALDEF concentrated most of its program activities. MALDEF was in search of an appropriate Texas federal-court vehicle to consolidate its modest victories in the many small state-court cases it had taken on in its first decade of existence. Unlike the laserlike focus of its role model, the NAACP Legal Defense Fund, which had strategically targeted desegregation as its reason for being, MALDEF had been somewhat behind the curve, in part due to its representation of ethnic and national-origin interests for Mexican Americans and in part due to the diffuse focus that derived from representing the linguistic, immigration, and even class interests of its variegated clients.

After all, Mexican Americans were not African Americans, although their histories of oppression and exclusion from American Anglo life were more similar than they were dissimilar, especially in "Jaime Crow" Texas, the Mexican American Mississippi. Historian Steven H. Wilson has noted the origins of the different litigation theories employed by the two groups to combat school segregation:

> The . . . creation of MALDEF had less to do with the shift in thinking [about school desegregation strategies] than might be expected. The upheavals brought by the black civil rights struggle, the farm workers' movement, and antiwar protests inspired many disaffected Mexican-descended youths to adopt similar goals and direct action tactics—such as walkouts and other disruptive demonstrations—in order to combat the inequities they encountered. As a result, however, activists frequently found themselves sanctioned by school administrators or even law enforcement agencies. Instead of suing schools to change the rules of desegregation, therefore, MALDEF undertook a number of cases that established the new organization as something of an un-official civil liberties bureau for militant Chicano students. Significantly, in these cases, MALDEF's attorneys did not argue—and in civil liberties cases had no reason to claim—that Mexican Americans were and ought to be considered a group distinct from Anglos. Nevertheless, MALDEF's early victories in this field helped to reestablish litigation as a tool for vindicating Mexican Americans' civil rights.[12]

Discussions with the various parties involved from the MALDEF side of this case clearly indicate that Roos and MALDEF president Vilma Martinez, a young Texas lawyer who had begun her civil rights career with the NAACP Legal Defense Fund, soon saw *Plyler* as the Mexican American *Brown v. Board of Education*: as a vehicle for consolidating attention to the various strands of social exclusions that kept Mexican-origin persons in subordinate status. This case promised to decide issues affecting Mexican migrant workers, who had been in the North American public imagination due to the charismatic leadership of César Chávez, head of the United Farm Workers union, who had organized a successful nationwide grape boycott.[13] It concerned education in Texas schools, long considered the most insensitive to Mexicans and Mexican Americans. It incorporated elements of school leadership and community relations, as the political powerlessness of Chicanos was evident even in geographic areas where they were the predominant population. The tuition dimension resurrected school-finance and governance issues, which had earlier been raised by Chicano plaintiffs seeking to have the radically unequal school financing scheme in Texas declared unconstitutional. After initial success, they had lost in a controversial and close 1973 decision by the U.S. Supreme Court, *San Antonio Independent School District v. Rodriguez*.[14] The 5–4 ruling seemed designed to call a halt to any expansions in the use of the equal protection doctrine, and it specifically declared that education was not a fundamental right that would trigger strict scrutiny under that clause. While MALDEF was not the architect of the *Rodriguez* litigation, the plaintiffs were Mexican American families in San Antonio. And finally, *Plyler* implicated immigration status, often dividing families on the basis merely of the side of the Rio Grande that the mother had given birth. *Plyler* even held out the promise to unite the class interests between immigrant Mexicans and the larger, more established Mexican American community in a way that earlier, important cases litigating jury selection, school finance, and desegregation had not been able to achieve.[15] Even though these cases all occurred in Texas over many years, and had even included some significant victories, they had not appreciably improved the status of Chicanos or broken down the barriers for large numbers of the community.

Historian Guadalupe San Miguel, Jr., in his pathbreaking study of Mexican American education litigation, analyzed the lawsuits undertaken by MALDEF in Texas in the years 1970–1981, its earliest record.[16] It undertook ninety-three federal and state court cases in Texas during those years and compiled a substantial record across several areas: seventy-one cases in the area of desegregation (76.3 percent), four in employment (4.3 percent), three in school finance (3.2 percent), seven in political rights (7.5 percent), six in voting (6.5 percent), and two other education cases (2.2 percent). In addition, a number of the cases included collateral issues such as language rights and bilingual education.[17] As an example of these cases, MALDEF undertook *United States v. Texas*, a comprehensive assault on the worst exclusionary practices by school districts, such as class-assignment practices and inadequate bilingual education.[18] The judge in that district court decision noted with some bite, "Serious flaws permeate every aspect of the state's efforts. . . . Since the defendants have not remedied the serious deficiencies, meaningful relief for the victims of unlawful discrimination must be instituted by court decree."[19] The case, which began in 1970, ended with a whimper on September 27, 2010, with a final order from the Eastern District of Texas, following the April 12, 2010, revised, modified order from the Fifth Circuit.

Over the years, MALDEF had joined forces with other Mexican American organizations, including more conservative groups such as the League of United Latin American Citizens (LULAC) and the GI Forum, organizations active over the years in assimilationist and citizenship issues and Latino military veteran issues. Thus, these national organizations, all founded in Texas to combat discrimination, merged their divergent interests in order to effect solidarity, and they have since served as plaintiffs in cases filed by MALDEF.[20]

Just as Thurgood Marshall had traveled the South to execute the Legal Defense Fund's strategic approach toward dismantling segregated schooling and the American apartheid system, seeking out the proper cases and plaintiffs, Martinez, Roos, and other MALDEF lawyers and board members had been seeking just the right federal case. They wanted to have a larger impact than they could expect from dozens of smaller cases in various state courts in the Southwest. If Mexican American plaintiffs could not win the school-finance case in *San Antonio Independent School District v. Rodriguez*, with such demonstrable economic disparities as had been evident in that trial, MALDEF needed to win a big one, both to establish its credibility within and without the Chicano community and to serve its clients. A case involving vulnerable school children in rural Texas being charged a thousand dollars for what was available to other children for free seemed to be that vehicle. The MALDEF lawyers found their Linda Brown in Tyler, Texas, where the brothers and sisters in the same family held different immigration status. Some had been born in Mexico, while those born in Texas held U.S. citizenship. Perhaps more important, they found their Earl Warren in federal district court judge William Wayne Justice, widely admired and reviled for his liberal views and progressive decisions.[21] Thus, in this small, rural town of Tyler, Texas, the stage was set.

The Plyler *Campaign*

The first issue to arise after the case was filed was whether the children could be styled in anonymous fashion in the caption and conduct of the case, so that their identities and those of their families would not be divulged. Use of the actual names of the plaintiffs in the *Hernandez* case against the Houston schools had placed all of them at risk of deportation. In the Tyler case, even though Judge Justice permitted the case to proceed with "John Doe" plaintiffs, the risk persisted. The U.S. attorney had apparently asked the Dallas district director of the Immigration and Naturalization Service (INS) to conduct immigration sweeps in the area, so as to intimidate the families into dropping their suit.[22] In response, Roos wrote to the head of the INS in Washington, DC, requesting that he call off any planned raids and characterizing them as trial tampering. As it happened, in this endeavor MALDEF enjoyed a run of luck, which is always an ingredient of successful trials. The INS commissioner at the time was Leonel Castillo, a native of Houston and a prominent Mexican American politician with progressive politics, himself a former Peace Corps volunteer who was married to an immigrant.[23] At his direction, the INS ultimately made no such raids. After these initial skirmishes, Judge Justice issued a preliminary injunction on September 11, 1977, enjoining the Tyler ISD from enforcing section 21.031 against any children on the basis of their immigration status.[24]

As a part of the overall trial strategy, Roos, Martinez, and other MALDEF officials began to press public-opinion leaders to "support the schoolchildren" and to develop a backdrop of public acceptance of their schooling and immigration status. As an example, Roos wrote leaders of the National Education Association (NEA), the progressive national teachers union, in October 1977, to request support and assistance; NEA later filed a brief and provided additional support to MALDEF.[25] In addition, MALDEF leaders traveled to meet with other Latino organizational leaders to enlist support and solicit resources and to encourage legal organizations to file amicus briefs on behalf of the plaintiff children. They asked for people to write editorials and to host fundraisers. I recall being a law student in the District of Columbia during this time and cutting class one night to attend a small fundraiser at a local hotel, an event sponsored by Latino organizations and Washington professionals.

On September 14, 1978, after a two-day hearing, Judge Justice issued his opinion, striking down section 21.031 as applied to the Tyler ISD. He found that the state's justifications for the statute were not rational and violated equal protection and that the attempt to regulate immigration at the state level violated the doctrine of preemption, which holds immigration to be a function solely of federal law.[26] Immediately after, the state moved for leave to reopen the case, citing the decision's implications for other school districts in the state and seeking a chance to bolster the record. Observers have suggested that the state had simply underestimated the plaintiffs' case, inasmuch as the judge in the *Hernandez* case in state court had sustained the statute fairly readily. But Judge Justice overruled the motion, because the "amended complaint does not state a cause of action against any school district other than the Tyler [ISD] and since this court intends to order relief only against [the Tyler ISD]."[27]

Case Management by MALDEF

During the federal trial, the issue of *Plyler*'s potential impact on other Texas school districts naturally arose, as word had spread to dozens of other communities, sparking many companion lawsuits. The original *Hernandez* decision had not spawned similar state court litigation; MALDEF and others turned to the federal courts so as to avoid having to litigate in multiple, hostile state venues, before elected state judges. MALDEF now confronted questions about how best to mesh its efforts, including its response to the *Plyler* appeals filed by the Tyler ISD and the State of Texas and proceedings in other · venues. Some of the issues became clearer when the state's largest school district, Houston ISD, faced a lawsuit in federal court in September 1978, filed by a group of local attorneys and another California-based public-interest law firm, with civil rights lawyer (and South African immigrant) Peter Schey as lead counsel. By this time, with the good news spreading from the Tyler case, four cases raising these issues had been filed in the Southern District of Texas and two in the Northern District. Moreover, the Eastern District court that had just decided *Plyler* faced six additional cases after the ruling. Rather than just suing the particular ISDs, these suits included as defendants the State of Texas, the Texas governor, the Texas Education Agency (the state agency that governed K–12 public education in the state), and that agency's commissioner. Eventually, all these fresh cases were consolidated into *In re Alien Children* and tried in the Southern District of Texas in Houston, before Judge Woodrow Seals. Judge Seals held a twenty-four-day trial.[28]

These sprawling cases presented an even broader assault on the system, whereas *Plyler* had been narrowly focused on section 21.031 and solely on the Tyler ISD. The various cases were brought by several different attorneys on many fronts, relying on several theories, hoping that they could replicate the victory Roos had carved out in his Tyler case. At this point, it became crucial that the various parties coordinate, because the defendants had deep pockets, legions of deputy attorneys general and private counsel, and other advantages, most importantly the staying power to mow down the plaintiffs at the trial and appellate levels. True, Roos had convinced the United States to intervene in his case on the side of the alien schoolchildren, but over the long haul, the federal government could not be wholly relied on in civil rights cases, as its interests could change, depending on the administration in office.[29] This scenario did occur in 1980–1981, when Governor Ronald Reagan defeated the incumbent president, Jimmy Carter, and took office.

In May 1979, after *Plyler* was decided at the trial level but before *In re Alien Children* was to go to trial, the local Houston counsel for the plaintiffs in the case before Judge Seals wrote Peter Roos, requesting that MALDEF consolidate its efforts into their case, which was more complex and comprehensive than the original case against the Tyler ISD. Roos responded to attorney Isaias Torres, a Texas native who had just graduated from law school and was working for the Houston Center for Immigrants, that MALDEF felt "quite strongly that consolidation would not be in the best interests of our mutual efforts."[30] After all, MALDEF had carefully selected Tyler as the perfect federal venue for arguing its case: a progressive judge, sympathetic clients, a rural area where the media glare would not be as great. In addition, in Tyler the case could be made that excluding the small number of undocumented children (the practical effect of charging each tuition of one thousand dollars) would actually lose money for the district, inasmuch as the State's school-funding formula based allocation amounts on overall head-count attendance. In a large urban school district or a border school district, the fact questions and statistical proofs would be more complex and expensive to litigate for both sides.[31] Moreover, because the Tyler trial had been a case of first impression at the federal level, the State's legal strategy had not been as sophisticated as it would be in another similar trial. The earlier *Hernandez* case in Texas state court had not involved the full panoply of legal and social science expertise and financial support available to a national effort such as that mounted by MALDEF.

Roos noted to Torres that the State had tried to make a late-in-the-day correction for its ineffective original efforts by seeking the leave to reopen the record, a request that Judge Justice had denied. State counsel would not likely make that mistake again and would mount a more aggressive strategy in their second go-round. Roos wrote, "While no doubt you have been incrementally able to improve upon our record [developed in the Tyler trial], consolidation would allow the state and other parties to buttress their record. I believe that one could only expect a narrowing of the present one-sideness [of the trial record in MALDEF's favor]. Consolidation would play right into th[e] hands of [the State's attorney] Mr. Arnett."[32]

Torres, on the other hand, worried that unless the cases were consolidated, the relief in *Plyler* might not extend beyond that small district. Tyler had folded, but what about Houston, Dallas, and the more important border districts? After all, Texas had over one thousand ISDs, and many of them had the same policies toward undocumented students as had Tyler; it was a state statute that gave them such permission. To this understandable concern, Roos indicated that his original strategy was aimed at winning once and then later applying it elsewhere, not joining up with other pending actions and thereby increasing the risk of losing on appeal: "Most importantly, I believe that once we have a Tyler victory, we will have started down a slippery slope which will make it impossible for the court to legally or logistically limit the ruling to Tyler."[33] This approach mirrors that of the NAACP on the road to *Brown*, in which Thurgood Marshall and his colleagues carefully picked their fights, each case incrementally building on the previous litigation.[34] Indeed, MALDEF General Counsel Vilma Martinez had worked at the Legal Defense Fund with Marshall's former colleague and successor, Jack Greenberg, and clearly understood the value of an overarching strategic vision and litigation plan.

But Roos had yet another reason for declining to join in the consolidated cases: he felt he had drawn ineffective opposing local counsel and wished to press his momentary advantage. He wrote, in a remarkable and candid private assessment, "A final, but important reason for believing consolidation unwise is, frankly, the quality of opposing counsel. Our [local] opposing counsel in Tyler is frankly not very good." He went on to say that this would likely not be the case in Houston, where the defense would include experienced attorneys from the specialized education law department of a major law firm, and where other districts would also contribute their efforts and resources. He added, "I believe it is our mutual interest to isolate the worst counsel to argue the case against us. Consolidation works against that. For the above-stated reasons, I would urge you not to seek consolidation. I just don't believe that it serves our mutual interest of getting this statute knocked out."[35]

The Results

Although Roos did not agree to combine forces at the crucial early stages, this issue was eventually taken out of his hands at the U.S. Supreme Court. At the request of the State of Texas, the Judicial Panel on Multidistrict Litigation eventually did consolidate a number of the cases—but, significantly, not *Plyler*—into the *In re Alien Children* litigation, and notwithstanding Roos's doubts about whether the Houston plaintiffs would succeed, Judge Seals rendered a favorable decision on the merits on July 21, 1980.[36] The plaintiff schoolchildren prevailed in a big way, most importantly on the issues of whether the State of Texas could enact a statute to limit inducements to immigration and whether equal protection applied to the undocumented in such an instance. Judge Seals determined that Texas's concern for fiscal integrity was not a compelling state interest and that charging tuition to the parents or removing the children from school had not been shown to be necessary to improve education within the state. Most important, he concluded that section 21.031 had not been carefully tailored to advance the state interest in a constitutional manner.

In the Fifth Circuit, meanwhile, Judge Justice's *Plyler* decision was affirmed in October 1980, and in May 1981, the U.S. Supreme Court agreed to hear the matter.[37] The Fifth Circuit issued a summary affirmance of the consolidated Houston cases a few months later, and the Supreme Court combined the Texas appeals of both cases under the styling of *Plyler v. Doe*, handing Peter Roos the lead vehicle over Peter Schey's cases.[38] Having developed fuller records and armed with Fifth Circuit wins, the two Peters worked out a stiff and formal truce, dividing the oral arguments down the middle, but with MALDEF's case leading the way.

Roos spent the time until the Supreme Court arguments shoring up political support. In March 1979, he had written to Drew Days, the assistant attorney general for civil rights, urging the government to join the litigation. Later he persuaded the secretary of Health, Education, and Welfare, Joseph Califano, to write the solicitor general urging him to enter into the fray on the side of the children, which side the government did take. Other MALDEF letters went to state officials in California and elsewhere, requesting their support. After the Reagan administration took office in January 1981, Roos wrote William Clohan, under secretary of the recently created Department of Education, to urge him to continue the actions of the Carter administration. Although the Reagan administration did not formally enter its amicus brief on the side of the plaintiffs (as had the Democrat lawyers) and took no position on the crucial equal protection issue, fortunately for Roos, it did not seek to overturn the lower court decisions. In fact, the brief stressed the primacy of the federal government in immigration, a position that favored the schoolchildren.[39]

The Supreme Court's Ruling

In June 1982, the Supreme Court gave Roos and Schey their win on all counts, by a 5–4 margin. Justice Brennan, in his majority opinion striking down the statute, characterized the Texas argument for charging tuition as "nothing more than an assertion that illegal entry, without more, prevents a person from becoming a resident for purposes of enrolling his children in the public schools." He employed an equal protection analysis to find that a State could not enact a discriminatory classification "merely by defining a disfavored group as non-resident."[40]

Justice Brennan dismissed the State's first argument that the classification or subclass of undocumented Mexican children was necessary to preserve the State's "limited resources for the education of its lawful residents."[41] This line of argumentation had been rejected in an earlier case, *Graham v. Richardson*, in which the court had held that the concern for preservation of Arizona's resources alone could not justify an alienage classification used in allocating welfare benefits.[42] In addition, Brennan relied on the findings of fact from the *Plyler* trial: although the exclusion of all undocumented children might eventually result in some small savings to the State, those savings would be uncertain (given that federal and state allocations depended primarily on the number of children enrolled),[43] and barring those children would "not necessarily improve the quality of education."[44]

The State also argued that it had enacted the legislation in order to protect itself from an influx of undocumented aliens.[45] The Court acknowledged the concern but found that the statute was not tailored to address it: "Charging tuition to undocumented children constitutes a ludicrously ineffectual attempt to stem the tide of illegal immigration."[46] The Court also noted that immigration and naturalization policy is within the exclusive powers of the federal government.[47]

Finally, the State maintained that it singled out undocumented children because their unlawful presence rendered them less likely to remain in the United States and therefore to be able to use the free public education they received in order to contribute to the social and political goals of the United States community.[48] Brennan distinguished the subclass of undocumented aliens who had lived in the United States as a family, and for all practical purposes permanently, from the subclass of adult aliens who enter the country alone, temporarily, to earn money. For those who remained with the intent of making the United States their home, "It is difficult to understand precisely what the State hopes to achieve by promoting the creation and perpetuation of a subclass of illiterates within our boundaries, surely adding to the problems and costs of unemployment, welfare, and crime."[49]

Prior to *Plyler*, the Supreme Court had never taken up the question of whether undocumented aliens could seek Fourteenth Amendment equal protection.[50] The Supreme Court had long held that aliens are "persons" for purposes of the Fourteenth Amendment[51] and that undocumented aliens are protected by the due process provisions of the Fifth Amendment.[52] However, Texas argued that because undocumented children were not "within its jurisdiction,"[53] they were not entitled to equal protection. Justice Brennan rejected this line of reasoning, concluding that there "is simply no support for [the] suggestion that 'due process' is somehow of greater stature than 'equal protection' and therefore available to a larger class of persons."[54]

After the *Rodriguez* school-finance decision, Justice Brennan had to walk a fine line to apply what amounted to scrutiny more demanding than the usual rational basis review. Although he rejected treating undocumented alienage as a suspect classification,[55] he concluded that the children were not responsible for their own citizenship status and that treating them as the Texas school-finance law envisioned would "not comport with fundamental conceptions of justice."[56] He was more emphatically concerned with education, however, carefully elaborating the nature of the entitlement to it. While he reaffirmed the earlier *Rodriguez* holding that public education was not a fundamental right (undoubtedly to attract the vote of Justice Powell, the author of the *Rodriguez* majority opinion), he recited a litany of cases holding education to occupy "a fundamental role in maintaining the fabric of our society."[57] He also noted that "[i]lliteracy is an enduring disability,"[58] one that would plague the individual and society. These observations enabled him to establish "the proper level of deference to be afforded § 21.031." He concluded, in light of the significant ongoing costs, that the measure "can hardly be considered rational unless it furthers some substantial goal of the State"— subtle and nuanced phrasing that nudged the level of scrutiny to what would be characterized as intermediate scrutiny.[59] Chief Justice Burger's dissent, in contrast, stuck with the customary formulation, requiring only "a rational relationship to a legitimate state purpose."[60] As a result of Brennan's careful construction, the Court rejected the claim, which the dissent had found persuasive, that the policy was sufficiently related to protecting the State's asserted interests.

Further, while the Court did not reach the claim of federal preemption,[61] it did draw a crucial distinction between what states and the federal government may do in legislating treatment of aliens.[62] The Court had upheld state statutes restricting alien employment[63] and access to welfare benefits,[64] largely because those state measures mirrored federal classifications and congressional action governing immigration. For example, in *De Canas v. Bica*, the Supreme Court had held that a state statute punishing employers for hiring aliens not authorized to work in the United States was not fully preempted by federal immigration law.[65] In public education, however, Brennan wrote, distinguishing *De Canas*, "we perceive no national policy that supports the State in denying these children an elementary education."[66]

Reactions

Much of the considerable scholarly response to the Court's reasoning in the case has evinced surprise that the majority went as far as it did in rejecting the state's sovereignty. Peter Schuck, for example, characterized the decision as a "conceptual watershed in immigration law, the most powerful rejection to date of classical immigration law's notion of plenary national sovereignty over our borders. . . . Courts are expositors of a constitutional tradition that increasingly emphasizes not the parochial and the situational, but the universal, transcendent values of equality and fairness [immanent] in the due process and equal protection principles. In that capacity, they have also asserted a larger role in the creation and distribution of opportunities and status in the administrative state. In *Plyler*, the Supreme Court moved boldly on both fronts."[67] Surveying the line of equal protection cases involving aliens from *Yick Wo* through *Graham* to *Plyler* and beyond, Linda Bosniak has summarized,

> [A]lienage as a legal status category means that the law of alienage discrimination is perennially burdened by the following questions: To what extent is such discrimination a legitimate expression, or extension, of the government's power to regulate the border and to control the composition of membership in the national community? On the other hand, how far does sovereignty reach before it must give way to equality; when, that is, does discrimination against aliens implicate a different kind of government power, subject to far more rigorous constraints? To what degree, in short, is the status of aliens to be understood as a matter of national borders, to what degree a matter of personhood, and how are we to tell the difference? These questions, I argue, shape the law's conflicted understandings of the difference that alienage makes.[68]

As was seen, Justice Brennan's majority opinion did not rely on the preemption doctrine, finding that the Texas legislation foundered even on lesser shoals, those of equal protection, stretching the children's status and their innocence to find the State's reasoning to be "ludicrously ineffectual."[69] Having turned the case over many times, I appreciate the extent to which Justice Brennan was carving out a safe haven for the children.

In a series of residency and immigration cases decided in the decade before *Plyler*, from approximately 1971 until 1982, and then immediately after *Plyler*, the Supreme Court developed the standard of scrutiny to be applied and the classification of persons for whom governmental benefits were to be conferred or withheld, determining which rights were fundamental and which groups were classified as suspect. Prior to *Graham* and after *Plyler*, government regulation in the context of who could make an entry into the country and who could be removed remained at the zenith of governmental discretion, "as it may see fit to prescribe," in the sweeping language of the 1892 case *Nishimura Ekiu v. United States*.[70] But from 1971's *Graham v. Richardson* through 1982's *Plyler* and *Toll*, the Court carved out decisions in more than a dozen cases involving alienage and public employment, benefits, civic participation, and program eligibility, broadening the reach of constitutional principles and the conditions that government could employ to advantage or disadvantage members of the political community who held less than citizenship status. Not each case turned on preemption or the power of the federal government to "forbid entrance," but led by varying majorities in a Court that was quite stable in its membership, the U.S. Supreme Court extended the protections afforded immigrants, particularly permanent residents, and limited the restrictions traditionally available to state and federal authorities. In cases ranging from welfare and program benefits (*Graham, Mathews v. Diaz, Nyquist v. Mauclet, Elkins v. Moreno, Plyler v. Doe, Toll v. Moreno,* and *Martinez v. Bynum*)[71] to employment and licensing (*Sugarman v. Dougall, In re Griffiths, De Canas v. Bica, Hampton v. Mow Sun Wong, Examining Board v. Flores de Otero, Foley v. Connelie, Ambach v. Norwick, Cabell v. Chavez-Salido,* and *Bernal v. Fainter*)[72] to civic participation (*Perkins v. Smith, Skafte v. Rorex*),[73] the Court expanded the rights of aliens within our midst and shrunk the ability of governmental authorities to direct substantive and unbridled prejudice against noncitizens. In addition, other similar cases involving durational eligibility criteria were decided during this period, and while the parties did not involve immigrants, similar issues were examined in the context of the apportionment of benefits and residency.[74]

Thus, the country moved from a world in which sovereignty trumped all else to a more complex view that once persons had joined the community, however temporarily and incompletely, the State would be required to proffer more nuanced and reasonable distinctions among groups of noncitizens, especially in areas where the authority of the State itself was not as directly implicated, as in choosing notaries or in apportioning benefits from taxes which all participants paid into the public fisc. Peter Schuck has aptly described the predominant view of the sovereign in near-absolute terms:

> In such a context, control over which strangers might enter was viewed as a powerful expression of the nation's identity and autonomy—in a word, of its sovereignty. Sovereignty entailed the unlimited power of the nation, like that of the free individual, to decide whether, under what conditions, and with what effects it would consent to enter into a relationship with a stranger. The power implied by that sovereignty was enjoyed by the Nation exclusively and was based wholly upon its explicit undertaking; the government simply owed no other legal obligation to those who sought to enter or remain without its consent. That a stranger was desperate to enter, and had invested a great deal in the effort, was as immaterial as the reasons that prompted the government to refuse her admittance. . . . In this sense, the classical idea of sovereignty implied a relationship between government and an alien that resembled the relationship in late nineteenth century private law between a landowner and a trespasser. The essential purpose of immigration law, then, like that of property law, was to pre-serve and enhance this sovereignty.[75]

Harold Koh assessed the law before *Graham* as essentially antediluvian:

> We sometimes forget how different the universe of equal protection looked back in March of 1971, when *Graham v. Richardson* came to the Court. In the seventeen years since *Brown v. Board of Education*, the most straightforward equal protection cases had already come and gone. The Court had declared race and national origin to be "suspect" classifications properly subject to judicial scrutiny and had deemed the rights to vote, to [undertake] interstate travel, and to appeal in criminal cases to be "fun-damental interests" whose burdening by legislative classifications similarly warranted heightened scrutiny.
>
> Harder cases, however, were yet to come. In 1971, the Court was just beginning to decide whether to extend heightened scrutiny to classifica-tions based on wealth, gender, and illegitimacy; it would be years before it would grapple with "quasi-suspect" classes or techniques of "intermediate" scrutiny. More than a year would elapse before Professor [Gerald] Gunther would announce to the word that the judicial scrutiny triggered by sus-pect classifications and fundamental interests, though "'strict' in theory," was "fatal in fact." More than two years would pass before the Court itself

would halt the expansion of the fundamental interests branch of the equal protection doctrine and fully embrace the two-tier approach to equal protection review. In short, as the Court heard arguments in *Graham v. Richardson*, it was by no means apparent how the Justices would adapt the Warren Court's "new" equal protection analysis to state laws placing peculiar burdens upon resident aliens. Indeed, it was not even certain that the Court would begin its inquiry by asking whether such restrictions deny those "persons" the "equal protection of the laws."[76]

The remarkable line of the cases leading from *Graham v. Richardson* to *Plyler* and *Toll* largely grew from Justice Blackmun's vision, a theory of alien equality, that the State cannot properly be allowed to invoke the very notion of citizenship to separate different members of the polity from full participation or to withhold the various incidents of community from all its participants. Koh, who served as Justice Blackmun's clerk, characterized this notion of citizenship as a communitarian approach: "Viewed in this light, states and courts that invoke 'citizenship' as a reason to deny permanent residents such rights subvert the very concept they invoke by using it as a barrier, rather than as an invitation, to participation. Similarly, states and courts that call on the image of 'community' as a reason to exclude, rather than include, individuals who seek membership in it despite their own objective—to give meaning to membership in that community—and thereby cheapen the very value they aim to preserve."[77]

Even if this view of the cases were widely accepted, it would not necessarily lead to incorporation of the undocumented into this vision of a fully formed and organic community in which all who legally constitute its membership should share equally in its largesse and reciprocal obligations. In this harsh light, *Plyler* does not perforce follow from this line of cases, under whatever theoretical approach was adopted. The powerful and generous impulse to fully incorporate all those who form the legal community need not extend to the undocumented, those whose entry without inspection and unauthorized presence or whose legal admission and transgressions render them out of status and who do not present themselves as deserving full benefit of the community's acceptance or constitutional protection. This "dirty hands" or "outlaw" version of immigration law is a powerful, indeed, all-encompassing trope. In its purest form, this view is the basis for all restrictionist and nativist worldviews, undergirding objections to the lawlessness and undeserving nature of seeking refuge in a community in which one has not met the test of admission or, once admitted, forfeits membership.[78]

It is this existential leap that is *Plyler's* singular contribution, that constitutional protection is extended to all persons who are sojourners into U.S. society and that under certain conditions, they may avail themselves of this exceedingly generous benefit for their children. Under *Plyler*, we do not place anyone beyond the reach of the Constitution: "[T]he protection of the Fourteenth Amendment extends to anyone, citizen or stranger, who *is* subject to the laws of a State, and reaches into every corner of a State's territory. That a person's initial entry into a State, or into the United States, was unlawful, and that he may for that reason be expelled, cannot negate the simple fact of his presence within the State's territorial perimeter. Given such presence, he is subject to the full range of obligations imposed by the State's civil and criminal laws. And until he leaves the jurisdiction—either voluntarily, or involuntarily in accordance with the Constitution and laws of the United States—he is entitled to the equal protection of the laws that a State may choose to establish."[79] Without finding that the children or their parents are a "suspect class,"[80] the majority held that the children could not be punished for the transgressions of their parents: "Persuasive arguments support the view that a State may withhold its beneficence from those whose very presence within the United States is the product of their own unlawful conduct. These arguments do not apply with the same force to classifications imposing disabilities on the minor *children* of such illegal entrants. At the least, those who elect to enter our territory by stealth and in violation of our law should be prepared to bear the consequences, including, but not limited to, deportation. But the children of those illegal entrants are not comparably situated."[81]

Under a traditional rational basis test, the statute would have only been required to be in furtherance of a legitimate governmental basis, much as the state court reasoning in the earlier case had upheld the legislation.[82] However, the heightened scrutiny standard enabled the majority to strike down the state statute, even without finding that the children were to be considered a suspect classification or that education was a fundamental right. Mark Tushnet, in a fascinating case study of the Court documents and deliberations, has concluded that the real story is how Justice Powell drew Justice Brennan, the author of the majority opinion, to his view that the Texas statutes were simply wrong-headed and harshly applicable to children who had done nothing wrong so as to warrant the treatment:

At the outset Brennan articulated a two-pronged theory to justify invalidating a statute that he and Powell firmly believed was a seriously misguided public policy. Powell insisted that Brennan first dilute one prong and then the other. What resulted was an opinion that on one level had almost no generative or doctrinal significance because it invoked too many considerations. On another level, the opinion had profound doctrinal significance because one could interpret it to hold that the Supreme Court will strike down statutes that are unconstitutional when a majority of the Court thinks those statutes are unwise social policy. Powell's jurisprudence produced an opinion that was almost nothing more than a direct reflection of his views of social policy. The Framers designed the Constitution, it appears, to allow judges to strike down statutes that are, to as reasonable a person as Powell, not sensible.[83]

Because Brennan was the author of the *Plyler* majority opinion, the role of Justice Powell was guised, but Tushnet reads the *Plyler* opinion as evidence of Powell's sensible hand; he characterizes Powell's approach in *Plyler* and in other cases as moderate, centrist, and balanced: "Moderation and balance characterized Powell's understanding of his centrist jurisprudence. Those terms, however, do not define themselves. In *Plyler*, the moderate position came down to treating a misguided social policy as unconstitutional. Powell did have doctrinal concerns, of course, but they were negative: he wanted to ensure that the Court's decision did not express a doctrine that might have troublesome implications for other cases. Powell's balancing was his bulwark against a rule-based formalism, but it did little to explain why the statute in *Plyler* was bad social policy, let alone unconstitutional."[84]

Indeed, this approach has drawn substantial criticism from scholars, including those who, as I am, are pleased with the result if not necessarily the route chosen.[85] Others, who do not view this case as a good result, are less accepting. Dennis Hutchinson, for example, has argued that the case "cut a remarkably messy path through other areas of the Court's jurisprudence"[86] and that the use of equal protection was "ad hoc and divorced from other related bodies of law created by the Court."[87] It is at this point that I believe that a different approach might have provided an alternative pathway, one that would have had more staying power and more narrative force. What is most interesting to me is why the dog did not bark and why Justice Brennan or, for that matter, his prod and provocateur in this instance, Justice Powell, chose not to decide the case on the grounds of preemption, either elaborating on or narrowing *De Canas v. Bica*,[88] clarifying its reach with regard to children and educational benefits, or striking down the Texas statute because, more plausibly, we do not want state or local school board policies that turn on federal immigration classifications. We do not want fifty-one currencies, fifty-one foreign policies, or fifty-one immigration regimes. The Court dismissed the preemption argument, which had figured in the lower courts' reasoning, in a simple footnote: "Appellees in both cases continue to press the argument that § 21.031 is pre-empted by federal law and policy. In light of our disposition of the Fourteenth Amendment issue, we have no occasion to reach this claim."[89]

Tushnet notes that Brennan did incorporate mention of the preemption doctrine but that it was glancing and not fully developed:

> Powell's argument was not enough, however, to stop Brennan. A month later Brennan sent Powell, but not his colleagues, a third version of the opinion. Structurally the first draft had two main parts: (i) a general discussion of why undocumented aliens might be a suspect classification followed by an application of general principles to the special case of children of undocumented aliens, and (ii) a general discussion of why education might be a fundamental right followed by an application to the special case of denying education to a group like those children. The second draft eliminates both the general discussion of suspect classifications and the general discussion of undocumented aliens. Brennan's third draft then eliminates the general discussion of education as a fundamental right. Claiming that he had incorporated Powell's analysis, Brennan concluded that he "no longer required any lengthy discussion of legislative material or any complex analytic framework." But, in response to an argument he found implicit in the proposed dissents, Brennan at last added a discussion of preemption. He told Powell that such a discussion was appropriate because the dissenters apparently believed that "undocumented status, without more, carried with it a State prerogative to deny these children an education," a belief that "rests, at heart, on the implications of federal law."[90]

This insider-baseball insight is fascinating, and all readers must be grateful to former Supreme Court clerks for their unique witness and privileged participant-observations. The longtime *New York Times* Supreme Court reporter Linda Greenhouse, who had many Court sources and carefully read the archival materials, also noted the tug-of-war among the justices and offered the view that Justices Blackmun and Stevens were working carefully to move Brennan to adopt Powell's views:

> Two months after argument, the effort to craft an opinion for the Court appeared to have foundered. At this point, two other members of the majority weighed in with letters to Justice Brennan. Both Blackmun and

Stevens urged him to move further in Powell's direction. The "class" of "illegal aliens" was a "poorly defined" one, Blackmun wrote, noting that one of the lower courts had found that a substantial number of the children were likely to remain in the United States and were not presently deportable; in any event, it was impossible to know which of the children might be found deportable or eventually be deported. Blackmun continued: "Thus, every child has a 'right' to be here until he actually is placed under a deportation order, and at every step of the immigration process a federal official still has the discretion to allow the child to remain in the United States. Many of these children, therefore, have, or will have, political and related rights, and there is no way for the State to determine which children do not have such rights." There was consequently no need to refer to the children as members of a suspect class, Blackmun said; rather, "one could say that the reason education is fundamental is that it is preservative of other rights" and "[t]he reason that it is fundamental to this group is that some of these children will be here permanently." It was, perhaps, a way out of the box, a way to get out of the suspect-category *cul de sac* without yielding much ground as a practical matter. In any event, Blackmun told Brennan, "I think it is desirable, if at all possible, to have a Court opinion, as well as a Court judgment." Stevens agreed. He told Brennan that "I am reasonably sure that any draft that is acceptable to you and to Lewis will be one that I will be able to join." Stevens added that "I agree completely with Harry's suggestion that it is extremely important to obtain a Court opinion if that is at all possible." He also said he agreed with Blackmun that "the reference to illegal aliens as a suspect class could well be deleted from the opinion." Perhaps, he said, the opinion could simply declare that what Texas was doing was irrational. But Blackmun's effort to reframe the question by centering an opinion around the "fundamental" nature of education, rather than on the nature of the excluded class, did not reassure Powell.[91]

I have better understood *Plyler* and other cases of its vintage by reading the work of Tushnet, Koh, and others who were there during deliberations with their Justices.[92] Here, though, I adopt and piggyback on the view of Peter Schuck (who was not there either), who accepts *Plyler* but who wishes it had been decided on a stronger or different constitutional footing:

Plyler could perhaps be understood and even defended as a case of federal preemption that merely reaffirms the exclusive, plenary power of Congress to regulate immigration. This view, however, is undercut by the Court's previous decision in *De Canas*. That case announced a broad tolerance for state legislation that discourages immigration in areas traditionally of local concern, such as labor markets and public education, in ways that are generally consistent with federal policy. Unless this aspect of *De Canas* has been overruled sub silentio, *Plyler* must be seen as the germination of a new and quite different principle. This principle seems to be that a state may not seek to discourage illegal entry by means of disincentives that may harm the children of those who, because the disincentives are ineffective, decide to enter anyway. This principle, of course, would have dictated a different result in *De Canas*, since it would have invalidated the statute in that case. Even more important, the principle would seem to require that result even if Congress, rather than a state, enacted the statute.[93]

Although *Plyler*'s incontestably bold reasoning has not substantially influenced subsequent Supreme Court immigration jurisprudence in the nearly thirty years since it was decided, the educational significance of the case is still clear, even if it is limited to this small subset of schoolchildren—largely Latinos—in the United States. Given the poor overall educational achievement evident in this population, even this one success story has significance.[94] Again, the parallel to *Brown* is striking: *Brown*'s legacy is questioned even after almost sixty years, largely due to Anglo racial intransigence and the failure of integration's promise.[95]

Postscript to Plyler: *The Education of the Polity*

In September 1982, the Court denied petitions to rehear the case, and the matter was over.[96] More than five years had passed since the issue had first appeared on the MALDEF radar screen, and the extraordinary skills and disciplined strategy of Roos and Martinez had prevailed. Indeed, their overarching strategic vision had enabled them to avoid the many centripetal political forces that threatened *Plyler* at every turn. To be sure, luck and the grace of God appeared to have intervened at all the key times: sympathetic clients with a straightforward story to tell, confronting an unpopular state statute that never had had its own compelling story, flying under big-city legal radar and lucking into poor opposing local counsel, federal and state officials at the early stages who were sympathetic and helpful, a change in the national administration that did not result in formal opposition, the ability to keep the Tyler case on track and for the Houston-based cases to prevail at their own speed and on their own legs, and the right array of judges hearing the cases as they wended their way through the system. This issue could have foundered at any one of the many turns, winding up like *Rodriguez*, with a similar gravitational pull but a more complex statistical calculus and worse luck. But the considerable legal and political skills of the MALDEF lawyers and the other lawyers served the schoolchildren well, as they had lawyers of color and Anglo lawyers on the path to *Brown*.

Soon after *Plyler*, both Vilma Martinez and Peter Roos left MALDEF, she to a Los Angeles law firm and he to the San Francisco–based public-interest organization META, where he continued education litigation on bilingual rights and immigrant rights. In 2009, she became President Barack Obama's ambassador to Argentina.[97] The original MALDEF San Antonio lawyer who had written the first *Plyler* memo, Joaquin Avila, succeeded Martinez as MALDEF's president and general counsel. In 1996, he won a MacArthur Foundation "genius" fellowship, after several years in private practice concentrating on voting rights; he now is a law teacher at Seattle University. Whatever became of the undocumented schoolchildren from Tyler, Texas? According to a newspaper story following up on them a dozen years later, nearly all of them graduated and, through various immigration provisions, obtained permission to stay in the United States and to regularize their status.[98] In 2007, on the twenty-fifth anniversary of the case, a number of reporters covered their lives for follow-up stories, and more have since appeared.[99]

The year after *Plyler* was decided, the U.S. Supreme Court took up a related case, *Martinez v. Bynum*[100] and upheld a different part of section 21.031, which provided that the parents or guardians of citizen and undocumented children had to reside in a school district before they could send their children to free public schools. Although this was the element of the statute that first drew Avila's attention and started the ball rolling toward MALDEF's filing of the *Plyler* lawsuit, *Martinez* does not amount to a significant narrowing of *Plyler*, in which the parents actually resided in the school districts, albeit in unauthorized immigration status. The student in *Martinez* was the U.S.-citizen child of undocumented parents who had returned to Mexico after his birth and left him in the care of his adult sister, who was not his legal guardian. The Court in *Martinez* sustained Texas's determination that the child did not "reside" in the district and thus did not qualify for free public schooling there, ruling that *Plyler* did not bar application of appropriately defined bona fide residence tests. The Court had indicated in passing that the undocumented may establish domicile in the country, a much larger issue than that presented in *Martinez*, in which the child's parents had not established the requisite residence in the district. Justice Brennan noted, "A

State may not . . . accomplish what would otherwise be prohibited by the Equal Protection Clause, merely by defining a disfavored group as nonresident. And illegal entry into the country would not, under traditional criteria, bar a person from obtaining domicile within a State."[101]

In 1994, an unpopular governor of California, Pete Wilson, revived his reelection campaign by backing a ballot initiative known as Proposition 187, which would have denied virtually all state-funded benefits, including public education, to undocumented aliens. Proposition 187 passed with nearly 60 percent of the vote, and Wilson was reelected, but the federal courts enjoined implementation of most of the ballot measure, relying prominently on *Plyler*. During the congressional debates that eventually led to the enactment of the Illegal Immigration and Immigrant Responsibility Act of 1996, Representative Elton Gallegly (R-CA) proposed an amendment that would have allowed states to charge tuition to undocumented students or to exclude them from public schools. He was banking that, in the wake of such federal legislation, the courts would distinguish *Plyler* and sustain the state measure. The provision became quite politicized, receiving prominent support from Republican presidential candidate Robert Dole. Gallegly might have been right that the Constitution would not be read by the Court of the 1990s to nullify a federal enactment of the kind he proposed, but he never got a chance to find out, because *Plyler* proved to have considerable strength in the political arena. The Gallegly amendment drew heated opposition in Congress and in the media, and critics relied heavily on the values and arguments highlighted in *Plyler*—and often on the decision itself. After months of contentious debate, the amendment was dropped from the final legislation, and no provisions became law that restricted alien children's right to attend school.[102] *Plyler* and the polity appear to have settled the question, although bills have been introduced in Congress over the years to deny birthright citizenship to children born to undocumented parents in the United States.[103]

Although *Plyler* had addressed the issue of public schoolchildren in the K–12 setting, almost immediately after the ruling, questions arose about how far the decision could be extended, notably whether it would protect undocumented college students. Before long, Peter Roos was going for the long ball again, litigating postsecondary *Plyler* cases in California and elsewhere.[104] The cases have mostly denied relief, although the record is mixed. That history is for a later chapter, but I will say this: the ultimate irony is that in 2001, just after Governor George W. Bush left Texas to become President George W. Bush, the State enacted H.B. 1403, establishing the right of undocumented college students to establish resident status and to pay in-state tuition in the state's public colleges.[105] In those twenty-five years since Texas had enacted section 21.031, this was silent testimony to the idea that you reside where you live, quite apart from your immigration status. Over a dozen states have acted since the Texas innovation.[106] And in Congress, the Development, Relief, and Education for Alien Minors (DREAM) Act has been considered in Congress and voted on more than once, as will be seen in chapter 4.[107] If enacted, it would remove a provision from federal law that addresses the issue of states providing in-state tuition status to undocumented college students and would also allow the students the opportunity to regularize their federal immigration status—an enormous benefit that would go well beyond what a state could provide.[108] *Plyler* clearly is alive and well in its adolescence.

3

The Implementation of *Plyler v. Doe*

I never even knew I was Mexican, I mean really Mexican. I thought I was born in Magnolia or the East End, since that's all I really remember. Except when my class went on a trip to NASA, I've never really left Houston. Except we went to Corpus [Christi] with my grandfather when the Aquarium opened. So I thought all along I was Mexican American, you know, Chicano, until "*la IRCA*" came along. My mother took me down to the "*Migra*," and we waited in line with a green bag full of papers, you know, with a twister tie on it like for grass and leaves. That was when I found out I was really Mexican, not Chicano. Born in Mexico. Except to talk to my grandfather and that, I don't even speak Spanish very well. Now I'm afraid to leave town, 'cause the "*Migra*" is, like, really coming down on illegals. Now, it turns out I'm illegal even though I've got my driver's license and that, even the SAT. If I'm illegal, what about these Mexicans who stand around the corners? I think the law should round them up, not me. I've been like a citizen up to now. It was "*la IRCA*" that made me illegal, but the lawyer said I could become a permanent resident and get a green card. I thought I could vote when I was 18, but now I have to become a citizen first. I'm gonna do it, but I'm not going to tell anybody, cause I want to go to college. I can go to college, can't I?[1]

It wasn't until they had the amnesty that I found out I wasn't born in Texas. We grew up in Laredo, but my parents got divorced and I moved to Houston with my mother and my sisters. She doesn't speak English, but she wants me to go to school. She cleans offices downtown, like law offices and a bank building. She can't help me with my homework, but she makes me do it before [I can watch] TV. If I can go to college, it's because she made me want to go. It's like for her. But now I found out I'm *mojado*, but we're going to get legal papers. [The lawyer] had me bring in my school grades to show that we were in the U.S. before the time. My sisters knew we were *mojados*, but I didn't. They said I was *pocho*, like tourists. But now I can go to college, maybe be a lawyer or doctor.[2]

It did not seem like a golden age at the time for me, for my clients, and for the undocumented community, but it surely was. In fact, if I were pressed, I would identify 1982's *Plyler v. Doe* as the true high-water mark of immigrant rights in the United States. Today, it is clear that the polity is more concerned with localized conditions than with extending immigrant rights, and in many respects, it likely would be harder for alien children to prevail. As one indicator, state legislatures are formally considering record levels of immigrant-related legislation. In the first six months of 2009, more than fourteen hundred bills were considered in all fifty states; in the same period, 144 laws and 115 resolutions had been enacted in forty-four states, with bills sent to governors in two additional states. A total of 285 bills and resolutions passed legislatures; twenty-three of these bills are pending governors' approval, and three bills were vetoed. No bills have been enacted in Alaska, Massachusetts, Michigan, or Ohio, the only four states not to have done so in this time frame.[3]

These recent statutes run the gamut, from enacting two pro-immigrant state programs for college tuition (one of which, in Wisconsin, even extends to the undocumented) to a number of blatantly restrictionist statutes, including ones in Georgia and Arizona that cover the waterfront: work authorization, human trafficking, enforcement provisions, regulation of immigration assistance services, penalties and deductions for business expenses and tax withholding, and overall benefit eligibility.[4] The Georgia state statute even exceeds California's restrictionist 1994 Proposition 187, virtually all of which was struck down in court.[5] These state statutes are mirrored by an increasing array of city, county, and regional laws and regulations also reaching immigration regulation, while a variety of long-existing (or dormant) codes are being dusted off, redeployed, and applied to aliens. Maricopa County, Arizona, has attempted to characterize alien entry into the country as a "conspiracy" to smuggle oneself, giving rise to enhanced criminal penalties.[6] This extraordinary rise in such legislative interests is undoubtedly due to overburdened locales, well-publicized and highly polarized federal attention to immigration, a sharp rise in conservative media regularly flogging the issue, and a decline in President Obama's popularity, all of which have led to a leadership vacuum in the field. Concerns about national security and terrorism in the world also contribute to this phenomenon, turning many discussions about immigration reform into referenda on border security and failed interdiction. It has been over two decades since the last national legalization reform of immigration, 1986's Immigration Reform and Control Act, signed into law by President Reagan.[7]

In some ways, it is a perfect storm of antialien factors. It is my thesis that state, county, and local ordinances aimed at regulating general immigration functions are unconstitutional as a function of exclusive federal preemptory powers. If purely state, county, or local interests are governed and if federal preemptory powers are not triggered, such ordinances may be properly enacted, provided they are not subterfuges for replacing or substituting federal authority; purely state benefits, as one example, can be extended or withheld to undocumented college students, as tuition benefits and state residency determinations are properly designated as state classifications, which reference but do not determine immigration status.[8] And the federal government has enacted statutes and promulgated regulations that subcontract or designate state or subfederal immigration enforcement; many examples include assorted memoranda of understanding (MOUs) that calibrate and regulate a proper role for effectuating federal obligations.[9] But a number of Supreme Court decisions and common law do not reserve a substantive role in immigration enforcement absent such delegation and carefully controlled, designated purposes.[10]

In this chapter, I examine one settled area in detail, noting how 1982's *Plyler v. Doe* has morphed beyond its original K–12 public-school-tuition moorings. This attestation to an important feature of immigrant life and the U.S. polity demonstrates that even thirty years of immigrant children's rights have not been fully resolved and have required additional litigation and additional vigilance to secure the Supreme Court's rulings. I believe this phenomenon can be observed by thick descriptions of a case in which more of an equilibrium has been reached, the case of undocumented schoolchildren, in which the record reveals substantial and longstanding accommodation to the 1982 case. However, even this settled case has been contested regularly in school board meetings and classroom buildings, and as this record will show, *Plyler* implementation issues have continued, sometimes necessitating additional litigation. Thus, the vigilance to secure these rights has stretched more than thirty years, since Texas enacted the state law in 1975 that enabled its public school districts to charge tuition to parents of undocumented schoolchildren. Although the underlying legislative history is unclear, and although no public hearings were ever held on the provision, certain border Texas school superintendents had urged the legislation which was enacted without controversy as a small piece of larger, routine education statutes.[11]

As discussed in chapter 2, in 1982, the Mexican American Legal Defense and Educational Fund (MALDEF) attorneys prevailed in the U.S. Supreme Court, in a 5–4 opinion authored by Justice William Brennan.[12] Justice Brennan struck down the Texas statute, finding the state's theory to be "nothing more than an assertion that illegal entry, without more, prevents a person from becoming a resident for purposes of enrolling his children in the public schools."[13] This holding has since driven restrictionist policy behavior and litigation, particularly in the auxiliary area of college tuition residency. Almost immediately after *Plyler*, a corollary issue was litigated, involving a U.S.-citizen child of undocumented Mexican parents, who had left the child in the care of his adult sister in a Texas town. This time, the Court determined that his domicile was not in Texas, a precept of traditional family law, which holds that the domicile of unemancipated children is that of their parents; in this instance, the child was not a legal charge of his sister and hence could not be considered a "resident" of the Texas school district.[14] (This is a legal infirmity that could be remedied by several means.) *Martinez v. Bynum* did not limit the earlier *Plyler*, and no other K–12 residency-related immigration case has been decided by the U.S. Supreme Court since 1983. A postsecondary residency case involving nonimmigrant visa holders was decided in 1982 for the alien college students on preemption grounds (*Toll v. Moreno*), but *Plyler* has remained in force, undisturbed since 1982.[15]

This is not to say that *Plyler* has not been attacked, at a variety of levels, in the nearly thirty years since it was decided. On the more quotidian level, MALDEF and other lawyers have had to file several dozen actions since the early 1980s to enforce *Plyler*'s clear holding, including school board actions to require Social Security numbers, school requests for driver's licenses to identify parents, additional "registration" of immigrant children, "safety notification" for immigrant parents, separate schools for immigrant children, and other policies and practices designed to identify immigration status or single out undocumented children. This chapter examines the range of these *Plyler* implementation issues, analyzing direct and indirect challenges that have arisen in the intervening quarter century, both in legislative reactions and in the many school-based policies that have eroded the blanket enrollment permission accorded the children by the original case. Some of these policies affect all children, Latino children disproportionately, but several of them have continued to single out children on immigration grounds and thus directly undermine their enrollment status. At the end of the day, it is difficult to ignore the petty nature and widespread harassment of the children, who, it must be remembered, have committed no crime of their own and who are innocent victims of behavior that might have been committed by their parents. This original-sin concept may have theological roots, but it is difficult to square with *Plyler*'s clear holding. Justice Brennan's majority opinion accurately characterized this situation as one "imposing special disabilities upon groups disfavored by virtue of circumstances beyond their control [and which] suggests the kind of 'class or caste' treatment that the Fourteenth Amendment was designed to abolish."[16]

In the first part of this chapter, I examine the direct challenges to *Plyler*: both those that have been federal legislative efforts—including those that appeared to have settled the matter in the mid-1990s in California and more current ones that have arisen—and state ballot initiatives and legislation that were enacted to address illegal immigration.[17] Direct challenges to undocumented students have also included "helicopter children," those whose parents sent them to study in the United States without parental residence; a subset of this complex issue, parents who have legally entered the country but whose behavior has resulted in their being out of status, rendering even citizen children removable; campus chase and policing policies; and nonlegislative, school-based initiatives such as the use of Social Security numbers and identification measures. I also examine cases and school district or state actions that indirectly implicate *Plyler* and analyze the various means by which restrictionist policies have attempted to extirpate the practice allowed by *Plyler* and to overturn its holding. Indirect measures include a variety of language issues, including bilingual education and English as a second language (ESL); building, siting, and attendance-zone concerns; undocumented students who become at risk when their achievements bring them into the spotlight or when they win national awards for academic prowess; the mean-spirited assault on programs that provide resources to undocumented children; separate immigrant schools and programs that concentrate the children in a special, circumscribed environment; college-preparation issues; and miscellaneous issues having to do with driver's licenses and school transportation. There is a long list of such topics that disproportionately affect these children, who are marginalized even within the difficult world of public and private schooling for immigrants in the modern United States. The original *Plyler* case has proven quite resilient, fending off litigation and federal and state legislative efforts to overturn it and nurturing efforts to extend its reach to college attendees who were allowed to stay in school by the original case. It has had to be reinforced by vigilant efforts, but it has proven more hardy than it first appeared.

Direct Challenges to Plyler

In November 1994, by nearly 60 percent, California's voters passed a popular state referendum, Proposition 187, which would have denied virtually all state-funded benefits (including public education) to undocumented Californians.[18] Immigration scholars Kevin Johnson and Ruben Garcia have carefully catalogued the many public comments that constituted the discourse over the passage of Proposition 187, and while reasonable people were on both sides of the issue, many unreasonable remarks and racist commentary coarsened the exchange. Johnson perceptively notes, "Proposition 187 is the product of a deeply complex, perhaps unique, set of political forces in the United States. As the solid support for the measure amply demonstrates, its backing did not split along classic liberal-conservative lines. The limited political power of noncitizens made it easier for one powerful politician [Governor Pete Wilson] to use Proposition 187 and anti-immigrant/anti-immigration sentiment to build a bipartisan coalition, ensuring his re-election and the initiative's passage. . . . Curiously enough, a much-debated aspect of the passage of Proposition 187—that it is nativistic and racist—in all probability will never be decided."[19] Garcia notes, after reviewing these strains in U.S. immigration history, culminating in Proposition 187, "immigration law and policy continue to be partially motivated by a drive for cultural and racial homogeneity."[20] The subsequent reappearance of state and local ordinances calls Johnson's "uniqueness" comment into question, but he is surely correct when he notes the "deeply complex" nature of the issue, and he was writing years before the issue of terrorism and attacks on the United States and its allies raised this dimension as a wellspring of immigration policy.

Proposition 187 was clearly intended by its sponsors to rescind *Plyler*, to restrict access to public benefits, and to expel aliens from the state. The preamble in section 1, for example, indicated, "[Californian citizens] have suffered and are suffering economic hardship, . . . personal injury and damage caused by the criminal conduct of illegal aliens in this state. [By enacting this legislation, Californians intend to] establish a system of required notification by and between such agencies to prevent illegal aliens in the United States from receiving benefits or public services in the State of California."[21] The proposition would have required law enforcement officials to ascertain the legal status of every person "suspected of being present in the United States" without proper immigration authorization and to notify federal and state authorities of their suspicions.[22] It would have extended the same affirmative notification obligation to state social service and health-care workers if that agency "determines or reasonably suspects" that the client was out of proper status.[23] While the details of these requirements were not fleshed out at the early stages, the overall scheme, if implemented, clearly would have placed certain obligations on various state, county, and local public officials and administrators to effectuate apprehension or notification requirements.

In a complex but authoritative opinion, the trial judge enjoined implementation and enforcement of sections 4, 5, 6, 7, and 9 of Proposition 187 and then subsequently struck down virtually all of the provisions, citing either preemption for the social service benefits or *Plyler* for the educational provisions.[24] During the pendency of these actions, Congress passed the Personal Responsibility and Work Opportunity Reconciliation Act of 1996 (PRWORA),[25] after which the judge held that the provisions of that law preempted any remaining provisions of the California proposition, as Congress had clearly "occupied the field," squeezing out any such role for states to act.[26]

Had these proposition provisions been able to stand, they would have gone even further than had the original Texas statute, which had allowed, but not required, school districts to charge tuition but had not banned students from attending Texas public schools. Proposition 187 would have enacted an absolute ban and would not have even allowed school districts to charge tuition for enrolling undocumented children. In addition, it would have required school authorities to report undocumented parents or guardians: "Each school district shall provide information to the State Superintendent of Public Instruction, the Attorney General of California, and [federal immigration authorities] regarding any enrollee or pupil, or parent or guardian, [of children] attending a public elementary or secondary school . . . determined or reasonably suspected to be in violation of federal immigration laws within forty-five days after becoming aware of an apparent violation."[27] The language even would have arguably required authorities to report undocumented (or, apparently, ostensibly undocumented) parents or guardians of enrolled citizen children. Careful scholars who examined these provisions also raised a number of other problems with them, including the state's constitutional right-to-education features, national-origin and race discrimination, and the obvious preemption issues.[28]

In 1997, the federal court hearing this dispute put an end to virtually all the remaining provisions of Proposition 187, its implementing regulations, and the interaction between the federal PRWORA and the state statute, when the trial judge concluded,

> After the Court's November 20, 1995 Opinion, Congress enacted the PRA [PRWORA], a comprehensive statutory scheme regulating alien eligibility for public benefits. The PRA states that it is the immigration policy of the United States to restrict alien access to substantially all public benefits. Further, the PRA ousts state power to legislate in the area of public benefits for aliens. When President Clinton signed the PRA, he effectively ended any further debate about what the states could do in this field. As the Court pointed out in its prior Opinion, California is powerless to enact its

own legislative scheme to regulate immigration. It is likewise powerless to enact its own legislative scheme to regulate alien access to public benefits. It can do what the PRA permits, and nothing more. Federal power in these areas was always exclusive and the PRA only serves to reinforce the Court's prior conclusion that substantially all of the provisions of Proposition 187 are preempted under *De Canas v. Bica*.[29]

There were some mopping-up details remaining, and when Wilson's successor, Gray Davis, came into office, he finally ended the matter by reaching a settlement with the litigants.[30] *Plyler*'s supporters breathed a sigh of relief as they realized that they had dodged the bullet. By the end of this protracted process, not only had a federal court comprehensively dealt with the various features of the proposition and the implementing regulations, but California statutes had been amended to safeguard *Plyler*: section 1643 of the California Education Code read, "Nothing in this chapter may be construed as addressing alien eligibility for a basic public education as determined by the Supreme Court of the United States under Plyler v. Doe."[31]

The challenges to Proposition 187 had occurred predominantly in one court, that of Judge Mariana R. Pfaelzer of the Central District of California, with some of the more technical and procedural issues being decided on appeal to the Ninth Circuit, including the consolidation of the many parties at interest and resolving the State's assertion that the law of abstention had been misapplied and whether the district court had abused its discretion in entering the original preliminary injunction.[32] She was upheld in the preliminary matters, and when Governor Davis conceded the issues and reached a settlement, the substantive matter never returned to the Ninth Circuit, from where an appeal might have gone to the United States Supreme Court. This meant that the original supporters of the proposition and Governor Wilson never got what it was they really wanted, an opportunity for the Supreme Court to accept certiorari and to overturn *Plyler*. Moreover, the Court taking up the issue would likely have held that 1996's PRWORA had preempted any such state initiative, whether enacted by a legislature or ballot measure. In addition, the California education statute itself had been amended to give ostensible authority to the original holding of *Plyler*, which would have made it difficult to repeal the central holding of the case through regulation or school board action.

The year 1996 had seen the enactment of restrictionist federal legislation (IIRIRA and PRWORA) and the efforts of Representative Elton Gallegly (R-CA) to amend federal law by allowing states to enact the type of legislation that Texas had passed in 1975, which had led to *Plyler*.[33] At the end of the process, the "Gallegly Amendment" was not added to the provisions that were signed into law. However, if the amendment had been enacted, the federal statute would have allowed states "to deny public education benefits to certain aliens not lawfully present in the United States" or to charge these students tuition for public school enrollment, as Texas had done. It drew sufficient negative attention to force its withdrawal from the other legislative proposals, a number of which were enacted.[34] But his hard line took on another, more symbolic role in the struggle between President Clinton, who genuinely wanted welfare reform, and the Republican Congress, which wanted to restrict immigrant rights and to tighten up what many legislators considered to be permissive loopholes in alien benefit eligibility.

In a fascinating and authoritative book by Philip Schrag on the refugee and asylum provisions of the 1995–1996 congressional debates, he wrote of the Gallegly proposals, "Agenda control worked for the Republican leadership in a more random way at a later stage of the process. Representative Gallegly was not able to make his public education amendment into law, but he was able to dominate the immigration agenda for months during the summer of 1996, so that other issues . . . were unable to break into most news stories. If the House had voted down the Gallegly amendment to begin with, Senator [Arlen] Specter or others might have had the attention or political capital available for other conflicts, and other sections of the final bill might have become more moderate."[35] While the provisions that did pass were draconian in other respects, removing much of the play in the joints for federal enforcement purposes and restricting immigrant benefits generally, Congress did not move to exclude schoolchildren. Even the two conservative Republican senators from Texas (Phil Gramm and Kay Bailey Hutchison) publicly signaled their opposition to repealing *Plyler*.[36] Prior to the final draft of the comprehensive bill, President Clinton indicated he would veto any version that would overturn *Plyler*'s holding.[37] In this very serious threat to *Plyler*, the children's story won over opponents, and luck once again played a substantial role.

The proposed Gallegly Amendment also did not appeal to the groups most closely identified with the issue, public school officials and teachers. By 1996, after more than a decade of living with *Plyler*, educators had made their peace with its requirements and had come to accept the decision. My own interaction with Houston-area school administrators, who had lost the original consolidated case and who had originally strongly opposed the decision, revealed relief that they would not have to play immigration police or attempt to identify which of the 220,000 schoolchildren were in proper immigration status and which were not.[38] In addition, more than thirty years after the original trial, the district has special programs for non-English speakers, migrants, and refugee children, as well as a special high school for undocumented students.[39] It also hired its first Mexican American school superintendent, who retired in late 2009.[40] Thus, the political process worked to remove any impediments to undocumented K–12 enrollments at the state and federal levels, even as severely tightened immigration restrictions were enacted into law; affirming *Plyler*'s holding as national policy exacted a high price in terms of immigration reform and welfare reform.

Dennis Hutchinson wrote soon after the 1982 decision that the case "cut a remarkably messy path through other areas of the [Supreme] Court's jurisprudence,"[41] and he and another scholar indicated that it was "ad hoc and divorced from other related bodies of law created by the Court."[42] Mark Tushnet, not as critical of the opinion as other critics have been, still regarded the majority opinion as containing "almost no generative or doctrinal significance because it invoked too many considerations";[43] however, Peter Schuck noted that the case had "epochal significance" in terms of immigrant rights.[44] María Pabón López, perhaps the most cynical of the many observers, has written of *Plyler*, "Because the nation's interest in maintaining a cheap and expendable labor force has converged with the expectation of an education for undocumented children, *Plyler* survives to this day."[45]

Arizona and Georgia are two of the states to have most recently passed comprehensive immigration statutes that undertake to regulate immigration in the state and to restrict benefits. Arizona's Proposition 100 would deny bail to undocumented immigrants, Proposition 102 would prohibit undocumented plaintiffs from receiving civil damages in Arizona litigation, Proposition 103 would establish English as the official state language, and Proposition 300 would restrict enrollment and resident tuition to undocumented public college students and persons enrolled in publicly funded adult-education instruction.[46] The four propositions were approved by over 70 percent of the voters in November 2006 and are not yet fully implemented by spring 2011, due to complexity, previous lawsuits over these issues, and new litigation filed after the referenda were passed.[47] In addition, authorities in Maricopa County (Phoenix) brought suit in novel applications of state law concerning human smuggling and general smuggling.[48] Although in the first case the defendant was acquitted, the larger enabling issue of the constitutionality of the statute as applied is looming, as it is for similar actions in Oklahoma.[49]

In April 2006, S.B. 529, the Georgia Security and Immigration Compliance Act, was signed into law, to take effect in July 2007.[50] Like the several Arizona propositions, it touched on many Georgia statutes, amending a number of them by adding reporting requirements, program eligibility guidelines, and detailed provisions for official transactions concerning aliens. It also added a new Registration of Immigration Assistance Act, which heavily regulates the legal services that may be provided to persons.[51] While it does not address the issue of public schooling for undocumented K–12 students or their parents and guardians, it does incorporate reference to the Immigration and Nationality Act, 8 U.S.C., sections 1621 and 1623, concerning undocumented college students.[52] It directs the state's higher-education authority to enact regulations for this topic, although it does so by incorporating provisions that, if drafted carefully, would not preclude undocumented students from receiving in-state tuition; it requires the state to "comply with all [applicable] federal law" in this area.[53] Hearings were conducted in spring 2007 by the Georgia Board of Regents, to receive public comment, and the State decided not to allow these students, even those who had resided in the state and attended public colleges, to receive in-state, resident tuition; a subsequent incident stemming from a 2010 traffic matter led the State to ban them entirely from public institutions.[54]

The passage of these comprehensive and restrictive state statutory schemes to regulate immigration shows how the grounds have shifted since 1994's Proposition 187, which singled out undocumented schoolchildren, even exceeding *Plyler*'s 1975 scheme. In the past dozen years, there has been a conscious effort by immigrant restrictionists not to touch the third rail of schoolchildren, at least not directly. After Proposition 187's failure and the doomed efforts of Representative Gallegly to enact *Plyler* at the federal level, the blowback has caused those who wish to expel these children to do so by making it harder for their parents to remain in the United States. While there are regular and ongoing efforts to educate Congress about the detrimental effects of *Plyler* and birthright citizenship, restrictionists have also taken a different tack by making the issue one of equity and fairness and couching their rhetoric as school-finance-reform and school-overcrowding issues.[55] In addition, they have ratcheted up the postsecondary *Plyler* pressure, as was evident in both these state efforts.[56] While Arizona has a substantial number of potential undocumented students and a longtime policy that permitted them to establish resident status for purposes of paying lower tuition, it is inconceivable that Georgia has such a problem or that it would, even over time.[57]

It is clear that squeezing out undocumented adults, especially parents, and removing them from the country has become a more viable and more widely employed stratagem, both by the local and state ordinances that attempt to restrict benefits generally and higher-education residency status in particular and by general efforts to enact omnibus nuisance measures. Even the traditional Americanizing efforts such as adult-education programs and ESL classes have been targeted in Arizona.[58] Workplace raids, arrests at work stations, and other widespread harassment measures have become the centerpiece of efforts to locate and remove undocumented adults, who will have to take their children, even their citizen children, with them when they are removed.[59] This has been a successful change of direction, as even the dissenters in *Plyler* indicated that they thought that removing innocent children was bad policy. Chief Justice Burger, as one example, wrote in his dissent, "Denying a free education to illegal alien children is not a choice I would make if I were a legislator. Apart from compassionate concerns, the long-range costs of excluding any children from the public schools may well outweigh the costs of educating them."[60]

While the children may have been innocent, restrictionists can claim, their parents surely have dirty hands. Although even this claim is problematic, it is a better sound bite for nativist discourse efforts, as infants are being characterized as "anchor babies," conveying putative citizenship benefits to their illegal and lawbreaking alien parents, who make illegal entries and foul our nest.[61] The *New York Times Style Manual* requires its reporters to use "illegal immigrant" in news coverage and headlines and bans "undocumented" as a preferred adjective; because the *Manual* is the widely employed arbiter for many other newspapers, these pejorative terms are regularly used and constitute the discourse even in the educated and literate population.[62] This Lou Dobbs/Fox-channel effect has achieved its intended purpose regarding public discourse about immigration, even if the taproot case has not been overturned or legislated away.

In reviewing the direct threats to *Plyler* and the enrollment of undocumented children, it is reassuring that the overall issue has become enshrined in law, practice, and politics. As was the case in the original litigation, in which the combination of the facts, excellent lawyering, and some luck blew the way of the children,[63] so it was with state threats such as the *LULAC* litigation, the timing of which found the more agreeable Governor Davis rather than the progenitor of the proposition, Pete Wilson, who never would have settled and would have likely appealed as far as the case would have allowed him. The case drew an exceptional federal judge who carefully reasoned her way through the exceedingly complex litigation: Judge Pfaelzer was appointed to the U.S. District Court for the Central District of California by President Jimmy Carter in 1978, and she assumed senior status later in the year she ruled on *LULAC*.[64] All her rulings that were appealed were upheld by the Ninth Circuit, but it need not have gone this way. On the federal stage, the Gallegly Amendment could have fallen on fertile ground, rather than facing a Congress that did not want to scapegoat children and a Democrat president who singled out that particular provision as the one he would not support and would veto if it made its way to his desk.

As noted, immigrant-rights advocates had reason to feel that a great deal was lost in the exchange leading to IIRIRA and PRWORA, but there have been no serious legislative threats to undocumented schoolchildren at the congressional level since 1996 or at the state level since *LULAC* was settled in 1997. Indeed, California incorporated *Plyler* language into its Education Code, and the Texas governor in 2007 indicated he would not support efforts to roll back the undocumented-college-student provisions he had signed into law earlier.[65] To be sure, more states have singled out postsecondary *Plyler* issues, some adding and some restricting residency, but if the DREAM Act gains any traction in Congress, it would, in part, resolve this issue as a part of comprehensive immigration reform.[66] Doing so would also allow immigrant advocates to concentrate on other issues rather than having to fight college issues, state legislature by state legislature—even having to protect statutes that were enacted that had to be defended again after enactment.[67] Of course, it would also mean not having to go to federal court or state court to defend state statutes, as was necessary in Kansas, Nebraska, and California, or to sue states, as in Virginia.[68]

The legislative and litigation issues have included direct attacks on the enrollment of undocumented schoolchildren and college students, but in terms of sheer advocacy, much of the shoring up and preservation of that right has taken place with regard to *Plyler*'s school implementation, unequal treatment of the children or their parents, and a large array of collateral and supporting issues at the school board, school, and classroom levels. Three of the more evident manifestations of problems with local administration of *Plyler* have been the treatment of students whose parents do not have legitimate Social Security numbers, school chase and access policies, and students whose presence implicates extraordinary immigration status.

To most adults and a large number of children in the United States, holding a Social Security number (SSN) is simply no big deal; I was issued an SSN card when I was four or five years old, when my parents established a bank account for me, after I received a savings bond from my grandparents as a birthday gift. It is a card issued to persons who work or who have work authorization and to persons who claim dependents on their income-tax returns.[69] Although undocumented persons who do not have proper papers or authorization to work are not eligible for an SSN, federal law requires everyone receiving income in the United States to file a tax return.[70] An important feature is that anyone who is not a U.S. citizen is considered a "resident alien" under the U.S. tax code, and all resident aliens—including those without immigration status—have the same tax obligations as do U.S. citizens.[71] As a result, three paths are available to undocumented workers in this circumstance. They can get a Taxpayer Identification Number (TIN), secure an SSN not their own, or engage in the underground economy and go bareback, without any number or documents. Further, while the undocumented are not able to secure a valid SSN, the TIN will not suffice for employment identification or authorization purposes.[72] Thus, virtually all undocumented workers, while required to pay taxes and to have withholding drawn from paychecks, engage in subterfuge and expose themselves to various fraud and tax-related problems. One thorough and useful analysis of this complex issue summarizes it as "the separate, unequal, and 'under-represented' federal income tax treatment of undocumented aliens"[73] and "a mismatch made in hell."[74] The details of tax law, an area as complex as immigration and nationality law itself, are beyond the scope of this chapter, but it is essential for observers to recognize that identifying numbers, paperwork details, and documentation are the linchpin, the quintessence of being "undocumented."[75]

Any use of an SSN or TIN by school officials will cause undocumented parents to avoid the transaction, when possible, and children often suffer as a result, such as when schools innocently, casually, and routinely employ these numbers for their own uses, as simple registration or identification of schoolchildren. Persons who are subjects of identification fraud or ones who lose a credit card or change banks come to realize the pervasiveness of private identification numbers and credit information; this is the closest civilian parallel to the experience of being undocumented. The quotidian use of SSNs far exceeds their legitimate, narrow purpose of tax and Social Security identification and authentication, as when bank, credit card, membership, registration, and a myriad of consumer transactions require the use of an SSN. Schools and colleges have routinely, and improperly, used SSNs for academic records, grade posting, and other inappropriate uses that violate federal or state laws ensuring privacy.[76] To be sure, such excesses are inconvenient and can implicate substantial credit risk and theft, but with undocumented parents and their children, the requirement that SSNs be used for school transactions puts the enrolled children at unnecessary risk and can force their parents to avoid school transactions or limit the children's participation in educational programs and activities.

Because this phenomenon has become so widespread, some states and school authorities have begun to exercise more care and caution in their requirements for identification and documentation in parent-school transactions. As one example, in 2003, Virginia amended its Education Code § 22.1-260, which had required that parents provide schools with an SSN for each student at the time of first enrollment; it was amended to permit school officials to use another individual-identifying number or to waive the requirement if parents were unwilling to disclose SSNs for their children.[77] Other states and school authorities have drafted policies for this issue, have printed materials and pamphlets to inform parents and to train school officials, and have maintained websites to provide information about these requirements.[78] Some jurisdictions also use similar federal or state law provisions for homeless children, who will often lack such formal identifiers, including home addresses and permanent phone numbers, and for whom special accommodations must be made.[79] It is also evident that maintaining contact with parents becomes much more difficult and time-consuming for regular parent-teacher transactions and school-community relations, which also means that support services and corollary informational interaction are diminished. And sometimes schools do not meet their obligations or do not properly take into account these features, even in programs designed and funded to address the special needs of such schoolchildren.

Even when school officials want to do the right thing, the lack of proper documentation can cause problems, such as authenticating parents or relatives who are authorized to pick up children after school, proving vaccinations and public health records, and maintaining proper contact with parents in the event of emergencies. The unavailability of driver's licenses for the undocumented, uneven availability of "consular matricular" cards or foreign documents, and fear of the use of banking services or credit unavailability all combine to make these identification issues difficult, even when school officials are disposed to take the necessary precautions or to have the requisite cultural sensitivity.[80] When they are not so disposed, it renders these transactions even more problematic. Until Congress acts to provide comprehensive immigration reform, with realistic and efficacious provisions concerning identification, Social Security participation, and driver's licenses, such issues will leach into the treatment of undocumented schoolchildren. In addition, issues of privacy, identity theft, data availability, and the proper balance between consumers and commercialized credit information will continue to affect the undocumented even more than they will the rest of U.S. society.[81]

The unavailability of proper documentation can extend to many other school-related attestations, such as proof of residence in the district. This is a complex matter, including constitutional concerns about domicile and custody. But is it also often a literal matter of documentation, as in the example of *Joel R. v. Mannheim Middle School District*, a 1997 Illinois state court case in which school authorities would not recognize the custody assertions in a matter of an undocumented child.[82] The school would not acknowledge the notarized document executed by Joel's parents before a judge in Mexico, who had granted a relative residing in the school district custody over Joel, on the grounds that "the Mexican document was not sufficient to enroll Joel because it did not establish, through an American court, that [the relative] was Joel's legal guardian."[83] The courts required the school district to admit the child and to accept the authenticated documents. Immigration authorities are conversant with the various forms of authentication and must deal with foreign documents as a matter of course, whereas campus officials may not have the expertise or experience in doing so, but failure to observe principles of comity and international law regularly implicates educational decision making, nowhere more commonly than in dealing with international children or undocumented parents of citizen children.[84]

Maintaining safety on campus and making sure that no unauthorized persons enter school grounds is a common and legitimate worry of educational officials and law enforcement authorities, and as a general rule, immigration authorities do not extend their dominion to schools, while school security personnel do not generally act as immigration-enforcement officials, carrying out immigration raids or searches. However, there are occasions where the twain do meet, as in *Murillo v. Musegades*, a 1992 case in El Paso, where INS authorities kept a too-watchful eye on the public high school on the U.S. side of the U.S.-Mexico border. In granting a request for a temporary restraining order against the INS, the federal judge noted,

> The El Paso Border Patrol has a regular, consistent, and prominent presence on the Bowie High School campus, whether their presence be by parking in the parking lots, speeding along the service roads, jumping across the curbs, or driving across concrete sidewalks and grassy areas. The El Paso Border Patrol's presence is further made known by their driving

over the football practice field and baseball diamond, entering the football locker rooms, surveilling with binoculars from the football stadium, and using binoculars to watch flag girls practicing on campus. Bowie High School provides an oasis of safety and freedom for the students and staff who reside within the School District. The continued harassment of Bowie High School students and staff by the El Paso Border Patrol is both an invasion of their civil rights and the oasis. . . . The El Paso Border Patrol does not comply with the policy issued by [the district director of the INS Service El Paso District], which states "that all law enforcement activities at all levels and types of schools is [*sic*] prohibited unless prior approval has been granted as provided." . . . Although the policy warns "failure to comply with this policy will lead to appropriate disciplinary action," Defendants produced no evidence of disciplinary actions for policy violators.[85]

Reviewing all the details in this complex case, including the school coach and students having been detained at gunpoint, the judge held, "[The] INS in this case discriminated against Plaintiffs in violation of their Fifth Amendment rights to equal protection. The INS has repeatedly and illegally stopped, questioned, detained, frisked, arrested, and searched Plaintiffs and numerous other students from the Bowie High School District. El Paso Border Patrol Agents have subjected Plaintiffs and others to indecent comments, obscene gestures, and humiliation in the presence of their co-workers, friends, family, and relevant community. The proffered evidence strongly supports this Court in its conclusion that the illegal and abusive conduct of the El Paso Border Patrol was directed against Plaintiffs, staff, and residents in the Bowie High School District solely because of their mere immutable appearances as Hispanics."[86] There had been a recent El Paso case concerning acceptable INS procedure, which the INS ignored in its Bowie police-pursuit policies. Following this case, all the parties entered into a stipulated agreement in which the INS agreed that it would not violate the "oasis" nature of the school and its students, irrespective of their immigration status.[87]

In the Bowie High School instance, it was school authorities and both undocumented and citizen students who were affected by the improper behavior of immigration authorities. In 2004, it was the school and police who initiated the inappropriate behavior, three hundred miles north in Albuquerque, New Mexico. Albuquerque Public Schools found three students outside the chain-link fence at Del Norte High School, adjacent to school property, and, suspecting them of being out of status, turned them over to the Border Patrol.[88] In federal court, the students filed *Gonzalez v.*

Albuquerque Public Schools, contending that Albuquerque Public School administrators, officers of the Albuquerque Police Department, and a Border Patrol agent violated the students' constitutional rights, including the right to a public education, when the boys were seized, interrogated, searched, and ultimately turned over to the Border Patrol.[89] The children were sent back to Mexico, although they were allowed to return to New Mexico to testify in the legal proceedings.[90]

In July 2006, all the claims against the school-district defendants were dropped as a result of a settlement,[91] which provided that the school district would implement new procedures and directives and conduct additional training of its personnel regarding the right of immigrant students to attend school, would provide a district liaison for immigrant parents, and would launch a public information campaign for immigrant parents to assure them that the district would not deny immigrant students an education.[92] The school-district defendants paid damages and attorneys' fees. By 2008, the City of Albuquerque and the Albuquerque Police Department had settled, and the action against them was resolved for the damages and fees.

In both the El Paso and Albuquerque cases, there had not been clear immigration-enforcement guidelines in place, even though there had been a recent case in El Paso, of which the INS authorities swore they were unaware.[93] For schools districts located in states along the U.S.-Mexico border, it is conceivable and foreseeable that there will be undocumented immigration, and school districts would do well to have model plans in place, both to regulate immigration enforcement and schools and to guide local police authorities. For example, there was evidence that the city's police officers would call in immigration authorities whenever there was a need for translation services or when persons apprehended could not converse in what was considered acceptable English.[94] At the time the children in Albuquerque were apprehended, they were students at the school, and their presence on the school grounds broke no civil law; there was no reason to have apprehended them and turned them over to anyone other than their parents or school authorities, except for their inchoate undocumented status, which police authorities are not in a position to presume or determine. Simply having stereotypical "Mexican" features in a state as Mexican dominant as New Mexico or even in rural Idaho or Vermont cannot be an articulable reason for police authorities to apprehend students in or near a school, "solely because of their mere immutable appearances as Hispanics."[95]

In 2006, several new *Plyler* threats arose at the school level, both of which ultimately resolved themselves; but they revealed the complexities generally associated with noncitizen enrollments. In March 2006, the school board in Elmwood Park, Illinois, refused to let an undocumented student enroll, on the grounds that she and her family had entered on B-2 tourist visas, long expired.[96] The State Board of Education threatened to remove funds, and the local board blinked, revising its attendance policies.[97] Even though persons can become undocumented either by surreptitious entry or by violating the terms of legal entry, no earlier decisions had turned on the means by which the original unauthorized status or entry had been effected; cases turned on undocumented status, not on exactly how the alien had entered the country or the particular state. As in so many of the immigration-related cases, the Elmwood Park case turned on complex technical immigration categories. It is necessary for schools to recognize that these categories can be fluid and confusing and that many noncitizen families are mixed, including some members who might be citizens or have permission to be in the country, while others might have entered surreptitiously or entered with proper permission, only to run afoul of visa requirements, intentionally or unintentionally. At the time of *Plyler*, immigration legal expertise might not have been widespread, but in recent times, such expertise is much more widely available and accessible. There is simply no reason why school districts must, through action or inaction, make mistakes concerning the immigration status of schoolchildren or parents. Nor is there a likely or adequate reason to act on these assumptions.

In the *Joel R.* case, cited earlier for purposes of discussion on the technical issue of documentation, the state appeals court held, for purposes of determining residency,

> Applying the law to the facts of the instant case, we find the circuit court did not err. First, it is uncontroverted that Joel lives indefinitely on a full-time basis with [his relative]. Second, it is also clear that [she] exercises complete control over Joel and is fully responsible for his care to the exclusion of Joel's parents who reside in another country. Third, [she] is Joel's legal guardian. Fourth, there was ample evidence of other non-educational factors being a part of the reason Joel moved to Melrose Park: the abject poverty and lack of social and economic opportunities he faced in Mexico; the desire to learn more about the country of his birth; and the need to eventually aid his parents financially. All of these factors support the circuit court's legal conclusion that Joel was a bona fide resident of District 83 and that his move to the district was not solely for educational purposes. Thus, we find no error in the circuit court's decision. In closing, we note

that defendants argued before the circuit court and this court that a deferential policy of experto credite should be adopted with regard to residency determinations made by school districts. To this end, defendants attempt, without citation to any relevant authority, to analogize school disciplinary cases, where courts have correctly afforded deference to a school's decision, to residency determinations. We find this argument to be wholly without merit and completely unsupported by the case law.[98]

Since losing this case, Illinois has been required to train its educators about such residency-requirement determinations, and it has posted these requirements online and made them publicly available.[99]

In 1996, Congress acted to eliminate the ability of parents to "helicopter" their children into school districts by simply sending them to live with other families, such as informal or even formal sponsors or noncustodial relatives.[100] These students are ineligible for F-1 nonimmigrant status on their own and may not attend a public school for more than a year and must pay the actual full cost of instruction for any such period of attendance.[101] The provision does not affect private schools, although it could affect charter schools and other private schools that are established and funded by public appropriations. Although this provision was enacted to keep more advantaged foreign families from sending their children abroad at the U.S. school's expense, this provision has been interpreted by some public school districts as affecting undocumented-student attendance.[102] Other corollary rulings concerning residency and domicile have also affected this issue, as in Elmwood Park, and the overall complexity has occasionally caught undocumented students in the snare.

In 2006, in Austin, Texas, hundreds of miles away from the Mexican border, there was mixed evidence that Immigration and Customs Enforcement (ICE) authorities were targeting schools and coming onto school grounds to apprehend children whose parents were arrested on the suspicion of being in the country without authorization.[103] School officials felt that they had to notify parents that such ICE actions would take place, so they sent out notices, warning, "Tell the students they are safe. That they have rights to not answer questions and to request to speak to attorney [sic] if they are picked up. . . . Some parents have come and withdrawn their children (students) today. We can't stop a lawful investigation, but we can certainly inquire as to their credentials and to the existence of a lawful investigation. We must also abide by any court orders, such as warrants, they present."[104] Of course, given such a notice, undocumented parents might withdraw their children out of a simple, undifferentiated fear of apprehension concerning their families. Such a situation places school districts in a similar conundrum: do they inform parents about any such pending acts by immigration authorities, knowing how parents might reasonably react, or do they not inform parents, on the chance that immigration authorities will only come onto a campus in the event a parent has been apprehended and ICE needs to notify and secure the children as well?

To observers who are familiar with the El Paso, Elmwood Park, and Albuquerque incidents, as well as other such occasions, it is not an idle or unreasonable fear on the part of undocumented adults, whose worst nightmares include not only their own arrest or apprehension but also being separated from their children. And schools have an obligation to communicate with parents, particularly parents who would be at risk, so this information is being disseminated out of a sense of duty and professional responsibility, the way that a school would notify parents of a new vaccination requirement or school functions or other such routine announcements. If school officials act badly and raise false specters or cry wolf in order not to have to deal with these children, which certainly can happen, that is one thing and is unforgivable. As taxpaying parents with legal obligations to place their children in schools, even undocumented parents deserve respect and consideration, the same as would any more advantaged parent. But it is clear that school-community relations have to be treated and conducted differently when the parents are undocumented and likely non-English-speaking, poor, and poorly educated. And this will be all the more true when parents are arrested en route to pick up their children, with ICE using the children as bait.

In Florida, a similar example of a nonimmigrant student surfaced, and while the case was correctly decided, it revealed the difficulty in determining the residency and domicile of persons who are not citizens or permanent residents. In this instance, it was a high school student who was the son of a treaty trader (a person with permission to engage in commerce under the terms of a treaty to which the United States is party), an E-2 nonimmigrant.[105]

Indirect Challenges: The Implementation of Plyler v. Doe

The evidence marshaled thus far has examined only the direct challenges to *Plyler*'s continued vitality and has indicated that the holding is alive and well. But the last direct challenge at the state level was in 1996–1997's *LULAC v. Wilson* holding in the challenge to California's Proposition 187,[106] and the last serious federal challenge was the ill-fated 1996 Gallegly Amendment, which was traded away by its supporters in exchange for restricting alien benefits and tightening up refugee and immigration provisions generally.[107] Viewed in this sense, there has not been a direct assault on *Plyler* since these attempts failed well over a decade ago. Even some conservative Republican senators were not willing to enlist in this effort—despite the issue's being contained in the national party's presidential platform[108]—and states appear to have resigned themselves to the policies derived from the case and to have found ways to accommodate the children. As additional evidence of acceptance, almost all the major receiver states and even other states have extended the reach of the case to the benefit of undocumented college students, permitted by the same 1996 legislation to which Representative Gallegly was trying to attach his restrictions.[109]

But the real contests have shifted to the more quotidian, everyday school level. In a variety of areas, it is the daily implementation of *Plyler* by school boards and school districts that poses the more potent threat, not only because this is the level at which individual children and families experience the policies but also because the national immigrants'-rights groups and advocates form networks that guard against state and federal predations and cannot always monitor or frame the issues at local flashpoints. When undocumented parents in Austin, Texas, pull their citizen children out of their school due to perceptions that school raids will be forthcoming, it is clear that *Plyler* as implemented requires constant monitoring and attention; when the parents are apprehended on a school stakeout or when parents are arrested when bringing their children to schools, as happened in Santa Fe, New Mexico, and in Detroit Michigan, the undocumented parents will have even more reasonable fears.[110]

Here, I consider a number of these local issues, including a sampler to show the many that have arisen: general issues of language instruction, building and zoning policies, publicity that arises when students do exceptionally well and draw attention to themselves, involvement in extracurricular programs, housing and local ordinances, separate schools and racial isolation, and miscellaneous practices that will disproportionately affect undocumented school children and their parents.

A number of states have availed themselves of federal funds to provide English-language instruction to immigrant and linguistic-minority children. As one example, in *Burgos v. Illinois Department of Children and Family Services*,[111] the Legal Assistance Foundation (LAF) filed suit against the Illinois Department of Children and Family Services (IDCFS) in 1975, well before *Plyler*. As a result of the suit, the parties entered into a settlement agreement to ensure that Spanish-speaking families are provided full and adequate services by IDCFS. The decree ordered IDCFS and its vendors to provide child-welfare services in Spanish to Latino clients whose primary language is Spanish, required children with Spanish-speaking parents to be placed with Spanish-speaking foster parents, and required individual or general written communications to Spanish-speaking clients to be in Spanish. In 1996, MAL-DEF assumed legal representation for plaintiffs because LAF could no longer handle class actions. A court-appointed monitor issued a report in 1997 and later became the implementation consultant. In 2006, MALDEF met with members of the community to address recent reports that IDCFS may not be in compliance with the consent decree. On July 13, 2006, MALDEF met with the Cook County public guardian regarding potential *Burgos* violations. On July 27, 2006, legislative public hearings were held on the *Burgos* consent decree, and discussions have continued to determine whether or not a federal monitor should be reappointed.[112]

It is not unusual for such systemic bilingual-education litigation to stretch out over many years, such as the 1974 *Aspira* consent decree between the New York City Board of Education and Aspira of New York, which established bilingual instruction as a legally enforceable federal entitlement for New York City's non-English-speaking Puerto Rican and Latino students.[113] The decree is still in place, although the governance landscape has changed considerably in the thirty-plus years, such as the mayor's office taking over direct supervision of the New York City schools.[114]

Some of these complex cases include other program features as well, such as teacher transfer, magnet programs, and racial assignments, as in the case of *American Civil Rights Foundation v. Los Angeles Unified School District*, a 2006 case that is still wending its way through the system.[115] In *Consortium for Adequate School Funding in Georgia, Inc. v. State of Georgia*, language courses and funding issues are at the heart of this case involving English for speakers of other languages (ESOL) students.[116] There are literally dozens of such cases in various stages of litigation in school districts across the country.[117]

Sometimes undocumented students surface when they have had extraordinary academic success. Highly publicized cases include one in which four students from Hayden High School in Phoenix went to the Niagara Falls area for a class trip, after they won a prestigious national robotics competition.[118] They were arrested as they crossed into Canada and returned with their class, and because Arizona no longer accords in-state tuition to undocumented college students, they have not been eligible to attend college in the state as residents. Another undocumented robotics student, this one from Senegal, was able to remain in the United States, due to enormous legal and politic pressure exerted on his behalf; in 2006, an undocumented Dominican student who had graduated with honors from Princeton surfaced when he won a scholarship to Oxford University, and others have surfaced as well, including extremely successful graduates.[119] When the 2010 DREAM Act did not clear the cloture hurdle, hundreds of potential DREAM Act undocumented would-be beneficiaries began to out themselves, in a courageous but dangerous fashion, bringing attention to them and their families in an attempt to draw attention to their plight; a number of favorable editorials appeared as well, although the effort eventually ended in bitter congressional politics—some of which was over immigration generally but which more likely involved the extreme power struggles between the political parties.[120]

One of the more remarkable developments is how Texas has been transformed by immigration a quarter century after *Plyler*. With rare exceptions, most of them along the Mexican border, virtually all the state's school districts have accommodated undocumented students or at least have not openly opposed their enrollments. Surely some of this is due to the rising electoral representation of Mexican American legislators and others who see no reason to oppose this development or to defy the Court's ruling; with a school-finance system that funds students on a complex formula that counts heads, some legislators have determined that it is foolish to vote against the fiscal interests of their constituents. Even Superintendent Plyler, long retired from the Tyler schools, has recanted his earlier opposition to the enrollment of the children.[121]

But it is all the more notable that only one Texas jurisdiction has engaged in enacting restrictionist local ordinances and that there has been no traction for any such statewide legislation. In Farmers Branch, Texas, city legislators have been the only officials to step up and single out undocumented renters and other residents. In this vein, they attempted to zero out city funding for a "Summer Funshine" child-care program, designed to keep young children from affiliating with gangs, because they suspected that some undocumented children were participating. The program, which serves 350 students each summer, has 110 places targeted for low-income children, whose families pay less for the program in conjunction with eligibility for federal free and reduced lunches.[122] In 2006, Farmers Branch, a rural suburb near Dallas, was the first local jurisdiction in Texas to have passed comprehensive immigration-reform provisions at the local level, which immediately were enjoined by the courts, and in 2010, four years later, the federal judge permanently enjoined the ordinance, bringing to a close the litigation.[123]

Plyler is essentially about residency requirements and who gets to go to school in what attendance zone. In the year after *Plyler*, the U.S. Supreme Court decided a companion case, *Martinez v. Bynum*, and held that parents or guardians of undocumented children (or for that matter, their citizen children) were required to reside in a school-district attendance zone. This was not a significant narrowing of *Plyler*, in which the Tyler and Houston and other parents had actually lived in the school districts in which their children attended, albeit in unauthorized status. The student in *Martinez* was a citizen child whose undocumented parents had left the country and left him the care of his adult sister, who was not his legal guardian.[124] The Court in *Martinez* sustained the State's determination that the child did not reside in the district and thus did not qualify for free public schooling there, ruling that *Plyler* did not bar application of an appropriately defined bona fide residence test.

There is growing evidence that this issue, long dormant, will rear its head, as a small number of U.S.-Mexico-border school districts have begun to police enrollments to ensure that the families are actually residing in the school boundaries, rather than sending their children into the schools from across the bridges that span the two countries. There is a small wedge between *Plyler* and *Bynum v. Martinez*, which would allow genuinely resident, albeit undocumented, or even mixed-nationality families to live in the district but would not protect similar children who do not live with their families in the district attendance zones or who are not fully or properly authorized to reside with families who do reside in the school zones.[125] The *Plyler* case had indicated that the undocumented may establish domicile in the country, a much larger issue than that presented in *Martinez*, in which the child's parents had not established the requisite residence in the school district.[126] This holding also loops back to *Joel R. v. Mannheim Middle School District*, the 1997 Illinois state court case mentioned earlier, in which school authorities would not recognize the custody assertions in a matter of an undocumented child.[127] Given the financial pressures that many border school districts find themselves in, school officials and local elected officials may feel that they can move against enrolling the children without risking electoral disapproval or bad press, especially should the issue become justified by or entwined with increased border-immigration security, the safety of the children, and the smoldering drug-interdiction violence and general militarization of the international border.

The Houston Independent School District, where one of the strands of *Plyler* arose, has begun a high school that concentrates on immigrant students, in order to provide them with the additional counseling and services they need to navigate school.[128] In 2000, the Urban Institute published a comprehensive review of the issue, *Overlooked and Underserved: Immigrant Students in U.S. Secondary Schools*, which investigated several such sites and reached very critical conclusions about the lack of coordination among schools, the poor achievement of these students, and the structural problems that school districts face in educating such large numbers of immigrant children who have not progressed and who are non-English-speakers.[129] Other reports have found similar massive problems; other school districts have also tried unusual means to reach and educate these children.[130]

Working in this field for many years has exposed me to a number of unusual problems, ones that I believe are sui generis with the undocumented. When I was recruiting agricultural-migrant students many years ago in Ohio, where I was first exposed to the issue, I recall migrant fathers holding me personally accountable after I had recruited their daughters to college, for their safety and security; I have had to bail out migrants whose cars attracted the attention of police and the immigration services, my first acquaintance with "driving while Mexican."[131] I have marveled at children who knew exactly how to calculate proper pesticide applications or do the arithmetic with gas money and mileage distances, even when they would likely fail traditional chemistry or math classes. Once, near my home in Houston, Texas, I saw two cars that obviously had just had a crash and were steaming wrecks, with no one sticking around; clearly, the owners would have rather abandoned their precious property than expose themselves to police authorities. In Santa Fe, New Mexico, an undocumented woman was unable to get a school parking permit due to the state's policy on driver's licenses, so she could not use her car to get to school.[132] Many of the various stories recounted here show the resilience and tenacity of these students.[133]

Conclusion: Plyler's Reach

In this chapter, I examined the direct and indirect challenges to *Plyler*, noting that many educators and legislators have accepted the original premise of the case, that innocent children should not be scapegoated for the actions of their parents, especially when the families are likely to join the community and remain. While the original case has proven quite supple, fending off litigation and federal and state legislative efforts to overturn it, and nurturing efforts to extend its reach to college attendees who were allowed to stay in school by the original case, it has had to be reinforced by vigilant efforts, and has proven sturdier than when it first appeared. Restrictionists have redirected their efforts, confronting birthright citizenship and focusing on the elimination of undocumented parents and unauthorized workers, rather than continuing their efforts at overturning *Plyler*. The many state efforts at regulating immigration have had the collateral effect of disrupting families and in a large number of cases have led to immigrant families being deported, even including the citizen children.[134] But the threats to the case remain and will likely increase until national politics enable a comprehensive resolution. There has also been a demonstrable rise in actual border enforcement, which spills over into educational access and transporting the children to schools where their families reside.

In all likelihood, at some point comprehensive immigration reform will occur and should alleviate some of these problems, particularly providing a form of legalization and extending some benefits. But parents and their children will keep coming, drawn by the possibilities of work and improving their lives. Such immigration reform will undoubtedly be a contentious and uncertain project, but until it occurs, these issues will continue to fester and will drive the practices even deeper, to become even more hidden in plain sight.

4

The Political Economy
of the DREAM Act and
the Legislative Process

Doe Goes to College

It looks like the long court saga against the Wilson Four is over.

A federal immigration appeals board on Nov. 29 concluded that the former Wilson Charter High School students in Phoenix had been wrongly targeted by immigration officials at the Canadian border because of their Hispanic appearance. As a result, a federal immigration judge in July 2005 was right to throw out the deportation cases against them, the board concluded in a statement rejecting the government's appeal.

Judy Flanagan, the students' lawyer, said Monday that she hopes the ruling puts an end to the case once and for all. "It's been four years now. It would be nice for it to end," she said. . . .

In June 2002, the students traveled to upstate New York to participate in a solar-powered boat competition. During a side trip to Niagara Falls, immigration officials at the Canadian border interrogated the students for nine hours and, after determining they were in the country illegally, began deportation proceedings. . . .

Although the so-called Wilson Four—Luis Nava, Jaime Damian, Yuliana Huicochea, and Oscar Corona—no longer have to worry about deportation, they face limited futures because they still don't have legal status, Flanagan said.

All four remain in the Phoenix area. Nava is completing a second bachelor's degree at Arizona State University, Damian is the father of twins, Corona has petitioned for a visa through his U.S. citizen wife. Huicochea is an advocate for undocumented students.[1]

Many developments have kept the Development, Relief, and Education for Alien Minors (DREAM) Act and the issue of undocumented college students in the news and on federal and state legislative agendas. Who would have thought that presidential candidates would be debating the issue, as they did in the Republican primaries of 2007 and 2008? Especially coming on the heels of a near miss months earlier, when the bill almost passed in the Senate, the topic is one that has all the earmarks of an agenda-building subject, situated in the complex and treacherous context of 21st-century U.S. domestic politics, especially those of comprehensive immigration reform. Inasmuch as this subset of much larger immigration, higher-education, and tuition policies commands recurrent attention, DREAM Act politics is a useful bellwether for observers of these domains.

This chapter builds on and amplifies several earlier studies of the DREAM Act and the general topic of undocumented college residency and, to a great extent, reveals the difficulty inherent in conducting research on pending legislation, especially one that is so fluid and so embedded in a larger, systemic regime. The first section includes the background for the DREAM Act, at the state and federal levels. I review the extensive litigation and legal developments, as well as the several state DREAM acts and other related issues concerning college residency and tuition. The second section reviews the federal DREAM Act and its failure to gain traction in its failed 2007 and 2010 U.S. Senate votes. The third section considers the politics of immigration reform that is the backdrop for these developments, and the conclusion assesses the prospects for enactment of the legislation, either as a standalone statute or, more likely, as one of many components in the larger comprehensive immigration-reform efforts. Considering how small this population of undocumented college students is in the larger scheme of things, never more than fifty thousand or sixty thousand by any estimates,[2] this extensive state and national legislative history reveals a surprising degree of attention in the polity and within U.S. legislative arenas. Nonetheless, as federal policy, it has not been able to stand on its own legs, and the odds have grown longer against its eventual enactment as a separate legislative program.

The DREAM Act

Litigation, Legal Developments

The first version of what became the DREAM Act was introduced into Congress in 2001, and many observers thought it would be easily enacted into law. But it did not enter the world naked. There had been many news stories about successful college students whose parents had brought them to the United States as children, who either entered without inspection or entered legally and then overstayed a visa or did one of the many things that can render a family out of status.[3] These children were able to stay in school by virtue of *Plyler v. Doe*, the 1982 Supreme Court case that struck down restrictive Texas laws that would have allowed school districts to charge tuition or to ban the students outright from the public schools.[4] Over the many years since *Plyler*, school districts have accommodated the children, who, against all odds, were graduating and applying to colleges and universities.

When their numbers began to grow and attention was paid, some public higher-education institutions and states began to impose or employ residency restrictions that precluded them from achieving domiciliary-based residency tuition, in effect creating a reprise of *Plyler* in postsecondary guise, or to charge them tuition rates as if they were international students without visas.[5] Other states and institutions allowed the students to establish residency and to pay the lower, in-state tuition; private institutions, which traditionally do not charge tuition based on state residency criteria, either allowed them to enroll or held that they could not do so, on the grounds that to do so would implicate their standing to issue I-20 visa documents, such as those employed by traditional F-1 or M-1 international students.[6] Given these students' many educational disadvantages, their ineligibility to receive most state aid and any federal financial assistance, and their inability to work while in school, it was a small number of students for whom this was even an issue.

Then, lightning struck with Proposition 187, California's 1994 ballot initiative designed to eliminate virtually all state benefits to undocumented immigrants.[7] This draconian measure, which was passed overwhelmingly by the state's electorate, would have stripped undocumented aliens of all but the most essential health and emergency medical services, would have overruled *Plyler* and denied educational benefits to undocumented children, and would have required public officials to report aliens thought to be undocumented to police and security authorities.[8] Almost immediately, declaratory and injunctive relief was granted by federal courts, and ultimately, almost all of Proposition 187's provisions were struck down by courts, although the bar on postsecondary residency was upheld.[9] By the mid-1990s, a number of states had also challenged what they considered failed federal immigration-enforcement policy and sought additional federal resources. Six of the major receiver states brought such suits, although all were eventually unsuccessful.[10]

At the same time, California Congressman Elton Gallegly (R-CA) intro-duced federal legislation to overturn *Plyler*, and while the "Gallegly Amend-ment" was unsuccessful,[11] the switch to a Republican-controlled Congress in 1995 resulted in two major 1996 laws restricting immigration and the status of immigrants: the Personal Responsibility and Work Opportunity Recon-ciliation Act of 1996 (PRWORA) and the Illegal Immigration Reform and Immigrant Responsibility Act of 1996 (IIRIRA).[12] These omnibus laws dra-matically changed the landscape, affecting federal benefits or status in many areas of health and welfare, including the requirement that if a state wished to accord resident tuition to the undocumented, it must do so "only through the enactment of a State law after August 22, 1996, which affirmatively pro-vides for such eligibility."[13] The enactment of these federal statutes led the judge in the challenge to Proposition 187 to determine that the federal gov-ernment had preempted state actions, expressing the "intention of Congress to occupy the field of regulation of government benefits to aliens."[14] When the State of California appealed this decision, the newly elected governor, Gray Davis, invoked the Ninth Circuit's special arbitration and mediation provision, which resulted in a July 1999 settlement.[15] This had the effect of undocumented California students' not being accorded resident tuition.

In 2001, Texas passed the first statute to accord the state-resident tuition allowed by IIRIRA and PRWORA, "affirmatively provid[ing] for such eligi-bility."[16] The same year, on September 11, the world fundamentally changed, and any immediate hopes for immigration reform were absorbed into the war on terrorism and the resultant overwhelming national-security con-cerns.[17] Even so, federal legislation was introduced in 2001, giving the DREAM Act its acronym.

Other states followed the lead of Texas, and through 2011, thirteen states had allowed undocumented students to establish residency and pay in-state tuition, including Maryland in 2011; one additional state (Wisconsin) had granted this status and then rescinded it; South Carolina voted to ban the undocumented from attending its public colleges; and other states allow them to enroll but charged them nonresident tuition.[18] Given these students' ineligibility to secure lawful employment, they do not qualify for jobs in col-lege or after graduation. As a general rule, they may not be licensed or gain authorization for skilled professions such as teaching, law, or medical fields.[19] As is evident from the narratives that follow, this is highly contested terrain, surprisingly so, especially considering how few such students there are in the context of over eighteen million college students. No estimates exceed fifty thousand to sixty thousand students nationally,[20] which would constitute the

TABLE 1.

State Legislation Allowing Undocumented
College Students to Establish Residency, 2011 (by Statute)

Texas, H.B. 1403, 77th Leg., Reg. Sess. (Tex. 2001) [amended by S.B. 1528, 79th Leg.,
   Reg. Sess. (Tex. 2005), relating to student financial aid]; TEX. EDUC. CODE ANN.
   § 54.052

California, A.B. 540, 2001-02 Cal. Sess. (Cal. 2001); CAL. EDUC. CODE §68130.5 [A.B.
   30 (2011), amending CAL. EDUC. CODE §68130.7 and   adding §66021.7, relating
   to student financial aid]

Utah, H.B. 144, 54th Leg., Gen. Sess. (Utah 2002); UTAH CODE ANN. § 53B-8-106

New York, S. B. 7784, 225th Leg., 2001 NY Sess. (NY 2002); N.Y. EDUC. LAW §355(2)
   (h)(8)

Washington, H.B. 1079, 58th Leg., Reg. Sess. (Wash. 2003); WASH. REV. CODE ANN
   § 28B. 15.012

Oklahoma, S.B. 596, 49th Leg., 1st Reg. Sess. (OK 2003) [financial assistance provisions
   rescinded, Oklahoma Taxpayer and Citizen Protection Act of 2007 (H.B. 1804)];
   OKLA. STAT.ANN.TIT. 70, § 3242

Illinois, H.B. 60, 93rd Gen. Assemb., Reg. Sess. (Ill. 2003); 110 ILL. COMP. STAT.
   ANN. [amended by S.B. 2085, 97th Gen. Assemb., Reg. Sess. (Ill. 2011); 110 ILL.
   COMP. STAT. ANN.]

Kansas, H.B. 2145, 2003-2004 Leg., Reg. Sess. (KS 2004); K.S.A. §76-731a

New Mexico, S.B. 582, 47th Leg. Reg. Sess. (2005); N.M.STAT. ANN. §21-1-1.

Nebraska, L.B. 239, 99th Leg. 1st Sess. (Neb. 2006); NEB REV. STAT. ANN. § 85-502

Wisconsin, 2009 Assembly Bill 75 (2009 WISCONSIN ACT 28); WIS. STAT. § 36.27
   [repealed by AB 40, June 26, 2011]

Maryland, S.B. 167, 2011 Leg., Reg. Sess. (Md. 2011); MD. CODE ANN. § 15-106.8 ["sus-
   pended," pending state referendum: MD Const. XVI, Sec. 2]

Connecticut, H.B. 6390, 2011 Leg., Reg. Sess. (Conn. 2011); CONN. GEN. STAT. § 10a-29

Source: http://www.law.uh.edu/ihelg/documents/Statute2011.pdf [current as of August 1, 2011]

entire enrollment at the main Columbus campus of The Ohio State University. In order to clear up the confusion on the issue, and to provide a path to
legalization for the affected students after their graduation, the DREAM Act
was introduced in 2001, in essentially its present form.

In 2005, the Washington Legal Foundation (WLF) filed a complaint with
the Department of Homeland Security (DHS) to challenge the Texas and
New York statutes, although it is not entirely clear why this agency would
have jurisdiction over these sections of IIRIRA. As of spring 2011 no action
had been taken on this matter by DHS, and discussions with attorneys and
officials involved indicated that there would be no action forthcoming.[21]

Indeed, the answer was provided in a response to a different question, one posed by North Carolina officials about their own admissions policies. In July 2008, the Department of Homeland Security wrote that any determinations of tuition residency or admissions policy by states were state matters, not in the federal domain: "[T]he individual states must decide for themselves whether or not to admit illegal aliens into their public post-secondary institutions. States may bar or admit illegal aliens from [*sic*] enrolling in public post-secondary institutions either as a matter of public policy or through legislation. Please note, however, that any state policy or legislation on this issue must use federal immigration status standards to identify which applicants are illegal aliens. In the absence of any state policy or legislation addressing this issue, it is up to the schools to decide whether or not to enroll illegal aliens, and the schools must similarly use federal immigration status standards to identify illegal alien applicants."[22] This would be the appropriate response to the WLF complaint as well, for state tuition and admissions policies have always been state issues, and it is surprising that a state entity would pose such a question, implicitly suggesting that the determination of a state status might turn on a federal determination; one wonders what the North Carolina response would have been had the federal department responded that the federal government actually would assert jurisdiction over the matter.

In *Day v. Sibelius*, lawyers challenged the Kansas statute that allowed undocumented college students to establish residency status for tuition.[23] The judge ruled for the state, finding that the plaintiffs did not have standing to bring suit.[24] The Federation for American Immigration Reform (FAIR) filed an appeal to the court of appeals, and on August 30, 2007, the Tenth Circuit affirmed the trial court decision in the case.[25] The United State Supreme Court denied the petition for certiorari, which had the result of upholding the statute.[26]

In December 2005, the same groups that filed the Kansas matter filed in California state court, *Martinez et al. v Regents of the University of California*, challenging AB 540, the California residency statute on a parallel track, and hoping to knock the practice out at both the federal and state levels. In October 2006, FAIR's attempt to bring the Kansas federal case to a California state court lost, when the trial judge ruled against it.[27] However, in fall 2008, an appeals court overturned the decision, ordered the matter back to trial, and found against the state.[28] In fall 2010, the state and university positions were upheld when the California Supreme Court overruled the state appeals court's ruling.[29]

In another higher-education immigration-residency case that occurred in California during this time period, a number of immigrant organizations filed suit in November 2006, bringing a challenge to state postsecondary-residency and financial-aid provisions in California: *Student Advocates for Higher Education et al. v Trustees, California State University et al.*[30] Citizen students with undocumented parents were being prevented from receiving the tuition and financial-aid benefits due them, at least in part because the California statute is not precisely drawn (or was being imperfectly administered). In addition, there is interaction among several overlapping features of the system: immigration, financial aid's independence of or dependence on parents, and the age of majority/domicile. The State agreed to discontinue the practice and entered into a consent decree, so the matter was resolved in favor of the plaintiffs. The order overturned California State University's odd take on undocumented-college-student residency—that if a citizen, majority-age college student had undocumented parents, he or she was not able to take advantage of the California statute according the undocumented in-state residence, even if the student were otherwise eligible. In a similar fashion, the Virginia attorney general and the Colorado attorney general also ruled that U.S.-citizen children could establish tuition-residency status on a case-by-case basis, even if their parents were undocumented.[31] These rulings made a virtue of necessity, inasmuch as citizen children who reach the age of majority by operation of law establish their own domicile, so that their parents' undocumented status is irrelevant to the ability of the children to demonstrate residency.

The DREAM Act in Congress and Federal Developments

Against this backdrop of considerable state activity, the federal stage was also active, following the introduction of the DREAM Act in 2001; in both 2003 and in 2005, the DREAM Act was reintroduced in Congress, and in 2004, Senate Judicial Committee hearings were held.[32] The bill languished there until comprehensive immigration-reform efforts failed in summer 2007. In July 2007, the Senate tried a different legislative approach and developed plans to attach the legislation to the Department of Defense authorization bill, but U.S. Senate majority leader Harry Reid (D-NV) pulled it from the floor when an Iraq-timetable amendment failed; as a result, the Senate never got to the DREAM vote.[33] The Department of Defense authorization bill was scheduled to return to the Senate floor in September 2007; however, in late fall 2007, there had been no additional movement on the proposal. The House Judiciary Committee held a DREAM Act hearing on May 18, 2007.[34] On September 6, 2007, the House held subcommittee hearings on the STRIVE Act, the comprehensive House immigration legislation that contained, among other provisions, post-secondary tuition and other features of the DREAM Act. In one last attempt

TABLE 2.
DREAM Act Congressional Legislative History

107th Congress *(2001–2002)*	S. 1291, DREAM Act of 2001 H.R. 1918, Student Adjustment Act of 2001
108th Congress *(2003–2004)*	S. 1545, DREAM Act of 2003 H.R. 1684, Student Adjustment Act of 2003
109th Congress *(2005–2006)*	S. 2075, DREAM Act of 2005 H.R. 5131, American Dream Act of 2006 S. 2611, Comprehensive Immigration Reform Act of 2006
110th Congress *(2007–2008)*	S. 1348, Comprehensive Immigration Reform Act of 2007 S. 774, A bill to amend the Illegal Immigration Reform and Immigrant Responsibility Act of 1996 to permit States to determine State residency for higher education purposes and to authorize the cancellation of removal and adjustment of status of certain alien students who are long-term United States residents and who entered the United States as children, and for other purposes H.R. 1221, To provide for cancellation of removal and adjustment of status for certain long-term residents who entered the United States as children H.R.1275, To amend the Illegal Immigration Reform and Immigrant Responsibility Act of 1996 to permit States to determine State residency for higher education purposes and to authorize the cancellation of removal and adjustment of status of certain alien students who are long-term United States residents and who entered the United States as children, and for other purposes S. 2205, A bill to authorize the cancellation of removal and adjustment of status of certain alien students who are long-term United States residents and who entered the United States as children, and for other purposes (voted on, 44–52, October 24, 2007) S. 2919, Department of Defense Authorization Bill (originated in House) H.R. 4986, Department of Defense Authorization Bill
111th Congress *(2009–2010)*	S. 729, DREAM Act of 2009 H.R. 1751, DREAM Act of 2009 S. 3827, DREAM Act of 2010

TABLE 2 *(continued)*
DREAM Act Congressional Legislative History

111th Congress *(continued)*	S. 3454, National Defense Authorization Act for FY 2011 (voted on, 43–56, September 21, 2010) S. 3932, Comprehensive Immigration Reform Act of 2010 S. 2992, DREAM Act of 2010 (introduced in 2010 lame-duck session) H.R. 5281, the Removal Clarification Act of 2010, amended by DREAM Act, H.R. 6497 (approved, 216–198, December 8, 2010) S. 3992, DREAM Act of 2010 (voted on, 59–40, to withdraw S. 3992 and vote on the Motion to Invoke Cloture on the Motion to Concur in the House Amendment to the Senate Amendment No. 3 to H.R. 5281; voted on, 41–55, December 18, 2010)
112th Congress *(2011–)*	H.R. 1842, Development, Relief, and Education for Alien Minors Act of 2011 S. 6, Reform America's Broken Immigration System Act S. 952, Development, Relief and Education for Minors (DREAM) Act of 2011 [Senate Hearing, June 28, 2011] S. 1258, Comprehensive Immigration Reform Act of 2011

in the session to enact legislation to address the status of the college students, on October 24, 2007, the Senate considered and voted down the stand-alone DREAM Act, 44–52, on the cloture motion; three years later, a similar cloture vote was defeated, when on September 21, 2010, the DREAM Act (S. 3454, the National Defense Authorization Act for Fiscal Year 2011) was defeated 43–56, with one senator not voting. Senator Reid voted no, so as to reserve the parliamentary right to call for a reconsideration in the same session, which he did by introducing the legislation during the lame-duck session in December 2010, after Democrats lost control of the House and kept a thin majority in the Senate. Not even one Republican senator voted for the legislation, even those who had supported and introduced it earlier; in a final gasp, on December 18, 2010, the Senate failed to overcome the cloture motion, and it failed a second time, effectively ending the matter.[35]

In addition, there were developments in other immigration categories, such as college developments for victims of human trafficking (T nonimmigrant visas).[36] And, as noted, the DHS in 2008 acted to situate the responsibility for state status as a state decision.[37] Even as the DREAM Act languished in Congress, dozens of national news stories, several small chapbooks on the subject, and many national studies drew attention to the issue, including reports by the Heritage Foundation in support of Kris W. Kobach's California state court litigation on in-state-tuition residency.[38] The Congressional Research Service published studies on the subject.[39] National professional associations have drawn attention to the issue, such as the National Association of College Admissions Counselors, making the DREAM Act an organizational priority.[40] The College Board also made it a priority, and in 2009 the board released a comprehensive report, drawing press attention.[41] The national and trade press regularly covered the subject, especially in 2010, before and after the congressional votes on versions of the legislation.[42]

Another national barometer of interest in this larger issue is the scorecard of how many legislatures have considered legislation on immigration-related issues. The National Conference of State Legislatures (NCSL) issued a report detailing the state-level immigration legislation in the first six months of 2009: more than fourteen hundred bills were considered in all fifty states.[43] Perhaps by definition, state legislators and their organizations are very conservative, as evident by the extraordinary data evident in the regular NCSL tabulations. But in an interesting overlap with liberal and progressive observers, the NCSL has taken the official position that federal law preempts state and local law immigration-enforcement efforts: "NCSL holds firmly that states do not have 'inherent authority' to enforce federal civil immigration law. We also oppose efforts to perpetuate this myth of 'inherent authority' indirectly by shifting federal responsibility of immigration enforcement to state and local law officers through the criminalization of any violation of federal immigration law."[44]

The Politics of Immigration Reform

Political scientists Benjamin Márquez and John Witte have written an exceptionally useful paper that maps out what they consider the varying and kaleidoscopic legislative strategies in recent immigration-reform efforts.[45] They grapple with the key issue in negotiating the complex and interlocking facets: whether to enact piecemeal statutes in the hope that varying coalitions will have different alignments in any complex regime, or to attempt a comprehensive solution that has many moving parts. They perceptively set out the basic tradeoffs inherent in comprehensive immigration-reform efforts in their conclusion:

A paper that sets out to discuss legislative strategies should in the end have some definitive recommendations, but we do not. That may be a function of the policy subject—immigration—or it may be because, when faced with complex policy issues, the road ahead depends on trying different strategies. And that is what we see for immigration policy. It is clear that, whatever occurs, moving down that road will be very difficult, as it has been in the past. For some issues such as amnesty, there seems to be strong support across a range of interest groups, yet no issue divides Congress more decisively. If that issue needs to be resolved, and the demand is pressing, it may be best to separate the issue and try to reach compromises with the backing of the interest groups. To include it instead in a large package of reforms is likely to sink the package along with amnesty.

On the other hand, other issues have formed natural combinations and compromises. Such has been the case on legal visa levels and in negotiations over types of visas. The Irish were even able to increase their numbers through a clever and indirect route as "diversity visas." In other contexts, diversity for Northern Europeans may well have been hard to sell. What we believe is essential is to keep the prospect of dealing with discrete and separable issues on the table. There is in Congress the powerful tendency to solve all the problems at one time in a huge complex bill that covers broad ranges of issues. This tendency has several possible failings. First, it may often produce nothing—as has been the case with immigration policy in the current century. Second, the results of large sets of compromises may make the resolution of individual issues less optimal than if they were handled in discrete legislation. We trust the skills and wisdom of leaders who work for years in a policy area to realize when one of these outcomes looms. At that point, it might be better simply to ask: "Can we make positive progress on issue x, always remembering that issue y can be dealt with on another day." Indeed, we also suspect that similar analyses on other issues, such as healthcare reform, would benefit from the same advice.[46]

My reading of this work agrees in large part, but the most interesting facet of Márquez and Witte's analysis is that it omits the DREAM Act from its consideration. This dog-that-does-not-bark dimension is interesting because it would have been the best test of their thesis—that incremental and severable legislative approaches to complex problems are preferable and, especially in immigration reform, likely the most efficacious political strategy. For example, they identify theoretical positions on "major policy issues on immigration": "Higher Immigration Totals," "Higher Family Unification," "Higher

Specialized Employment," "Amnesty—Path to Citizenship," "Guest Worker Program," "Social Services for Illegals [*sic*]," "Employer Sanctions/IDs," and "Border Security."[47] In these core areas, they chart interest-group salience, probe the resistance each position triggers, and indicate the extent to which there are possibilities for compromise. They also helpfully measure the additional partisan and ideological implications of particular salience to analyses of immigration, and highlight two: "the effects on members of both parties of representing districts in southwestern border states, and, independently, districts with high levels of foreign-born constituents."[48]

Although Márquez and Witte do not focus on the DREAM Act or the area of undocumented postsecondary students, they might profitably have done so, as there has been substantial subfederal legislative activity in the field, there is an evident tug-of-war among advocates and restrictionists, there is a large body of literature and public focus on the subject, there is the categorical precedent of related U.S. Supreme Court decisions with bearing on the issue, there is a growing litigation record in other federal and state courts, and more to their point, the issue is severable (what they characterize as "discrete and separable") and has already been contested in the Congress. Thus, it would have been the perfect test case for their thesis and a useful case-study proxy for contesting the efficacy of comprehensive immigration reform.

This chapter has documented the extensive previous legislative activity, the dramatis personae of contestants, and the considerable research and policy literature and media attention paid to the postsecondary *Plyler* issue. The holding of *Plyler v. Doe* that allowed undocumented schoolchildren to enroll freely in elementary and secondary schools has been challenged but has remained good law nearly thirty years after the 1982 decision.[49] Indeed, except for a mid-1990s dustup that threatened congressional action to overturn the holding, *Plyler* has become accepted and accommodated by a substantial majority of school districts and policymakers, making a virtue of necessity and holding the innocent children harmless for what may have been the transgressions of their undocumented parents. However, *Plyler* does not extend to high school graduates and their admission to college or other postcompulsory schooling, and a number of cases have arisen, including an important one that wended its way through California courts until it was resolved in favor of the undocumented and other resident students, and one still dormant in Texas state court.[50]

This section details the final two facets of undocumented college students as a component of comprehensive immigration reform: the severability of the issue and the legislative history of the DREAM Act in Congress. The near misses of the 2007 and 2010 legislation (both 2010 occasions), the unusual provenance, and likely recurrence all make this issue a bellwether for the likelihood of a more omnibus legislative strategy. Recalling Márquez and Witte's framing question ("At that point, it might be better simply to ask: 'Can we make positive progress on issue x, always remembering that issue y can be dealt with on another day'"),[51] one might usefully ask, can the DREAM Act pass as a standalone bill, if at all, or must it be a part of a larger legislative strategy?

Here, it is useful to recall in more detail the original status and introduction of the DREAM Act. As noted in table 2, it was first introduced on August 1, 2001, by Senator Orrin Hatch (R-UT); the bill had broad, bipartisan support, with Senator Hatch being among the most conservative members of the Senate, and Senator Richard Durbin (D-IL) being among the most liberal.[52] The DREAM Act in its various versions languished in Congress, until comprehensive immigration-reform efforts failed in summer 2007.[53] In July 2007, Senator Reid attempted to attach the legislation to the Department of Defense authorization bill, but the Senate never got to the DREAM vote in this vehicle.[54]

Nonetheless, the tactic to use the Department of Defense bill as a vehicle was quite clever and was possible and germane because of provisions in the legislation that would have facilitated the legalization of undocumented members of the U.S. military. By 2007, the growing unpopularity of the war in Iraq made the issue a political tar baby, too divisive to provide the ground cover that might have been available had the tactic been used sooner after 2001's "war on terror" or in the early stages of the Iraq or Afghanistan military actions. The House moved the legislation forward but, by 2007, had never actually brought the legislation forward for a vote; it was not until late 2010 that the House ever voted on a version of the DREAM Act, when it passed in that chamber.[55] On October 24, 2007, the Senate voted down the stand-alone DREAM Act, 44–52.[56] The one possible aperture closed and its moment had passed.

Even the major actors in this 2007 vote were an odd array. In a situation where sixty votes were needed and every vote counted, four voters who were on record as supporting the legislation did not show up to vote. Senator John McCain (R-AZ), who had been instrumental in the failed Kennedy-McCain effort at comprehensive immigration reform, did not vote, as he was in the midst of his presidential campaign, which turned out to be unsuccessful; Senator Edward Kennedy (D-MA) was unavailable for the vote, as his health had taken a turn for the worse, and he ultimately died in the summer of 2009.[57] Senator Barbara Boxer (D-CA) was unavailable, as extensive fires had broken out in her state, and she was attending to business there; Senator Christopher Dodd (D-CT), an early DREAM Act supporter, was also unavailable and did not vote.[58]

Most unusual and remarkable was the action of Senator Arlen Specter (R-PA), who had been a supporter of the DREAM Act and who was considered among the most liberal Republicans in the Senate. He voted against the bill, on the credulity-straining grounds that if it were enacted, it would impede the larger goal of comprehensive immigration reform. On the Senate floor on October 24, 2007, he read the following remarks:

> Mr. SPECTER. Mr. President, I believe that the DREAM Act is a good act, and I believe that its purposes are beneficial. I think it ought to be enacted. But I have grave reservations about seeing a part of comprehensive immigration reform go forward because it weakens our position to get a comprehensive bill.
>
> Right now, we are witnessing a national disaster, a governmental disaster, as States and counties and cities and townships and boroughs and municipalities—every level of government—are legislating on immigration because the Congress of the United States is derelict in its duty to proceed.
>
> We passed an immigration bill out of both Houses last year. It was not conferenced. It was a disgrace that we couldn't get the people's business done. We were unsuccessful in June in trying to pass an immigration bill. I think we ought to be going back to it. I have discussed it with my colleagues.
>
> I had proposed a modification to the bill defeated in June, which, much as I dislike it, would not have granted citizenship as part of the bill, but would have removed fugitive status only. That means someone could not be arrested if the only violation was being in the country illegally. That would eliminate the opportunity for unscrupulous employers to blackmail employees with squalid living conditions and low wages, and it would enable people to come out of the shadows, to register within a year.
>
> We cannot support 12 to 20 million undocumented immigrants, but we could deport the criminal element if we could segregate those who would be granted amnesty only.
>
> I believe we ought to proceed with hearings in the Judiciary Committee. We ought to set up legislation. If we cannot act this year because of the appropriations logjam, we will have time in late January. But as reluctant as I am to oppose this excellent idea of the Senator from Illinois, I do

not think we ought to cherry-pick. It would take the pressure off of comprehensive immigration reform, which is the responsibility of the Federal Government. We ought to act on it, and we ought to act on it now.[59]

This defection of a previously supportive senior Republican senator, combined with the White House's efforts to defeat passage, essentially on the same grounds, was the kiss of death to the bill. The White House issued a press release just prior to the DREAM Act Senate vote, acknowledging the need for overall immigration reform but suggesting that the legislation was too generous:

> The Administration continues to believe that the Nation's broken immigration system requires comprehensive reform. This reform should include strong border and interior enforcement, a temporary worker program, a program to bring the millions of undocumented aliens out of the shadows without amnesty and without animosity, and assistance that helps newcomers assimilate into American society. Unless it provides additional authorities in all of these areas, Congress will do little more than perpetuate the unfortunate status quo.
>
> The Administration is sympathetic to the position of young people who were brought here illegally as children and have come to know the United States as home. Any resolution of their status, however, must be careful not to provide incentives for recurrence of the illegal conduct that has brought the Nation to this point.[60]

Senator Specter had been widely considered a safe vote on the issue, and his politics had evolved to the point where he even switched parties in 2008 and became a Democrat.[61] Senator Kay Bailey Hutchison (R-TX), who anticipated running for governor of Texas against the incumbent Republican, Rick Perry (who had signed into law the first state legislation to grant in-state tuition to the undocumented), voted for the DREAM Act and thereby reduced the risk of alienating Latino voters in her home state, who would now have to choose in the primary between two candidates who had both supported the issue.[62] Observers, including Senate staff, noted that there had been several other possible votes that would have been available for the legislation if the required sixty votes were within shouting distance; these senators were only willing to risk the wrath of critical voters if the game were worth the candle and their votes would actually count.[63] The absences of Senators McCain and Kennedy, both champions of immigration reform generally, the absences of Senators Dodd and Boxer, the defection of Specter, and the White House's withholding support clearly doomed the star-crossed bill at the very last stages of the maneuvering. There was evidence that many Republicans, all of whom except McCain voted, also had not wanted to give what would likely have been viewed as a legislative immigration "victory" to the Democrats, or to appear to do so, with the national presidential elections coming soon afterward. Given that the DREAM Act had bipartisan sponsorship from the outset, there were signals that its enactment would be able to garner the sixty votes necessary to avoid the filibuster, under the structural and operating cloture rules of Congress. On this point, political scientist Barbara Sinclair has noted of this complex institutional ecosystem, especially the role of the filibuster and other procedural tactics,

> The minority party—and quite a few independent observers—argues that rules barring any germane amendments are undemocratic, but such rules are often necessary to prevent carefully constructed compromises from coming unraveled on the floor. If allowed to offer any and all germane amendments, the minority may well come up with ones that repeatedly place some of the majority in the politically perilous position of choosing between "the popular" and "the responsible" vote. Forcing the most vulnerable members of the majority to take such votes is often the minority's aim. An important facet of the job of the congressional party leadership—one that a strong party leadership has a much better chance of carrying out—is protecting and enhancing the party's reputation. This means bringing a broader perspective to bear, and restrictive rules can be a valuable leadership tool for making it easier for members to take a broader perspective. In thinking about reform, we need to remember both that a geographically-based electoral system builds in a certain parochialism— also known as responsiveness and accountability to the constituency—and that how the legislature is organized internally can either accentuate or attenuate that parochialism.[64]

This was the final nail in the coffin, especially when the Republican presidential candidates began in earnest to accuse each other of weakness on immigration and of favoring an amnesty to the affected students.[65] By this time, FAIR, the Heritage Foundation, and restrictionist lawyers had also added to the thermodynamics, making it impossible for supporters to bring up the issue.[66] The fleeting, best opportunity for enacting the DREAM Act had passed, caught in the ironic pincers of being too much (for conservative legislators who feared being tarred as supporting an "amnesty") and too little (enacting it would torpedo the larger strategy of reforming overall immigration problems). In this scenario, the initiative died both by fire and by ice, and even was too little, too late, being tarnished by the increasingly unpopular Iraq war association; it likely would have passed had the Department of Defense strategy been attempted either immediately after September 11, 2001, or soon after, when support for the Afghan and Iraqi war efforts was greater on both sides of the aisle. Even more ironically, several of the terrorists involved in the deadly attacks were themselves college students out of status, and the predictable reaction to the acts of terrorism also entangled the issue.[67] It is all the more remarkable that the various state DREAM acts were all undertaken after 2001, save the original statute, signed into Texas state law before September 11 by Governor Bush's successor.

After President Barack Obama, an early cosponsor of the bill when he was in the U.S. Senate, was elected to the presidency and assumed office in January 2009, his first major legislative initiatives were dealing with the economic meltdown that had begun to surface politically in the late summer and fall of 2008[68] and then with comprehensive health-care and insurance reform,[69] which were brought forward in the omnibus fashion that Márquez and Witte had suggested was less likely to succeed. Senator Reid indicated that he would not proceed with the next major legislative subjects in piecemeal fashion, forcing climate change, banking regulation, and immigration reform to evolve as omnibus projects.[70] There was also a substantial wait until the Obama administration made its own immigration-reform design clear. It was not until mid-November 2009 that DHS Secretary Janet Napolitano made her first address on the subject of comprehensive immigration reform, and while she stressed the need to incorporate the undocumented "shadow" population through legalization provisions, the major emphasis appeared to be on border security and employment verification:

> Let me be clear: when I talk about "immigration reform," I'm referring to what I call the "three-legged stool" that includes a commitment to serious and effective enforcement, improved legal flows for families and workers, and a firm but fair way to deal with those who are already here. That's the way that this problem has to be solved, because we need all three aspects to build a successful system. This approach has at its heart the conviction that we must demand responsibility and accountability from everyone involved in the system: immigrants, employers and government. And that begins with fair, reliable enforcement.[71]

Until the actual proposals to be voted on are introduced, whether by Congress or by President Obama and the executive branch, the full contours will not be evident, but everything points to an omnibus approach. And the convolutions of the 2009–2010 health-care-reform strategy suggest that the most salient consideration will be which of the large-scale systemic initiatives is able to move forward and under what timing and calendar constraints it will emerge: can climate control, taxation reform, immigration, and the continuing war efforts all move to the front burner, or will they compete for the political resources in serial fashion?

The first year of the Obama presidency, as everyone knows, was spent putting out economic fires and enacting health-care reform. It was not until health-care legislation appeared to be passing in late March 2010 that President Obama indicated his intention to move forward with immigration reform, and, burned by Republican intransigence on health-care and insurance reform, he did so by indicating that both parties would have to put forward bipartisan legislation, even as it had become clear that Republicans would not provide any votes in the Senate for the Democratic health-care legislation that was passed, with last-minute student-loan reform tacked onto it.[72]

Senator Charles Schumer (D-NY) assumed the responsibility for shepherding immigration reform through the Senate, following the death of Senator Kennedy, and his remarks have shown him to be much more conservative than was the late senator. For example, in his public remarks, he has adopted restrictionist code words and rhetoric (e.g., "force-multiplier," "border security"), has made it clear that his first priority is to "secure the border" and to change the discourse of the issue. For example, in summer 2009, he gave a public lecture in which he laid out his first principle, objecting to widely employed terminology such as "undocumented workers."

> The first of these seven principles is that illegal immigration is wrong—plain and simple. When we use phrases like "undocumented workers," we convey a message to the American people that their Government is not serious about combating illegal immigration, which the American people overwhelmingly oppose.
>
> Above all else, the American people want their Government to be serious about protecting the public, enforcing the rule of law, and creating a rational system of legal immigration that will proactively fit our needs rather than reactively responding to future waves of illegal immigration.

People who enter the United States without our permission are illegal aliens, and illegal aliens should not be treated the same as people who entered the United States legally.[73]

On the subject of the DREAM Act, his principles did not include specific reference to the topic, but he did vote for the bill in 2007 and both times in 2010, suggesting his inclination and support for this part of the larger issue. The draft versions of reform legislation have included DREAM Act provisions, buried in larger, omnibus overhaul approaches, drawing attention away from their "legalization" or "amnesty" features.[74]

Conclusion

Despite my own personal preference that the DREAM Act be enacted on its own, because once enacted, it would clear the decks and show that bipartisan differences could be resolved, leading to the larger, more comprehensive overhaul, this is likely not how the wheel has turned. There was a brief window in time, in 2007, when this might have occurred, and the narrative recounted here shows that a little luck might have helped turn the corner: had Senator Kennedy been well, had Senator Specter not backed away, had the fires not broken out in California, had Senator Dodd not taken a walk, had there not been a presidential election looming, all for want of a nail. But all legislation, not just that affecting immigration, has to face the cards in play on the table at the time of its consideration. The 2010 efforts were also doomed, this time by extremely partisan politics and the crowded calendar of events in the 111th Congress, especially with voting just before and just after the midterm 2010 elections.

President Obama has undertaken so many major initiatives, especially an agonizing and bitter year on health-care reform and including an early and unexpected vacancy on the Supreme Court and then a second vacancy,[75] that there may be a situation where all the oxygen in the room has been inhaled. As one observer has noted, "On February 24, [2009], Obama addressed Congress to explain his budget priorities and urge Congressional action on three key priorities: energy, health care, and education. . . . This three-part agenda, combined with other pending legislative initiatives (immigration reform, highway programs, banking system regulation) not mentioned in the address, was remarkably ambitious. President Obama's strategy was to begin by pushing for several major initiatives at once."[76] The agenda items are not only "remarkably ambitious," but they are inextricably interrelated. In another setting where

President Obama was addressing the entire Congress, it was during his discussion of health-care proposals that Representative Joe Wilson (R-SC) famously shouted out, "You lie!" concerning putative immigrant benefits.[77] If there ever had been a need to demonstrate the relationship among several volatile topics, surely this unprecedented breach of protocol was Exhibit A.[78]

It is this final reason why comprehensive immigration reform will likely require an omnibus and overarching legislative strategy: because the issue is simply one of such transcendent complexity, with so many interrelated moving parts, that it cannot be incrementally reformed. While partisan politics will always be present, the bedfellows of immigration reform cannot be easily identified by the traditional scorecards. In 2001, I would have taken any bets that immigration postsecondary legislation introduced by Senator Hatch and the late Senator Kennedy would have been enacted into law; indeed, I did take that bet, and in print.[79] If cosponsorship is a signaling device or leading indicator, the DREAM Act would be law today, and these young adults would be working their way through a form of legalization. However, even if the legislation were passed tomorrow, it would not affect the ability of states to grant resident-tuition status, to enable them to award state scholarships or grants, or to allow them to withhold enrollment. Thus, no matter the fate of omnibus immigration reform or the DREAM Act, this issue will remain an agenda item at the state level. Gary Reich and Alvar Ayala Mendoza, in their thoughtful study of the unlikely passage of state-resident-tuition legislation in Kansas, noted that its successful enactment was due, in a traditional sense, to the careful, *Plyler*-like framing of the issue as one of educating a vulnerable population and to the persistence and skill of its advocates:

> Given the conservative bent of the Kansas legislature and the generally negative perception of undocumented workers among Kansas residents, the state would appear to be a least-likely case for adoption of a policy granting undocumented students in-state college tuition status. However, in spite of the odds against adoption of a pro-immigrant policy in a generally anti-immigrant state, advocates were successful. As argued here, that success stems in large measure from the ability of advocates to reframe the issue as one of educational opportunities for public school students, an issue frame that was more likely to garner bipartisan support within the Kansas legislature. The results in this paper are consistent with the view that issue framing can be an effective, low-cost resource by which policy advocates may influence policymaking, even in inhospitable environments.

How is the issue framing used in Kansas applicable to other states in which in-state tuition for undocumented students has become part of the legislative agenda? The Kansas case suggests two factors that are key for framing such legislation in other states. First, the presentation of cost-benefit ratios is crucial. In Kansas, proponents of HB 2008 were able to credibly present the argument that the legislation involved low costs to taxpayers and that the benefits applied to a broad group of state residents. However, in states where the population of undocumented workers is growing at even faster rates than Kansas (such as North Carolina, Alabama, Georgia, or Tennessee) the effectiveness of this argument becomes less clear. On the one hand, voters and legislators in the new high immigrant growth states may be more likely to perceive immigration as contributing to socioeconomic upheaval; this perception may be more acute because these states lack a history of integrating immigrant communities into social service networks, as has occurred in traditional immigrant destination states such as Texas, California, New York, and Illinois. Thus, the cost of in-state tuition may be more readily perceived (and framed) as a broad redistribution of tax revenue benefiting newly-arrived immigrant families at the expense of native taxpayers. On the other hand, where immigration is growing most rapidly, local businesses are more dependent on immigrant labor. In such a situation, the business community may be more receptive to in-state tuition as a labor training and retention tool.

Second, the local framing of in-state tuition is crucial. Advocates of instate tuition in Kansas consistently couched their arguments in the local terms of Kansan children desiring an education. By contrast, the main opponent of HB 2008 employed an issue frame based on national immigration policy and terrorism to argue against the bill. The appeals to national immigration policy and terrorism did not appear to resonate with state legislators, nor were they supported by any major elected state official (for example, neither the Governor nor the Attorney General played a role in the debate over the bill). However, where concerns about immigration law and the threat of terrorism have more local salience for voters and elected officials (Arizona may be a relevant example), we would expect FAIR's arguments to be more effective. In this regard, national immigration debates may work against proponents of in-state tuition in the future. In Kansas, debates about HB 2008 occurred in a climate in which illegal immigration was not as prominent a public policy issue as it would become just a year later, when the Bush Administration's immigration reform bill prompted extensive media attention.[80]

Of course, there are a million stories in the naked city-state, and there are features evident in Kansas that were simultaneously unique and generic, as there have been in every state where the issue has been taken up, whether successfully, unsuccessfully, or both, as in the case of Oklahoma, where both the thrill of victory and the agony of defeat were evident in the rescission of a part of the statute.[81] In this sense, the legislative strategy will have a different playbook in every state, even as the toolkit will have certain common instruments that may be deployed or not, as the localized circumstances require. Indeed, this is the case of every statute ever enacted and is unremarkable in one very real sense.

However, at the federal level, where immigration fundamentals reside, the basics of the system are so complex, the policy issues are so politicized and so intertwined, and the different coalitions are so evanescent that the polity cannot feed all the smaller parts through the legislative scheme and process one component at a time.[82] This is the view that the Immigration Policy Center has urged, and it may have the final word:

> It is misleading to characterize our immigration crisis as solely a question of what to do about the 11 to 12 million unauthorized immigrants living in the United States. Our problems extend to a much broader range of issues. For instance: Insufficient numbers of visas are made available to bring in either high-skilled or less-skilled workers at the levels needed to meet the changing needs of the U.S. economy and labor market. Arbitrary visa caps have created long backlogs of family members who must wait up to 20 years to be reunited with family living in the United States. Wage and workplace violations by unscrupulous employers who exploit immigrant workers are undercutting honest businesses and harming all workers. Inadequate government infrastructure is delaying the integration of unauthorized immigrants who want to legalize and become U.S. citizens. Furthermore, the lack of a comprehensive federal solution has created a range of lopsided, enforcement-only initiatives that have cost the country billions of dollars, while doing little to impede the flow of unauthorized immigrants. In fact, the current immigration system's structural failures, and the inadequate or misguided responses to these failures, have led to the largest unauthorized population in our nation's history.[83]

In fall 2010, at the urging of Latino groups and to jump-start comprehensive immigration reform, Senator Reid changed his mind and brought forward a bill. Facing a substantial challenge in his reelection to the U.S. Senate, he opted for a down-payment approach, with DREAM being the first building block toward future comprehensive reforms, and with AGJOBS legislation as the likely next step. The DREAM Act became an amendment to a Department of Defense bill, S. 3454, the "National Defense Authorization Act for Fiscal Year 2011." Reid also added two other amendments: a repeal of "Don't Ask, Don't Tell" (DADT), regarding the enlistment of gays and lesbian soldiers in the military, and an overhaul of the "secret hold" tradition in the Senate, to require public disclosure in order to move legislative actions forward. On September 21, 2010, the vote became hostage to the DADT controversy, and the Republicans voted as a bloc, rather than accord President Obama and the Democrats a victory on this issue; the cloture motion was rejected 43–56 (with one absence). Senator Reid voted no after it was clear that he did not have the required sixty votes. (The no vote for his own motion would allow him to call for reconsideration.) Even Republican supporters of the legislation in the 2007 vote did not support the overall package in the 2010 effort, and two Democrats crossed over to vote against it as well.[84] Once again, the DREAM Act was tantalizingly close, and its consideration gave rise to many public stories about undocumented college students in the media; these continued through the lame-duck session, when once again the votes were not there.[85]

The third time may be the proverbial charm, but not in this subject matter. In the final days of the same Congress, the greatest disappointment occurred. On December 8, 2010, the House attached the DREAM Act (H.R. 6497) to another moving House bill, H.R. 5281, and passed it: 216 to 198. This was the first time that the House had ever voted on a version of the DREAM Act since its introduction in 2001. Initially, the Senate was scheduled to take a procedural vote on its version of DREAM (S. 3992), but instead, Senate Democrats voted 59–40 to withdraw S. 3992 and focus on the bill passed on December 8 by the House. On December 18, 2010, the Senate took up the cloture motion (technically, the "Motion to Invoke Cloture on the Motion to Concur in the House Amendment to the Senate Amendment No. 3 to H.R. 5281, the Removal Clarification Act of 2010"). Democratic backers of the legislation fell short of the sixty votes required to move the DREAM Act legislation forward, with a vote of 55–41 in favor. Five Democrats—Senators Max Baucus (MT), Kay Hagan (NC), Ben Nelson (NE), Mark Pryor (AR), and Jon Tester (MT)—joined most Republicans in voting against the measure. Three Republicans—Senators Bob Bennett (UT), Richard Lugar (IN), and Lisa Murkowski (AK)—voted yes. Four members—Senators Jim Bunning (R-KY), Judd Gregg (R-NH), Orrin Hatch (R-UT), and Joe Manchin

(D-WV)—were not present for the vote. The ultimate irony was that in a separate vote, the "Don't Ask, Don't Tell" policy was repealed and that Senator Hatch, who introduced the original DREAM Act legislation a decade earlier, did not vote for his original bill.[86]

At some point and by all indications, it is likely this legislation will pass in one form or another, and then the next in the never-ending line of complex problems will be taken up. These issues will have their own narratives and legislative histories and their own arcs and trajectories. Immigration will continue to claim a permanent place in the congressional agenda, especially in a globalized world where the United States will require immigrants, and they will come. When a DREAM Act becomes law, the structural features of federal immigration legislation and state college-tuition policies will still necessitate coordinated and integrated state legislation for full implementation at the institutional level, guaranteeing continued attention to the issue. If perfect federal legislation were enacted tomorrow, there would still be many roadblocks for the students, as many of them reside in California, a state where higher-education institutions are extremely crowded, where college costs have risen rapidly,[87] and where a state supreme court case hung like a sword of Damocles over the issue of resident tuition status, until it was resolved in 2010 in favor of the statute.[88] The students would still be ineligible for state financial aid and, depending on the details of the federal legislation, may remain ineligible for Title IV financial assistance. As always, both God and the Devil will be in the legislative details.

Paradoxically, the wall-to-wall blare of talk radio, cable television, and electronic and digital technologies in the universal media market will both facilitate communication and atomize our ability to form a discourse in which comprehensive legislative solutions are called for. But the republic will survive, legislative work will get done, and our experiment in representative democracy will continue to evolve. And these *Plyler* children among us will have graduated from college and taken up their place in the larger community.[89]

5

Conclusion

*The Discourse and the Danger
(or, Why* Plyler *Should Have Been
Decided on Preemption Grounds)*

Stinky is one ugly robot, a raggedy contraption constructed of crudely painted, cheap plastic pipes pasted together with gobs of the foul-smelling glue that gave the monstrosity its name.

Stinky's creators didn't look all that impressive, either—four teenage guys in baggy pants and sneakers, all of them illegal Mexican immigrants attending Carl Hayden High School in funky West Phoenix.

When Stinky arrived at last year's Marine Advanced Technology Remotely Operated Vehicle Competition—an underwater robotics contest sponsored by NASA and the Office of Naval Research—it was greeted with barely suppressed snickers. Nobody expected Stinky to compete with the robot from MIT, a handsome machine created by 12 elite engineering and computer science students and decorated with a sticker from ExxonMobil, the company that donated $5,000 to the MIT team.

But the kids from Hayden High beat MIT and the rest of the competition—an amazing upset chronicled in an inspiring story in the April issue of *Wired* magazine. Americans love a tale of scrappy underdogs triumphing against long odds, and "La Vida Robot" by Joshua Davis is a classic. It's got all the ingredients of a feel-good movie of the week—colorful characters, high drama, low comedy and a happy ending.

Well, a sort of happy ending.[1]

I have been actively involved in residency reform and study since 1975, when I was a doctoral student and campus recruiter at Ohio State University. As a Chicano student, I was drawn to recruit other Latinos to campus, but in Ohio, the only communities with residents of Mexican origin were located in the northern part of the state, where tomatoes and other perishable crops were grown and processed. I discovered that a number of talented Mexican American and Puerto Rican farmworkers were interested in attending college, especially since the tomato and pickle crops were being mechanized and Latinos were not being hired in the canneries that ringed the northern border of the state. However, each year these students and their families followed the crops, from Texas melons and onions up through the Midwest vegetables to tree fruits in northern Michigan. These travels meant they could not establish residency in any state, even those at either end of the migrant stream (Texas or Ohio or Michigan) where they maintained a legal domicile. In my typical graduate-student way, I did not know the complexity of the interstate residency systems, and so I asked, "Why not?" I formed a ragtag group of advocates in Columbus, and we convinced the legislature and the Higher Education Coordinating Board to enact a change in Ohio law that enabled agricultural workers to accumulate the residence period of twelve months over the space of three years.[2] Breaking up the time period seemed, in my amateur's way at the time, a fair way to allow these farmworkers a chance at college.

To this day, I remember our big meeting with Ohio Board of Regents officers. We even showed them the television movie *Harvest of Shame*, the classic Edward R. Murrow investigation into the plight of U.S. farmworkers. The Board of Regents' biggest fear was that nonfarmworkers would pose as the new "protected class" in order to avail themselves of this residency benefit. That someone, not a migrant, would try and pass for one had never occurred to me: not even César Chávez had ever glamorized the profession enough to make it fashionable. I earnestly whipped out an application I had brought in my files, and showed the administrators what a migrant academic transcript looked like: grading periods for the same seven high schools, for the same four weeks, over each of four years. Once administrators saw the transcript, once the evidence and discourse were in terms they could understand, their concerns were allayed. Moreover, once the migrant students were admitted, they were entitled to other grants and curricular benefits as well and, through a formal interstate compact agreement, to residency status in other reciprocal states.[3] And these students were U.S. citizens, not even the undocumented field hands of today, lured by the backbreaking jobs no one else wants to undertake.

This was my first professional taste of how benefits and status are accorded by place and duration and my first high-level political organizing success. (Actually, it was my second: as an undergraduate, I had convinced my college seminary officials to do away with Saturday-morning classes, which had made me a hero with classmates and faculty alike.) In the years since, I have established residency as my subfield of study by conducting research, litigating cases, serving on campus residency appeals committees, and being an expert witness in residency cases.[4] In an ironic twist, I was once sued for my university committee's denial of the residency appeal by one of my law students and defended by another former student; I also served both as a hostile fact witness and expert in that case.[5] I know residency.

But others do not, or they misperceive it. These undocumented students at issue have met all admissions criteria, have met all traditional residence requirements, and displace no one on academic grounds. Except for the different fee bills they receive, they are indistinguishable from other college students. Even in California, where 40 percent of all undocumented residents are assumed to live, undocumented college students constitute an almost invisible minority of students. Colleges in the United States have accustomed themselves to the students' presence and have administered their enrollment without incident—even though federal financial-aid funds are unavailable to this population.[6] No study has shown them to be a substantial number, even in border-area colleges. Through expert testimony and research, it is evident that the lure of college is not a "pull" factor to attract illegal immigration.[7]

Nonetheless, attorney Ralph W. Kasarda, who has filed briefs in the *Martinez* case, exemplifies how strident the restrictionist rhetoric can appear:

In outright defiance of federal laws, politicians from states that do offer in-state tuition to illegal aliens argue with a straight face that granting eligibility for in-state tuition is not a postsecondary education benefit as contemplated by the federal statutes. . . . Since *Plyler* does not require states to provide a college education to adult illegal aliens, state taxpayers should mercifully be spared this unnecessary expense. But driven by political ideology rather than concern for their state's fiscal well-being, some state politicians have enacted legislation that forces their constituents to subsidize the post-secondary education of adult illegal aliens. . . . Numerous policy reasons forcefully argue against offering in-state tuition to adult illegal aliens in order to subsidize their college education, including the added burden that must be borne by taxpayers and the likelihood that offering this benefit to illegal aliens will encourage more illegal immigration. State action to encourage and condone illegal immigration is contrary to federal laws that make it a crime to immigrate to the United States illegally, stay in the country illegally, and to hire illegal aliens. The end result is the weakening of the rule of law, particularly since illegal aliens must resort to the violation of other laws to secure employment such as identity theft, and offering false documents to their employers.[8]

Similarly, Kris W. Kobach has argued that states and legislators offering admission and resident tuition are engaging in "nullification,"[9] "defiance,"[10] and "lawbreaking."[11] But these objections to undocumented alienage and higher-education enrollments are not rooted in careful research and analytic study. My reading of the discourse leads me to believe that those who object do not do so on meritocratic or substantive grounds: Governor Mitt Romney's objections that the money used for serving undocumented aliens deprives lawfully resident aliens of their benefits ring hollow, even as presidential politics.[12]

Not only is there considerable resistance that extends even to permanent residents receiving benefits—so much so that there is an entire legal literature devoted to the topic of nativism[13]—but the imprecise, undifferentiated, and broad-brush swipes at "illegals" and "aliens" generally tar all the groups. Free-floating racial animus often leads to a generalized resentment against all people of color, or "others."[14] Some legislation has even been so mean-spirited as to advocate a repealing of *Plyler v. Doe* and the constitutional provisions that enable native-born children to be U.S. citizens,[15] irrespective of their parents' immigration status. All of these arguments, mixed in a cauldron amid shrill warnings about the rights of "real Americans," lead inevitably to a sense of divisiveness, racial superiority, and undifferentiated prejudice. Thus, hundreds of anti-alien bills have been introduced and enacted,[16] as if these workers were the source of the sputtering economy, even though government studies have shown that immigrants—however defined—are net economic contributors and will be more so after their incorporation through comprehensive immigration reform.[17]

Much is made of the detrimental effects of immigration: that criminals are not deterred from entering or remaining in the country, that aliens are stubbornly monolingual in languages other than English, that they take jobs and services from citizens, that they undercut or depress wages, that they do not understand the American character, that their unlawful presence is itself a sign of an unwillingness to abide by rules or to accept responsibility for their actions.[18] Of course, these traits, to the extent that they are accurate, do describe some immigrants in legal status or in undocumented status, just as they surely describe some natives. However, if there were a group that holds promise to become productive, long-term residents and citizens, alien college students would surely be that group. With the generally dismal schooling available to these students,[19] that even a small percentage could meet the standards of the University of California or of other selective colleges and universities is extraordinary. Given their status and struggle, each represents a success story of substantial accomplishment.

In a fascinating ethnographic study of a number of undocumented students in California who navigated the complex requirements and who risked revealing themselves to immigration authorities, sociologist Leisy Abrego wrote,

> The case of AB 540 in California strongly suggests that unintended constitutive functions of law may sometimes have more transformative effects on the daily lives of targeted subjects than the intended instrumental objectives of law. Instrumentally, AB 540 has been partially successful; the exemption from out-of-state tuition makes community college more accessible, but fails to make a university education affordable for most undocumented students. In comparison, however, the constitutive effects of the law are considerably more far reaching. Despite the narrow actionable aspects of AB 540, the law is powerfully symbolic for the students who benefit from it. To them, the law represents a statement about their earned belonging in this society; it signals support for their endeavors and affirmation of their legitimacy.
>
> While courts and other state actors play important roles in the production of law, the constitutive approach underscores that ordinary citizens and subjects also contribute greatly to the meaning and outcomes of law. Law's constitutive power is relational and leaves room for contestation. Although marginalized groups have been known to stand against the law, the relational nature of law's constitutive power opens up the potential for innovative actions to exploit law's possibilities and invoke its power and protection. In this way, law may be invoked and utilized in ways never intended by legislators.[20]

Abrego's observations of these successful survivors mirror my own many interactions with these communities over the years. While I do not wish to seem or to be reductionist, or to generalize beyond recognition, it has been my experience that most of these students are high-achieving strivers, with a resilience and persistence held by few native citizens—who are born to advantage relative to these students—and most have parents who struggled to bring them to this country and exercised considerable risk to enable them to achieve. That they do so under extraordinary circumstances is remarkable to virtually all who observe them, and partially explains why so many educators and legislators have accepted *Plyler* and worked to assist them in navigating the complexities of school and college. Despite the success of anti-immigrant rhetoric in shaping a discourse and of restrictionists in fashioning resentments, reasonable legislators of both parties have actually seen through the fog and attempted to address these issues, notwithstanding the political blowback. This underlying support to remedy the failures of national immigration policy are better barometers of the country's acceptance of this shadow population and generosity than are even the bleatings of the Lou Dobbses of the world.

The narratives of chapter 2 show how tenuous the *Plyler* decision was in the first place, with a substantial dose of luck and persistence and a powerful backstory of innocent children. Scholars who have looked carefully and thoughtfully at the case have determined it to be sui generis, not so much as limited to its facts but as possessing weak doctrinal force and little constitutional significance. Its gravitational pull has not affected many subsequent cases, as none has come before the Court since then on all fours. The political events since 1982 have not led to serious challenges on legislative fronts, even as *Plyler* has always been vulnerable to federal legislating on the issue of the education of undocumented children. The Gallegly proposal to turn back the clock was the one serious attempt to overturn *Plyler* at the federal level, and such efforts have not surfaced in a serious vein since then. With the one exception of the successful challenge to California's ballot initiative, which, like the original case, had good winds blow the way of the children, no serious state actions have threatened their educational access in the nearly two decades since *LULAC v. Wilson*. Notwithstanding, chapter 3 chronicled the many permutations that have arisen in lower federal and state courts, revealing that immigrant advocates have had to relitigate and shore up a number of corollary and subsidiary issues flowing from the touchstone *Plyler*; but on the whole, they have beaten back most of the secondary direct and diagonal threats, such as policies affecting immigrant youth. Indeed, the record shows wide and deep accommodation to these children at individual school, district, and state levels—even as federal and state efforts to enact stricter employment legislation have increased. Chapter 4 records the broad range of postsecondary *Plyler* issues, where most of the states with larger numbers of undocumented schoolchildren, and even some with fewer such students, have facilitated their enrollment in the public colleges and universities. While the number of such students has always been small, it has not been inconsiderable, and federal law addressing such college achievement came very close to enactment, suggesting the widespread public acceptance of these children in the polity, even past the point where they were innocent children brought here surreptitiously by their parents.

When comprehensive immigration reform is eventually enacted, these *Plyler* legacies will be first in line to take advantage of the transformative powers of citizenship. Even as states have ratcheted up the efforts to apprehend undocumented parents and unauthorized workers, safe havens for the college children were carved out and maintained, not universally but widely. As but one example, Utah—not thought of as a particularly hospitable climate to immigrants—moved to enact significant restrictionist employment and benefit legislation but retained its earlier postsecondary residency-tuition status for undocumented college students. While several states did enact harsh measures against these college students, such as South Carolina, which banned them in 2009, and others such as Virginia, Missouri, and Arizona have not accorded them in-state-residency eligibility, major receiver states have extended them this status, as have unusual venues from Nebraska to Kansas. If Florida were to move in this direction, all the major immigrant states save Arizona would allow undocumented students to enroll and receive resident tuition status. These are surely markers of how deeply the roots of *Plyler* have reached into the country's soil.

The truth is that the United States needs this talent pool. In many highly technical fields, foreign scholars enroll in high numbers and, after consuming the benefit, return to their countries.[21] This is as it should be, as learning respects no borders, and U.S. institutions are surely enriched by recruiting internationally. However, the undocumented have every incentive to remain in the United States, to adjust their status through formal or discretionary means, and to contribute to the U.S. economy and polity. My own experiences over the years with these students are that they are extremely loyal to the United States. Despite their undocumented status, most are more Americanized than are many native-born students. They believe in the immigrant success story, having lived it in most instances. Some, like "Jose" and "Manuel," the two students quoted at the beginning of chapter 3, have literally never known any other life. Why deny these students college admissions and resident tuition, when they are likely to become full-fledged members of the U.S. community, following the inevitable provisions of immigration reform? In my native New Mexico each year, Santa Feans ritualistically burn Zozobra, or "Old Man Gloom," a forty-foot straw figure, to expiate the year's accumulation of grief and indignities.[22] After examining all the arguments raised by immigration restrictionists on the issues of undocumented college residence, I have come to believe that those who raise objections, particularly those who act on these beliefs, do so to burn Zozobra and thus to expiate their own fear and loathing of the unknown. Just as 19th-century California officials banned pigtails on prisoners and oppressed them through a series of measures to keep Chinese immigrants in their place,[23] these storytellers have resorted to false stories and scapegoating in their campaign to vilify immigrants. Kevin R. Johnson, with a long history of thoughtful immigration scholarship, labels this phenomenon of waging metaphorical wars as "The Hijacking of the Debate over Immigration Reform by Monsters, Ghosts, and Goblins (or the War on Drugs, War on Terror, Narcoterrorists, Etc.)," noting the rhetorical devices advanced to thwart substantive improvements in immigration laws, even as all observers acknowledge the pressing need for change.[24]

All the available data show negligible undocumented participation in the country's vast higher-education system. Unconcerned with the true data, immigration opponents have told tales out of school, of massive displacement and lawlessness. Neither of these tales is true. On balance, immigrants, whether lawfully admitted or undocumented, are present and future contributors. Our society benefits tremendously by their stories and loyalties. Precluding their incorporation into the community through higher education is a foolishly short-sighted policy, and those who actively oppose the integration of long-term undocumented elementary and college students should be ashamed of themselves for their actions. Important public policy should not be premised on such prejudice.

When I consider the hydraulics of immigration, about which I have thought for a long time, and the likely downsides of the nativist proposals, and when I count the rise of immigration-related proposals at the local and state level, I am convinced that no good can come from subfederal assumption of immigration powers. Some of the inefficiencies in the current system are incontestably dysfunctional, but so would be the result of increased overlap in immigration enforcement. Most important, these changes would not appreciably improve the current system, which already has coordinating provisions built in, if not widely adopted.

Blowback in affected communities and increased prejudice are sure to follow from, among many examples, enforcing raids on workplaces and labor stations,[25] requiring Spanish-language preachers not to proselytize in their congregants' language,[26] or necessitating landlords in Hazleton, Pennsylvania, or Farmers Branch, Texas,[27] to check the immigration status of renters.

All of these are sure signs of a racial, ethnic, and national-origin "tax" that will only be levied on certain groups, certain to be Mexicans in particular or, equally likely, Mexican Americans. These more-than-petty nuisances are reminiscent of our inglorious immigration history of racial exclusion and are pigtail ordinances in modern guise. Despite their surface attractiveness and thin veneer, they should be resisted as fixes.

On occasion, the centrist view prevails, as it did in *Plyler*. When the case was wending its way through courts, encountering the fortuitous events and forces on its way to the Supreme Court, the recent history of *Rodriguez* was in evidence, a case with equally compelling circumstances and even more far-reaching implications for the education of Latino children and, indeed, of poor children throughout the country, for whom property-tax-driven school-funding practices consistently have led to underachievement and longstanding poverty. If education were not a fundamental right for citizen children, as the 5–4 decision in 1973 had held, how could undocumented children, whose parents were unable to organize politically or involve themselves in school issues, hope to prevail in 1982? In short, how did our country travel the long road from *Rodriguez* to *Plyler*, and in less than a decade?

Writing in 2009, Linda Greenhouse supplies the most plausible explanation, in the dynamics of the Supreme Court decision making, particularly that of Justice Lewis Powell, who had authored the disastrous *Rodriguez* majority opinion: she paints him as a decent person, moved by the plight of the innocent children:

Notes taken at the conference by both Justices Brennan and Blackmun confirm that Powell's participation followed his outline as he cast one of the five votes to affirm the judgment of the United States Court of Appeals for the Fifth Circuit that the statute was unconstitutional. The Mexican-born children on whose behalf the class-action lawsuit had been brought "have no responsibility for being there," Powell said, according to Brennan's notes. It was "hard to think of [a] category more helpless than children of illegal aliens." Powell then stated, however, what was certainly obvious to his colleagues: that he did not view education as a "fundamental right," a position he had expressed for the Court eight years earlier in his majority opinion in *San Antonio Independent School District v. Rodriguez*. But, he added, as long as the state chose to provide an education to "some children," he did not see how it could deny the same benefit to others. . . . In *Plyler*, he struggled to reconcile a profound sense of fairness with a tightly bound view of the judicial function. Born in 1907, a gentleman of the old South, Lewis Powell may appear to us now as someone from a long-ago era, a kind of judicial Everyman whose response to *Plyler v. Doe* can be seen as a mirror of how a basically conservative, fair minded citizen of his day, who happened to be a Supreme Court Justice, might have responded to the policy concerns that animated the case.

Today's Supreme Court, of course, is very different, deeply polarized and lacking a single Justice who had not previously served as a judge on a federal court of appeals. Insistence on doctrinal purity seems to be the order of the day, as reflected in the inability of Chief Justice Roberts, for the plurality, and Justice Kennedy, concurring in the judgment, to reach common ground in the 2006 Term's school integration case, *Parents Involved in Community Schools v. Seattle School District No. 1*. When a major immigration case next reaches the Court, as one will, we shall see whether the story of *Plyler v. Doe* is of more than merely historical interest. But it is surely at least that.

Justice Powell responded to the Texas statute not only as a Supreme Court Justice, but as one who had devoted years of his life to education, which he regarded as essential to the democratic enterprise. "It is difficult to conceive of someone who could have had a more intimate knowledge of all facets of American education than the Honorable Lewis Franklin Powell, Jr.," in the words of one scholar of education law who deemed Powell "the education Justice" in a published appraisal in 2001. Powell's interest in the subject was manifest throughout his judicial career; he wrote either for the Court or separately in 51 education-related cases, including, most famously, his controlling separate opinion in *Bakke*, four years before *Plyler*. A lifetime of experience told him that the Texas law was fundamentally misconceived: mean-spirited, hurtful to the individuals affected, and spectacularly counter-productive for society as a whole. The state's interest in educating the children, he noted in his pre-conference outline, was "strong—perhaps stronger than those advanced for not educating." And indeed, his opinion in *Rodriguez* had anticipated just such a situation, absent the immigration context. *Rodriguez* rejected the notion that disparities in wealth among a state's public school districts presented a problem of constitutional dimension. But if a state were actually to charge tuition to attend public school, meaning that those who were too poor to pay were "absolutely precluded from receiving an education," Powell had observed in a footnote, "that case would present a far more compelling set of circumstances for judicial assistance than the case before us today."[28]

For many of the reasons that have been evident in this book project, it is difficult to reimagine or re-create the time and place of the pre-IRCA 1980s as the high-water mark of the liberal polity, resulting in the bipartisan 1986 legislation that allowed *Plyler* children to become citizens, as they did. Reading the record of the case, one missing feature is the highly polarizing debate and interest-group mobilization so much in evidence today. While the issue in the 1970s was hardly under the radar, it did not draw the sting of restrictionists or the attention of progressive/ethnic partisans that have arisen since. As unimaginable was a breach by a congressman heckling the president of the United States about immigrant health care in a televised congressional session ("You Lie!") in 2009, it would have been simply unfathomable in 1982.

Even so, and despite the intermittent restrictionist impulses in the United States polity, there has been wide and deep acceptance of these children in the nation's schools. Many, although not all, of the thousands of school districts and states have accommodated their enrollment, facilitated their schooling, celebrated their achievements, and extended them college acceptance and resources. The one serious federal challenge to *Plyler*, the Gallegly Amendment, failed to gain traction, and even though the DREAM Act has been stalled as stand-alone national enactment, comprehensive immigration reform of some stripe is a likely eventual development.

Paradoxically, *Plyler*'s wide-scale acceptance, even in a time of increased authorized and unauthorized immigration, has occurred in the context of unprecedented nativism and restrictionism, and in the face of unmatched concerns about national security and terrorism. And the rise of employment-related legislation and enforcement is a much more salient feature than the issue has been since 1986, when, after all, the hiring of unauthorized workers was made illegal for the first time. Therefore, much of today's attention has been paid to rooting out the core reason for the undocumented workers who come to our factories, homes, and workplaces. That they have children, including U.S.-citizen children, is less the dominant focus than is the original sin of the parents following the siren call of work.

As the stories shown here have revealed, *Plyler* was always a close call: the decision was surprising, inasmuch as it followed the hapless experience of *Rodriguez*, and close readings of the decision have shown it never commanded widespread constitutional attention or gained the weight accorded other doctrinal developments. It is widely understood to be one of a kind, perhaps high moral ground, iconic but limited in its application. Peter Schuck, among the case's most thoughtful observers, takes this view: "Some of the manifest difficulties of devising a new constitutional order in an area of law that has long defied one are revealed in *Plyler v. Doe*, in which the Court felt obliged to turn conventional legal categories and precedents inside out in order to reach a morally appealing result."[29]

● Much as *Brown v. Board of Education* (*Brown I*) could not authoritatively cite Fourteenth Amendment framers or ratifiers as being unsympathetic to segregated public schooling, for the historical evidence either did not apply or more likely accepted the status quo, the Fourteenth Amendment's ratification could not fully apprehend or accommodate a view of unauthorized aliens in the community, as there was no such legal construct until much later in the 20th century. In *Brown I*, Chief Justice Warren wrote, concerning Reconstruction history, the "most avid proponents of the post-War Amendments undoubtedly intended them to remove all legal distinctions among 'all persons born or naturalized in the United States,'" while the "opponents, just as certainly, were antagonistic to both the letter and the spirit of the Amendments and wished them to have the most limited effect." He noted, further, that "free common schools, supported by general taxation, had not yet taken hold" at the time the amendment was adopted and that white children were educated by private groups, while the education of black children "was almost nonexistent, and practically all of the race were illiterate. In fact, any education of Negroes was forbidden by law in some states."[30] Such was also the case with undocumented children at the time, to the extent that any such children were being schooled at all in the southwestern United States, even after the 1846–1847 U.S.-Mexican War or the 1848 Treaty of Guadalupe Hidalgo (and New Mexico and Arizona were not admitted fully into the Union until 1912).[31] And the extensive work of historian Mae Ngai has convincingly demonstrated that national immigration policy did not admit or envision concepts of "the undocumented," especially along what was to become the U.S.-Mexican border, until the middle of the 20th century.[32]

Plyler v. Doe transformed immigration law in both broad and narrow fashion. For the many reasons examined here, the case can be considered one of many in a developing line of residency cases reaching back to *Graham*, in which the states and Congress were required to draw lines with more specificity and nuance than any of the legislative bodies had done by the broad, unvariegated brush strokes that did not distinguish among the many categories of citizens (residents of Alaska for oil-revenue sharing), permanent residents (Arizona Medicare and Medicaid patients who met durational tests), nonimmigrants (G-4 treaty-organization dependents who wished to gain Maryland resident-tuition status), and even the undocumented. Thus, legislators simply could not convince the Court that there was even a "substantial purpose" being employed in carving out the classes for eligibility—which would normally be the minimal standard for upholding such classifications.

In this sense, all aliens "within" the borders of the country, no matter their legal status, are eligible for certain constitutional protection, a principle of long standing. That the Texas statute singled out the children, innocent even if their parents had "dirty" hands, convinced the lower courts and Justice Brennan all the more that the State could not meet even this minimal test. That it was educational eligibility convinced the Court to employ the level of scrutiny it chose and to fashion the extent of the right to be accorded. *Plyler*, read soon after its ruling with the *Bynum* and *Toll* cases, suggests that the Supreme Court was willing to examine more carefully the benefits or statuses to be withheld or extended by states or Congress: even citizen schoolchildren must reside in the attendance zone with their parents or guardians, and even adult dependents legally in the country with nonimmigrant visas that require maintenance of a foreign domicile can lay claim to college residency for tuition purposes. Henceforth, durational benefits and status distinctions would have to withstand more searching scrutiny and delineate immigration classifications more carefully and with nuance. That said, the decision's incorporation of "inchoate" federal policy and lack of efficacy failed to generate clear doctrine or guidelines, issues that have surfaced in the current debates over the extent to which local or state authorities may regulate immigration by means similar to the Texas school-attendance zones, such as renter laws, work authorization, policing powers, and other municipal ordinances.

As a general proposition, I would be reluctant to grant extraordinary, unreviewable deference to immigration authorities, as I would be to giving unbridled power to any governmental actors. The sad and sorry record of immigration policy's reflecting prejudice rather than our better angels is manifest in virtually every footnote I have fashioned for this project. In the collective brainstem of most Mexican Americans, we need hear no more than mention of "Operation Wetback," the Bracero Program, or the "Secure Border Initiative [*sic*]" to flinch at increased federal authority or congressional delegation of power and authority to the executive branch. Whether the power accrues by the doctrine of enforcing sovereign external relations or by giving extraordinary *Chevron, U.S.A.*-style deference to administrative-agency decision making, including statutory interpretation and administrative rule making, on the presumption that this branch of government is elected by the voting public, these underlying rationales assume full and robust participation in the polity by the affected and interested parties, who then bind themselves to this process.[33] This electoral algebra, of course, does not apply to the undocumented, whose presence is unauthorized, liminal, and contested.

The suggestion that proxies and advocates for the political stakes of the unauthorized population can carry these interests forward and assert them as others would in the traditional fashion is ludicrous. Immigration and administrative law scholar Kevin R. Johnson has summarized this paradox. By his calculus, administering immigration laws and programs pose

> a fundamental problem for the democratic rationale for deference: if we entrust agencies with making and enforcing the laws because of their political accountability, what should we do if a specific agency is only accountable to part of the group of people affected, directly or indirectly, by its decisions? Both lawful and undocumented immigrants, barred from having any formal political input, namely, a vote, in the administrative state are deeply affected, and often injured, by decisions of the bureaucracy. Citizens, whose interests often diverge from those of noncitizens, are indirectly affected by the decisions of the immigration agencies, but, whatever the limitations of their input, have a full voice in the national political system about the general policy direction of the bureaucracy through election of the President.

As a result, he writes, "immigrants and their advocates lack the hard political capital of the ordinary citizen constituency of an administrative agency. One would expect that the imbalance in political input between the affected communities results in agency rulings and decisions on immigration matters that fail to fully consider or appropriately weigh the interests of immigrants. This fact helps explain why the rights of immigrants have been marginalized by the immigration agencies, as well as by Congress, throughout U.S. history, but especially in times of social stress."[34] He was referring to the specifics of immigrants in the Hurricane Katrina debacle, but his point can be made with equal force to virtually all federal immigration-agency administrative decisions.

Peter Schuck is equally dubious of why judicial deference is so manifest in immigration decision making, a longstanding practice that he chalks up to the inherent nature of sovereignty:

> It is worthwhile pausing to consider why this deference persisted for so long. One might suspect that judicial reluctance to challenge the power of the other branches reflected the weak political support for aliens. Yet even the Warren Court, whose case reports are filled with decisions check-

ing governmental authorities on behalf of politically vulnerable groups, was abjectly deferential in the context of immigration law and thus firmly within the classical tradition. A lack of political influence, therefore, fails to explain why courts that eagerly picked up the cudgels to protect convicted criminals did not do so for aliens.

Other possible explanations for judicial deference seem equally dubious. The Immigration and Naturalization Service (INS), whose administrative competence and fairness have often been harshly criticized, would seem an odd repository for judicial trust. Nor has the congressional record in the immigration area been one to inspire much judicial confidence; legislative threats to constitutional values have been common. Another rationale for extraordinary judicial deference in classical immigration cases—the presence of foreign policy, national security, or other questions of an essentially nonadjudicatory nature—has explicitly been disavowed by the Court. And even if one remains skeptical of this disclaimer—even if one believes that immigration cases often present questions of legislative fact and foreign policy with which courts are and should be profoundly uncomfortable—that rationale can hardly explain the striking pattern of judicial deference in cases decided as late as the 1970's in which daunting questions of that kind were either inconsequential or wholly absent. Indeed, judicial deference cannot even be explained on the grounds that only the claims of aliens are involved: the plaintiffs in some of these decisions asserted claims—unsuccessfully, as it turned out—based primarily upon the rights of United States citizens, not of aliens. . . .

Other considerations reinforce the power of the sovereignty concept as an explanation for judicial deference. For over a century, the states have been consistently excluded from any significant role in the administration of immigration policy. Moreover, immigration policy has enjoyed a considerable consensus as among the President, Congress and the bureaucracy; one searches the immigration cases in vain for a titanic interbranch struggle like those that have occurred in other areas of public law. One measure of this consensus is that Congress has chosen to confer exceedingly broad discretion over the most farreaching immigration decisions, has delegated this discretion not merely to the executive branch but to a cabinet official who traditionally is a close political confidant of the President, and has done so not only for matters obviously requiring the weighing of many administrative considerations but also for those impinging upon fundamental civil liberties.[35]

I am persuaded that these loosely woven threads of unfettered discretion and distrust of the process can be stitched solely by a robust sense and application of the preemption doctrine. Although I share the distrust aimed at lodging so much authority for immigration policy and procedure at the federal level, I am more loathe to allow it to cascade down to the state and local level. To employ another metaphor, I would not let immigration policy or, more important, enforcement norms regress to the mean. For every state that has accorded resident tuition status to undocumented college students, there has been a South Carolina or Georgia or Arizona to take a step backward. For every regrettable federal action, there have been several yahoo local and state ordinances, either sprouting in regional restrictionist soil or as part of a national agenda to turn the clock back. In *INS v. Chadha*, a case decided within a year of *Plyler*, and in many other cases, the Supreme Court has made clear "the plenary authority of Congress over aliens."[36] To turn back the only Texas local anti-immigrant ordinance, in Farmers Branch, near Dallas, MALDEF had to secure three temporary restraining orders and eventually won a permanent injunction, making it the Dutch-boy legal-defense fund, requiring fingers in too many local and state dikes.[37] To undertake and finance all the litigation required of MALDEF in Arizona, the organization had to close its Atlanta office, despite the many incidents of discrimination against Latinos in the southeastern United States.[38]

Earlier, in my review of the various legal strands of *Plyler*, I suggested why I thought that the preemption doctrine would have been more useful even than that of equal protection, especially in the current nativist climate. By deciding on the fresh equal protection grounds and by unpersuasively distinguishing (or by finessing) *De Canas v. Bica*'s ostensible application, the Court never squared up the question of the extent to which preemption was implicated. The Court could have held that the employment-related provisions of *De Canas*'s California unemployment-program administration were not on all fours with the Texas school statute. Justice Brennan could have persuasively revealed the extensive regulatory structure and legislative detail that had erected the mixed federal-state benefit regime upheld in *De Canas*, contrasting it with the lack of a federal role in governing state and local elementary-secondary schooling. He could have noted the absence of a Texas legislative history that reversed the longstanding practice of not allowing "free public schooling" but still requiring such attendance of the children in the state's truancy statutes, which never were reformulated to address the status of their attendance obligation. He could have noted the Hobson's choice facing the undocumented parents, whose children were required by Texas law to attend school, even as the Tyler and Houston Independent School Districts were charging large fees for the obligatory attendance. That he did not attempt such an analysis has frustrated the alien-benefits question since, or at least made the conflated mix of preemption doctrine and equal protection difficult to discern, even if in practical terms, observers may not care which constitutional theory drives the decision making or jurisprudential inquiry. The transcendent, glorious meaning of *Plyler* surely is its equal protection principles, applied to innocent sojourners in the larger community, but also its place in the complex assignment equation of who apportions benefits and status and to whom and under what constraints. Having decided *Plyler* on its preemption grounds would have assisted courts today that are deciding similar attempts to regulate immigration policy at the state and local level; such rulings would then shore up *Plyler's* stature as timely and relevant, reaffirming it as the robust and supple decision it has revealed itself to be.

The communitarian seeds of *Plyler* may not have rooted in the sterile nativistic and restrictionist soil, but a "morally appealing result" is surely preferable to its antonym. And it may be difficult for immigrant activists and defenders to remain vigilant when threats do occur, either the direct Gallegly-like or Proposition 187 threats or the more oblique practices identified here, such as heightened attendance-zone enforcement or driver's license and Social Security identification policies. I prefer to cast my lot with the generous impulses of communitarian traits in the American character, trusting and verifying the challenges and recognizing the long view. However these children arrived here, most of them are our newest family members, and we ignore this at our peril.[39] For this reason, if for no other, *Plyler v. Doe* should be celebrated and noted as the salutary event it surely is.

Notes

1. Quoted in Amy Thompson, *A Child Alone and without Papers* 14 (Center for Public Policy Priorities 2008) [translation by Michael A. Olivas; Spanish misspellings in original].

2. For comprehensive analyses and different approaches to these complex topics, see Michael A. Olivas, *Immigration-Related State Statutes and Local Ordinances: Preemption, Prejudice, and the Proper Role for Enforcement*, 2007 U. Chi. Legal F. 27 (2007); Peter J. Spiro, *Beyond Citizenship: American Identity after Globalization* (Oxford Univ. Press 2008); Catherine Dauvergne, *Making People Illegal: What Globalization Means for Migration and Law* (Cambridge Univ. Press 2008); Roxanne L. Doty, *The Law into Their Own Hands: Immigration and the Politics of Exceptionalism* (Univ. Ariz. Press 2009); Elizabeth McCormick, *The Oklahoma Taxpayer and Citizen Protection Act: Blowing off Steam or Setting Wildfires?*, 23 Geo. Immigr. L.J. 293 (2009); D. Carolina Núñez, *Fractured Membership: Deconstructing Territoriality to Secure Rights and Remedies for the Undocumented Worker*, 2010 Wis. L. Rev. 817 (2010).

3. Regrettably, there is a substantial literature on these developments. On the small shelf of the best of these chronicles, see Steven W. Bender, *Greasers and Gringos: Latinos, Law, and the American Imagination* (NYU Press 2003); Kevin R. Johnson, *The "Huddled Masses" Myth: Immigration and Civil Rights* (Temple Univ. Press 2004); Marcos Pizarro, *Chicanas and Chicanos in School: Racial Profiling, Identity Battles, and Empowerment* (Univ. Texas Press 2005); Laura E. Gomez, *Manifest Destinies: The Making of the Mexican American Race* (NYU Press 2007); Leo R. Chavez, *The Latino Threat: Constructing Immigrants, Citizens, and the Nation* (Stanford Univ. Press 2008); Richard R. Valencia, *Chicano Students and the Courts: The Mexican American Struggle for Educational Equality* (NYU Press 2008). For many of the details about these cases, see generally Olivas, *Immigration-Related State Statutes*, and the litigation docket of the Mexican American Legal Defense and Education Fund: *Providing Access to a Quality Education*, available at http://www.maldef.org/education/litigation/index.html (accessed Mar. 15, 2010). See also Maria Sacchetti, *Lynn's Immigrants and Police Share a Gulf*, Boston Globe, Sept. 25, 2009, at Metro-1 (In Lynn, Massachusetts, a "Guatemalan man was brutally beaten," who "police say was targeted because of his ethnicity"). For details of the Marcelo Lucero trial, see Manny Fernandez, *In Jury Selection for Hate Crime, a Struggle to Find Tolerance*, N.Y. Times, Mar. 9, 2010, at A20; Manny Fernandez, *L.I. Teenagers Hunted Latinos for "Sport," Prosecutor Says*, N.Y. Times, Mar. 19, 2010, at A18. Manny Fernandez, *Racial Slurs Preceded L.I. Attack, Victim's Friend Testifies*, N.Y. Times, Mar. 25, 2010, at A24; Manny Fernandez, *Lawsuit Filed by*

Estate of Immigrant Killed on Long Island, N.Y. Times, Nov. 22, 2010, A27 (convicted killer received twenty-five-year prison term for "beaner hopping").

NOTES TO CHAPTER 2

1. Barbara Belejack, *A Lesson in Equal Protection: The Texas Cases That Opened the Schoolhouse Door to Undocumented Immigrant Children*, Texas Observer, July 13, 2007, at 14–21.

2. The historian Mae M. Ngai, in a perceptive study concerning the history of undocumented immigration and the way in which different nationalities have been racialized by the immigration process, has concluded,

> [The process of how the nation constituted immigration] had an important racial dimension because the application and reform of deportation policy had disparate effects on Europeans and Canadians, on the one hand, and Mexicans, on the other hand. But, the disparity was not simply the result of existing racism. Rather, the processes of territorial redefinition and administrative enforcement informed divergent paths of immigrant racialization. Europeans and Canadians tended to be disassociated from the real and imagined category of illegal alien, which facilitated their national and racial assimilation as white American citizens. In contrast, Mexicans emerged as iconic illegal aliens. Illegal status became constitutive of a racialized Mexican identity and of Mexicans' exclusion from the national community and polity.

Mae M. Ngai, *The Strange Career of the Illegal Alien: Immigration Restriction and Deportation Policy in the United States, 1924–1965*, 21 Law & Hist. Rev. 69, 72 (2003). Her full-length book, *Impossible Subjects: Illegal Aliens and the Making of Modern America* (Princeton Univ. Press 2004), outlines these differentiated developments in considerable detail, and this background elaborates on why "illegal alienage" has developed in immigration policy and practice as essentially a concept of guarding our southern border (our *"frontera"*) from undesirables. See Carl Gutiérrez-Jones, *Rethinking the Borderlands: Between Chicano Culture and Legal Discourse* (Univ. California Press 1995); Steven W. Bender, *Greasers and Gringos: Latinos, Law, and the American Imagination* (NYU Press 2003); Juan F. Perea, *A Brief History of Race and the U.S.-Mexican Border: Tracing the Trajectories of Conquest*, 51 UCLA L. Rev. 283 (2003); Laura E. Gómez, *Manifest Destinies: The Making of the Mexican American Race* (NYU Press 2007).

3. Peter H. Schuck, *The Transformation of Immigration Law*, 84 Colum. L. Rev. 1, 54 (1984).

4. Plyler v. Doe, 457 U.S. 202 (1982).

5. In the Houston case challenging this statute, the federal-court trial judge said,

> The court cannot state with absolute certainty what the Legislature intended when passing the amendment to 21.031. Neither the court nor the parties have uncovered a shred of legislative history accompanying the 1975 amendment. There was no debate in the Legislature before the amendment was passed by a voice vote. There were no studies preceding the introduction of the legislation to determine the impact that undocumented children were having on the schools or to project the fiscal implications of the amendment.

In re Alien Children Education Litigation, 501 F. Supp. 544, 555 n.19 (1980). The record, such as it is, showed that the legislation likely arose after a Texas attorney general opinion held that prior to 1975, the Texas education law did not differentiate among children on the basis of their immigration status. Att'y Gen. Op. H-586 (1975), p. 3.

6. Tex. Educ. Code Ann. § 21.031 (Vernon Supp. 1981).

7. The *In re Alien Children* record included considerable statistical testimony, including the data in this paragraph, prepared by then law student Laura Oren and Houston lawyer Joseph Vail; I found copies of the original hand-tabulated data in Oren's files on this subject (copies on file with author). Both Oren and Vail became my colleagues at the University of Houston Law Center, where both migrated after local law careers, including Vail's later service as an immigration judge. Vail died in spring 2008. See Michael A. Olivas, *In Memoriam: Joe Vail*, 13 Bender's Immigr. Bull. 267 (2008).

8. Hernandez v. Houston Independent School District, 558 S.W.2d 121 (Tex. Civ. App.-Austin 1977). The case was tried in Austin rather than Houston because of the administrative proceedings required to challenge the state administrative agency.

9. *Hernandez*, 558 S.W.2d at 125.

10. Avila to Roos, Sept. 26, 1977, MALDEF Files, M0673, Box 115, Folder 5, Stanford University. I found a copy of the letter in the Stanford University Green Library Special Collections Room. The concordance to these records is Theresa Mesa Casey & Pedro Hernández, eds., *Research Guide to the Records of MALDEF/PRLDEF* (Stanford Univ. Libraries 1996). Additional files from early MALDEF work in Houston are available in the archives of the Houston Metropolitan Research Center (HMRC), particularly the Abraham Ramirez collection, used extensively by Guadalupe San Miguel, Jr., to explain earlier Houston school-desegregation cases and bilingual-education issues in his excellent study *Brown, Not White: School Integration and the Chicano Movement in Houston* (Texas A&M Univ. Press 2001). Ramirez was a local civil rights attorney who was affiliated with MALDEF in its early years, although he was not an employee. For additional studies of Houston schooling, see William H. Kellar, *Make Haste Slowly: Moderates, Conservatives, and School Desegregation in Houston* (Texas A&M Univ. Press 1999); Angela Valenzuela, *Subtractive Schooling: U.S.-Mexican Youth and the Politics of Caring* (SUNY Press, 1999).

11. Martinez v. Bynum, 461 U.S. 321 (1983). In order to stop this practice, Congress in 1996 enacted what is now INA § 214(m), 8 U.S.C. § 1184(m).

12. Steven H. Wilson, *Brown over "Other White": Mexican Americans' Legal Arguments and Litigation Strategy in School Desegregation Lawsuits*, 21 Law & Hist. Rev. 145, 193 (2003) (citations omitted). See Vicki L. Ruiz, *"We Always Tell Our Children They Are Americans"*: Mendez v. Westminster *and the California Road to* Brown v. Board of Education, 200 Coll. Board Rev. 20 (Fall 2003); Margaret E. Montoya, *A Brief History of Chicana/o School Segregation: One Rationale for Affirmative Action*, 12 Berk. La Raza L.J. 159 (2001); Ian F. Haney López, *Race, Ethnicity, Erasure: The Salience of Race to LatCrit Theory*, 85 Cal. L. Rev. 57 (1998); Ian F. Haney López, *White by Law: The Legal Construction of Race* (NYU Press 1996); Clare Sheridan, *"Another White Race": Mexican Americans and the Paradox of Whiteness in Jury Selection*, 21 Law & Hist. Rev. 109 (2003).

13. Richard Griswold del Castillo & Anthony Accardo, *César Chávez: The Struggle for Justice* (Piñata Books 2002).

14. San Antonio Independent School District v. Rodriguez, 411 U.S. 1 (1973). For a detailed history of the case, see Michael Heise, *The Story of* San Antonio Independent

School Dist. v. Rodriguez: *School Finance, Local Control, and Constitutional Limits*, in *Education Law Stories* 51–82 (Michael A. Olivas & Ronna Greff Schneider, eds., Foundation 2008).

15. George A. Martinez, *Legal Indeterminacy, Judicial Discretion, and the Mexican American Litigation Experience: 1930–1980*, 27 U.C. Davis L. Rev. 555 (1994); Mario T. García, *Mexican Americans: Leadership, Ideology, and Identity, 1930–1960* (Yale Univ. Press, 1989); Gary A. Greenfield & Don B. Kates, Jr., *Mexican Americans, Racial Discrimination, and the Civil Rights Act of 1866*, 63 Cal. L. Rev. 662 (1975); Richard Delgado & Victoria Palacios, *Mexican Americans as a Legally Cognizable Class under Rule 23 and the Equal Protection Clause*, 50 Notre Dame Law. 393 (1975); George J. Sánchez, *Becoming Mexican American: Ethnicity, Culture and Identity in Chicano Los Angeles, 1900–1945* (Oxford Univ. Press 1993); Christopher Arriola, *Knocking on the Schoolhouse Door:* Mendez v. Westminster, *Equal Protection, Public Education, and Mexican Americans in the 1940's*, 8 La Raza L.J. 166 (1995); Neil Foley, *The White Scourge: Mexicans, Blacks, and Poor Whites in Texas Cotton Culture* (Univ. California Press 1997); Juan F. Perea, Buscando *America: Why Integration and Equal Protection Fail to Protect Latinos*, 117 Harv. L. Rev. 1420 (2004).

16. Guadalupe San Miguel, Jr., *"Let All of Them Take Heed": Mexican Americans and the Campaign for Educational Equality in Texas, 1910–1981* (Univ. Texas Press 1987). I also examined all MALDEF board minutes and annual reports, stored in the Los Angeles national headquarters, Apr. 2007.

17. San Miguel, *"Let All of Them Take Heed,"* 174 tbl. 10; see Jorge C. Rangel & Carlos M. Alcala, *De Jure Segregation of Chicanos in Texas Schools*, 7 Harv. C.R.-C.L. L. Rev. 307 (1972).

18. United States v. Texas, 506 F. Supp. 405 (E.D. Tex. 1981), rev'd, 680 F.2d 356 (5th Cir. 1982). It is not surprising that such anti-Mexican legislation and practices would have originated in Texas, a jurisdiction widely regarded to be officially inhospitable to its Mexican-origin population. See Arnoldo De León, *They Called Them Greasers: Anglo Attitudes toward Mexicans in Texas, 1821–1900* (Univ. Texas Press 1983); David Montejano, *Anglos and Mexicans in the Making of Texas, 1836–1986* (Univ. Texas Press 1987); Marcos Pizarro, *Chicanas and Chicanos in School: Racial Profiling, Identity Battles, and Empowerment* (Univ. Texas Press 2005); Richard R. Valencia, *Chicano Students and the Courts: The Mexican American Struggle for Educational Equality* (NYU Press 2008); Cynthia E. Orozco, *No Mexicans, Women, or Dogs Allowed: The Rise of the Mexican American Civil Rights Movement* (Univ. Texas Press 2009).

19. United States v. Texas, 506 F. Supp. at 428. The final order ending the case came in September 2010, in 601 F.3d 354 (5th Cir. 2010).

20. For example, the *U.S. v. Texas* case was formally styled *United States of America, Plaintiff, Mexican American Legal Defense Fund, LULAC, and G.I. Forum, Plaintiffs-Intervenors v. State of Texas et al., Defendants.* For histories of these organizations, see Carl Allsup, *The American G.I. Forum: Origins and Evolution* (Univ. Texas Press 1982); Benjamin Márquez, *LULAC: The Evolution of a Mexican American Organization* (Univ. Texas Press 1993); Henry A. J. Ramos, *The American GI Forum: In Pursuit of the Dream, 1948–1983* (Arte Público Press 1998); Laura E. Gómez, *The Birth of the "Hispanic" Generation: Attitudes of Mexican-American Political Elites toward the Hispanic Label*, 75 Latin Am. Persp. 45 (1992); Suzanne Oboler, *The Politics of Labeling: Latino/a Cultural Identities of Self and Others*, 75 Latin Am. Persp. 18 (1992); Suzanne Oboler, *Ethnic Labels, Latino Lives* (Univ. Minnesota Press, 1995); Orozco, *No Mexicans*.

21. For example, Judge Justice was the trial judge in *U.S. v. Texas*, in which he found Texas and the school districts to have been out of compliance with regard to school-desegregation and English-language-instruction obligations under federal law. 506 F. Supp. 405 (E.D. Tex. 1981); rev'd, 680 F.2d 356 (5th Cir. 1982). The case finally ended in 2010, by which time Justice had died. 601 F.3d 354 (5th Cir. 2010). For examples of his long record of progressive decisions, see John J. DiIulio, *Governing Prisons* (Free Press 1987) (longstanding prison litigation). For this record, he earned an impeachment bill, introduced on June 24, 1981, but never passed. H.R. 168, 97th Cong. (1981). See Frank R. Kemerer, *William Wayne Justice: A Judicial Biography* (Univ. Texas Press 1991). He died in October 2009, with virtually all the obituaries citing his role in the *Plyler* case. See Albert H. Kauffman, *Judge William Wayne Justice: A Life of Human Dignity and Refractory Mules*, 41 St. Mary's L.J. 215 (2009). On the twenty-fifth anniversary of the case, the judge said of his ruling, "I think it's the most important case I ever decided." Katherine Leal Unmuth, *25 Years Ago, Tyler Case Opened Schools to Illegal Migrants*, Dall. Morn. News, June 11, 2007, at A1.

22. The plaintiff in that early case was named Carlos Hernandez. See the letter from Peter Roos to Leonel Castillo, in which he warns, "We have been informed that the local United States Attorney, John Hannah, has requested the Director of [the Dallas INS] to take steps to deport the plaintiffs in this case and possibly to conduct a sweep in the Tyler region." Roos to Castillo, Sept. 13, 1977, MALDEF Files, M0673, Box 115, Folder 5, Stanford University. This issue arose in a recent case in which undocumented college students in Virginia who brought an action concerning a state statute that denied state college access to undocumented students sought to file their case anonymously. The judge ruled against them on this issue. Doe 1 et al. v. Merten, 219 F.R.D. 387, 184 Ed. Law Rep. 843 (E.D. Va. 2004). And then he ruled against them on the larger issue, once alternative plaintiff organizations were enlisted as substitutes, holding that the state of Virginia could enact practices which denied undocumented students admission or residency status. Equal Access Education v. Merten, 305 F. Supp. 2d 585 (E.D. Va. 2004), 325 F. Supp. 2d 655 (E.D. Va. 2004) (finding that students did not have standing, absent evidence that institution denied admission on perceived immigration status).

23. In the *Plyler* trial court case and at the Fifth Circuit, the U.S. Department of Justice and the U.S. attorney intervened on the side of the schoolchildren. After Castillo left office, he returned to Houston. In 1983, he wrote in a foreword to a special immigration issue of a law review: "[T]he authors are all persons of recognized ability and concern. . . . [Among others, Isaias Torres and Peter Schey] have all been involved in the daily battles of making the INA [Immigration and Nationality Act] fit a particular individual's situation at a particular time. During the time that I served as Commissioner (1977–79), it was my privilege to be sued by some of these individuals. I knew that regardless of the outcome, the ultimate goal of justice for immigrants would prevail because effective advocates help cure improper procedures and faulty legislation." Leonel Castillo, *Foreword*, 5 Hous. J. Int'l L. 191 (1983).

24. See Doe v. Plyler, 628 F.2d 448, 450 (5th Cir. 1980).

25. Roos to Roy Fuentes, Oct. 18, 1977, MALDEF Files, M0673, Box 115, Folder 6, Stanford University. Roos was also trying at this time to address similar issues in California, as a series of letters in the MALDEF files revealed. He wrote California school districts that their attendance practices violated state guidelines for undocumented children. See, e.g.,

Mar. 12, 1979, MALDEF Files, M0673, Box 61, Folder 8, Stanford University; Oct. 29, 1979, MALDEF Files, M0673, Box 62, Folder 1, Stanford University; Oct. 19, 1979, M0673, Box 62, Folder 1, Stanford University.

26. Doe v. Plyler, 458 F. Supp. 569 (E.D. Tex. 1978).

27. See *In re Alien Children*, 501 F. Supp. at 552.

28. The federal case became a veritable magnet, as various plaintiffs and defendants were added, requiring many pages of explanation for these procedural issues. A playbill would include (1) from the Southern District: Martinez v. Reagen, C.A. No. H-78-1797, filed Sept. 18, 1978; Cardenas v. Meyer, C.A. No. H-78-1862, filed Sept. 27, 1978; Garza v. Reagen, C.A. No. H-78-2132, filed Nov. 6, 1978; Mendoza v. Clark, C.A. No. H-78-1831, filed Sept. 22, 1978; (2) from the Northern District: Doe v. Wright, C.A. No. 3-79-0440-D; and (3) from the Western District: Roe v. Holm, MO-79-CA-49; Coe v. Holm, MO-78-CA-54. What the court termed "tag-along actions," originally filed in the Southern District, were also consolidated: Cortes v. Wheeler, C.A. H-79-1926, filed Sept. 20, 1979; Rodrigues v. Meyer, C.A. H-79-1927, filed Sept. 20, 1979; Adamo v. Reagen, C.A. H-79-1928, filed Sept. 20, 1979; and Arguelles v. Meyer, C.A. H-79-2071, filed Oct. 4, 1979. Six additional cases originally filed in the Eastern District of Texas were likewise consolidated: Doe v. Sulphur Springs, P-79-31-CA, filed Oct. 29, 1979; Doe v. Lodestro, B-79-618-CA, filed Sept. 18, 1979; Doe v. Ford, TY-79-351-CA, filed Sept. 28, 1979; Roe v. Horn, TY-79-338-CA, filed Sept. 24, 1979; Roe v. Como-Pickton, P-79-234-CA, filed Oct. 19, 1979; and Poe v. Chappel Hill, TY-79-449-CA, filed Dec. 10, 1979.

Observers of this trial have reported that Judge Woodrow Seals committed an interesting gaffe during arguments when he asked "whether anything of worldwide importance had ever been written in Spanish," or words to that effect. (Apparently he had not heard of the classic works by Miguel Cervantes, Octavio Paz, José Vasconcelos, Gabriel García Márquez, Pablo Neruda, Sor Juana, or the many other Latino and Latina writers.) Witnesses report that it was an electric moment, one he sensed and after which he publicly apologized. See Juan R. Palomo, *Judge Seals Calls Spanish Comment "Senseless, Dreadful,"* Hous. Post, Mar. 7, 1980, at 3B.

29. A good example of this unreliability appeared in connection with a long-running dispute involving public colleges in Nashville, Tennessee. The U.S. Department of Justice supported the plaintiffs over the course of many years, and after working out the dispute among the many parties, the judge entered a final order that included racially specific remedies. Later, after the Reagan administration took office, the Department of Justice attempted to switch horses and get the court to strike down the agreement. The judge refused to accept this too-little-too-late intervention. Geier v. Alexander, 801 F.2d 799 (6th Cir. 1986); see also Geier v. Blanton, 427 F. Supp. 644 (1977). The original case finally wound down on June 18, 2004, when the issue of attorney fees was decided. Geier v. Sundquist, 372 F.3d 784 (6th Cir. 2004).

30. Roos to Isaias Torres, May 17, 1979, MALDEF Files, M0673, Box 61, Folder 10, Stanford University. In the interest of full disclosure, I note that Torres was a Georgetown University Law Center classmate of mine. I also note that I relied on insider-baseball conversations with Augustina H. Reyes, who was a senior Houston ISD administrator and then a member of the Houston ISD board as an elected official. I married her in 1984.

31. These were some of the problems that had doomed the educational finance case. See Michael Heise, *State Constitutional Litigation, Educational Finance, and Legal Impact: An*

Empirical Analysis, 63 U. Cin. L. Rev. 1735 (1995); Augustina H. Reyes, *Does Money Make a Difference for Hispanic Students in Urban Schools?*, 36 Educ. & Urb. Soc'y 353 (2003).

32. Roos to Torres, May 17, 1979.

33. *Id.*

34. Mark V. Tushnet, *The NAACP's Legal Strategy against Segregated Education, 1925–1950* (Univ. North Carolina Press 1987); Mark V. Tushnet, *Making Civil Rights Law: Thurgood Marshall and the Supreme Court, 1936–1961* (Oxford Univ. Press 1994); Robert J. Cottrol, Raymond T. Diamond & Leland B. Ware, Brown v. Board of Education: *Caste, Culture, and the Constitution* (Univ. Press Kansas 2003); Amilcar Shabazz, *Advancing Democracy: African Americans and the Struggle for Access and Equity in Higher Education in Texas* (Univ. North Carolina Press 2004); William C. Kidder, *The Struggle for Access from* Sweatt to Grutter: *A History of African American, Latino, and American Indian Law School Admissions, 1950–2000*, 19 Harv. BlackLetter L.J. 1 (2003). For the history of earlier Mexican American trial strategies, see Lisa Lizette Barrera, *Minorities and the University of Texas Law School (1950–1980)*, 4 Tex. Hisp. J.L. & Pol'y 99 (1998); Guadalupe Salinas, *Mexican-Americans and the Desegregation of Schools in the Southwest*, 8 Hous. L. Rev. 929 (1971); Ricardo Romo, *Southern California and the Origins of Latino Civil Rights Activism*, 3 W. Legal Hist. 379 (1990); George A. Martinez, *The Legal Construction of Race: Mexican-Americans and Whiteness*, 2 Harv. Latino L. Rev. 321 (1997); Michael A. Olivas, ed., *"Colored Men" and "Hombres Aquí"*: Hernandez v. Texas *and the Emergence of Mexican-American Lawyering* (Arte Público 2006); Michael A. Olivas, *The "Trial of the Century" That Never Was: Staff Sgt. Macario Garcia, the Congressional Medal of Honor, and the Oasis Café*, 83 Ind. L.J. 1391 (2008); Valencia, *Chicano Students*.

35. Roos to Torres, May 17, 1979.

36. *In re Alien Children*, 501 F. Supp. at 596–597. His remarks about the Spanish language had occurred on the final day of the plaintiffs' testimony.

37. Plyler v. Doe, 451 U.S. 968 (1981) (noting probable jurisdiction in the *Plyler* litigation).

38. Texas v. Certain Named and Unnamed Undocumented Alien Children, 452 U.S. 937 (1981) (noting probable jurisdiction in *In re Alien Children*). The procedural sequence is more fully explained in the *Plyler* merits decision, *Plyler*, 457 U.S. at 207–210.

39. Although the Carter administration officials had actually supported MALDEF and the Houston children's attorneys in the earlier stages of the cases, including both the trial court and Fifth Circuit phases, the Reagan administration did not side with the appellee children when the cases finally made their way to the Supreme Court, filing instead only as amicus curiae. 1981 WL 390001. As examples of the support MALDEF tried to line up for its side, the MALDEF files include numerous letters written by Roos. Roos to Peter Schilla, May 19, 1981, Western Center on Law and Poverty, Sacramento; Roos to Schilla, May 14, 1981, M0673, Box 63, Folder 6, Stanford University; Roos to Norella Beni Hall (urging her support but focusing on education issue), M0673, Box 63, Folder 6, Stanford University; Roos to Lorenza Schmidt, Member, California Board of Education, June 25, 1981, M0673, Box 63, Folder 7, Stanford University; Roos to Associate Attorney General Drew Days, Mar. 28, 1979, M0673, Box 61, Folder 8, Stanford University; and Roos to William Clohan, Under Secretary, U.S. Dept. of Education, May 20, 1981, M0673, Box 63, Folder 6, Stanford University. The files also include a letter from HEW Secretary Joseph Califano to U.S. Solicitor General Wade McCree, urging the United States to enter the

case on behalf of the children plaintiffs. Califano to McCree, July 17, 1979, M0673, Box 907, Folder 9, Stanford University. These letters and dozens more show the extent to which Roos and MALDEF sought and then shored up support for their clients. Veteran Supreme Court observer Linda Greenhouse has carefully reviewed the notes and files from the case deliberations and has captured the dynamics of the transitions between DOJ administrations, which likely accounted for the unusual silence. See Linda Greenhouse, *What Would Justice Powell Do? The "Alien Children" Case and the Meaning of Equal Protection*, 25 Const. Comment. 29, 30–33 (2008) (citations omitted). At footnote number 10, noting the inconsistencies, she characterized it this way: "The brief the Solicitor General filed was an extremely odd, even tortured, document." At the end of the day, and at the margins, this ambivalence likely worked to the advantage of the children's case.

40. *Plyler*, 457 U.S. at 227.

41. *Id.*

42. Graham v. Richardson, 403 U.S. 365, 375 (1971).

43. *Doe*, 628 F.2d at 576–577.

44. *Plyler*, 457 U.S. at 229.

45. *Id.* at 229–230.

46. *Id.* at 228.

47. *Id.* at 225–226.

48. *Id.* at 229–230.

49. *Id.* at 230

50. "No State shall . . . deprive any person of life, liberty, or property, without due process of law; nor deny to any person within its jurisdiction the equal protection of the laws." U.S. Const. amend. XIV, § 1.

51. Yick Wo v. Hopkins, 118 U.S. 356, 369 (1886) (stating that Fourteenth Amendment provisions "are universal in their application to all persons within the territorial jurisdiction, without regard to any differences of race, of color, or of nationality").

52. Wong Wing v. United States, 163 U.S. 228 (1896).

53. *Plyler*, 457 U.S. at 211.

54. *Id.* at 213. In the dissent, Chief Justice Burger concurred that the equal protection clause applies to undocumented aliens. *Id.* at 243.

55. *Id.* at 219 n.19.

56. *Id.* at 220 (citing Trimble v. Gordon, 430 U.S. 762, 770 (1977), an important case applying greater scrutiny to classifications disadvantaging children born out of wedlock).

57. *Id.* at 221 (citations omitted).

58. *Id.* at 222.

59. *Id.* at 223–224.

60. *Id.* at 248.

61. *Id.* at 210 n.8. In a postsecondary-education alienage case decided soon after *Plyler*, Toll v. Moreno, 458 U.S. 1 (1982), the decision turned on preemption. See Michael A. Olivas, Plyler v. Doe, Toll v. Moreno, *and Postsecondary Admissions: Undocumented Adults and "Enduring Disability,"* 15 J.L. & Educ. 19 (1986).

62. *Plyler*, 457 U.S. at 224–226.

63. De Canas v. Bica, 424 U.S. 351 (1976).

64. Mathews v. Diaz, 426 U.S. 67 (1976).

65. *De Canas*, 424 U.S. at 356.

66. *Plyler*, 457 U.S. at 226. This sentence became the focus of efforts to change federal law in 1996, led by Representative Elton Gallegly (R-CA), to incorporate an explicit provision authorizing exclusion of undocumented children from public schools.

67. Peter H. Schuck, *The Transformation of Immigration Law*, 84 Colum. L. Rev. 1, 58 (1984).

68. Linda S. Bosniak, *Membership, Equality, and the Difference That Alienage Makes*, 69 N.Y.U. L. Rev. 1047, 1057 (1994). See also Kevin R. Johnson, *Civil Rights and Immigration: Challenges for the Latino Community in the Twenty-First Century*, 8 La Raza L.J. 42 (1995); Harold H. Koh, *Equality with a Human Face: Justice Blackmun and the Equal Protection of Aliens*, 8 Hamline L. Rev. 51 (1985).

69. *Plyler*, 457 U.S. at 228.

70. Nishimura Ekiu v. United States, 142 U.S. 651, 659 (1982).

71. Graham v. Richardson, 403 U.S. 365 (1971) (state welfare benefits); Mathews v. Diaz, 426 U.S. 67 (1976) (federal medical insurance); Nyquist v. Mauclet, 432 U.S. 1 (1977) (state tuition assistance); Elkins v. Moreno, 435 U.S. 647 (1978) (state resident tuition); Plyler v. Doe, 457 U.S. 202 (1982) (K–12 public school enrollment); Toll v. Moreno, 458 U.S. 1 (1982) (state resident tuition); Martinez v. Bynum, 461 U.S. 321 (1983) (K–12 public school enrollment).

72. Sugarman v. Dougall, 413 U.S. 634 (1973) (state civil service); In re Griffiths, 413 U.S. 717 (1973) (state bar examination); De Canas v. Bica, 424 U.S. 351 (1976) (state employment authorization); Hampton v. Mow Sun Wong, 426 U.S. 88 (1976) (federal civil service, even though an identical requirement); Examining Bd. of Engineers, Architects and Surveyors v. Flores de Otero, 426 U.S. 572 (1976) (state engineering licensing); Foley v. Connelie, 435 U.S. 291 (1978) (state troopers); Ambach v. Norwick, 441 U.S. 68 (1979) (state public schoolteachers); Cabell v. Chavez-Salido, 454 U.S. 432 (1982) (state probation officers); Bernal v. Fainter, 467 U.S. 216 (1984) (state notary public).

73. Perkins v. Smith, 426 U.S. 913 (1976) (jury service); Skafte v. Rorex, 430 U.S. 961 (1977) (dismissing appeal from Rorex v. Skafte, 553 P.2d 830 (Colo. 1976) [local school board voting]).

74. E.g., Shapiro v. Thompson, 394 U.S. 618 (1969) (right to travel violated by state and D.C. durational requirements); Vlandis v. Kline, 412 U.S. 441 (1973) (out-of-state applicants cannot be irrebuttably presumed to be nonresidents for state tuition); U.S. Dep't of Agriculture v. Moreno, 413 U.S. 528 (1973) (provision of the Food Stamp Act which excludes from participation any household containing an individual who is unrelated to any other member of the household creates an irrational classification in violation of the equal protection component of the due process clause of the Fifth Amendment); Zobel v. Williams, 457 U.S. 55 (1982) (dividend distribution plan under which Alaska apportioned benefits to adult citizens in varying amounts based on length of each citizen's residence violated equal protection clause).

75. Schuck, *Transformation of Immigration Law*, 6–7 (citations omitted).

76. Koh, *Equality*, 57–58.

77. *Id.*, 95 (citations omitted).

78. See, e.g., Peter Brimelow, *Alien Nation: Common Sense about America's Immigration Disaster* (HarperPerennial 1995); Samuel P. Huntington, *Who Are We: The Challenges to America's National Identity* (Simon & Schuster 2004); Kris W. Kobach, *The Quintessential Force Multiplier: The Inherent Authority of Local Police to Make Immigration Arrests*, 69 Alb.

L. Rev. 179 (2005) (arguing that the undocumented have no equitable claims on polity). But see Julian L. Simon, *The Economic Consequences of Immigration* (Univ. Michigan Press 1999); Kevin R. Johnson, *Opening the Floodgates: Why America Needs to Rethink Its Borders and Immigration Laws* (NYU Press 2007) (refuting thesis).

79. *Plyler*, 457 U.S. at 215 (emphasis in the original) (citations omitted).

80. "We reject the claim that 'illegal aliens' are a 'suspect class.'" *Id.* at n.19.

81. *Id.* at 219–220 (emphasis in the original).

82. "The determination to share [the State's] bounty, in this instance tuition-free education, may take into account the character of the relationship between the alien and this country." *Hernandez*, 558 S.W.2d at 125.

83. Mark V. Tushnet, *Justice Lewis F. Powell and the Jurisprudence of Centrism*, 93 Mich. L. Rev. 1854, 1873–1874 (1995).

84. *Id.*

85. See, e.g., Maria L. Ontiveros & Joshua R. Drexler, *The Thirteenth Amendment and Access to Education for Children of Undocumented Workers: A New Look at* Plyler v. Doe, 42 U.S.F. L. Rev. 1045 (2008).

86. Dennis J. Hutchinson, *More Substantive Equal Protection? A Note on* Plyler v. Doe, 1982 Sup. Ct. Rev. 167, 184 (1982). I learned a great deal from this brilliant article, especially about back-handed and left-handed compliments. For example, I had always thought that *tour de force* was a complimentary term. I now know it need not be: "As substantive due process, Plyler is of a piece with Carey; as equal protection, Plyler is simply a *tour de force*." *Id.*, 182.

87. This is a snarky little gem, hidden in the final throes of a review of the 1982 Supreme Court term, in which the authors ridicule *Plyler* as a "particularly troubling recent example" of "the Court's mismanagement of its own resources in the face of higher demands on its time" and characterize it as "worst of all." Yikes. Phillip B. Kurland & Dennis J. Hutchinson, *The Business of the Supreme Court*, [October Term] 1982, 50 U. Chi. L. Rev. 628, 650 n.61 (1983).

88. I had begun my research on the case before I read the work of Hutchinson, so no one was more surprised than I when we both employed the same metaphor of the silent dog. The sound he did not hear was *Shapiro v. Thompson*, 394 U.S. 618 (1969), a right-to-travel case, while mine is *De Canas v. Bica*, 424 U.S. 634 (1976). "The problem was not so much of unsatisfactory analysis, but of silence. The most important dog that did not bark in the opinion of the Court was Shapiro v. Thompson." Hutchinson, *More Substantive Equal Protection?*, 184. In the context of the local and state ordinances that have grown up in the 21st century, I believe that *De Canas* has barked, or not barked, louder.

89. *Plyler*, 457 U.S. at 210 n.8.

90. Tushnet, *Justice Lewis F. Powell*, 1871–1872.

91. Greenhouse, *What Would Justice Powell Do?*, 42–43 (citations omitted).

92. Others would include, e.g., John C. Jeffries, Jr., *Justice Lewis F. Powell, Jr.* (Scribner's 1994); and Tushnet, *Making Civil Rights Law*.

93. Schuck, *Transformation of Immigration Law*, 57 (citations omitted). This language suggests that preemption lurks deep within *Plyler*, even if it was not articulated. Hutchinson also considered whether preemption applies: "Although Justice Brennan's opinion in Plyler reaffirms De Canas v. Bica and analyzes the State's interests in light of the federal immigration scheme, the opinion does not explain why what appears to be preemption

analysis is relevant to the Equal Protection Clause." Hutchinson, *More Substantive Equal Protection?*, 189.

94. See San Miguel, *"Let All of Them Take Heed"*; Rangel & Alcala, *De Jure Segregation*; Gilbert G. Gonzalez, *Chicano Education in the Era of Segregation* (Balch Institute Press 1990); Valencia, *Chicano Students*; Carlos K. Blanton, *From Intellectual Deficiency to Cultural Deficiency: Mexican Americans, Testing, and Public School Policy in the American Southwest, 1920–1940*, 72 Pac. Hist. Rev. 39 (2003). For an interesting online reference for a Mexican American woman who was involved in the important school-finance litigation in San Antonio, labor and education activist Alberta Zepeda Snid, see Virginia Raymond, *Snid, Alberta Zepeda*, Handbook of Texas Online, available at http://www.tshaonline. org/handbook/online/articles/SS/fsn12.html (accessed Aug. 30, 2009). Snid, inaccurately referred to as Alberta Sneed, is already in the *Handbook of Texas Online* in the article on *Rodríguez et al. v. San Antonio ISD*: Cynthia E. Orozco, *Rodríguez et al. v. San Antonio ISD*, Handbook of Texas Online, available at http://www.tshaonline.org/handbook/online/ articles/RR/jrrht.html (accessed Aug. 30, 2009). While there is an increasing amount of attention to this complex history of Latino/a schooling, there is still much that needs attention by future scholars. And if there is too little we know about the schooling of Chicanos, we know less yet of the education litigation undertaken by Puerto Ricans or of other Latino populations. See Antonia Pantoja, *The Making of a Nuyorican: A Memoir* (Arte Público 2002).

95. For critiques of *Brown*, citing its promise and the failure of white communities to implement its holding, see, among others, Alex M. Johnson, Jr., *Bid Whist, Tonk, and United States v. Fordice: Why Integrationism Fails African-Americans Again*, 81 Cal. L. Rev. 1401 (1993); Kimberlé Williams Crenshaw, *Race, Reform, and Retrenchment: Transformation and Legitimation in Antidiscrimination Law*, 101 Harv. L. Rev. 1331 (1988); Richard Delgado & Jean Stefancic, *The Social Construction of* Brown v. Board of Education: *Law Reform and the Reconstructive Paradox*, 36 Wm. & Mary L. Rev. 547 (1995); Jack M. Balkin, ed., *What* Brown v. Board of Education *Should Have Said* (NYU Press 2001).

96. Plyler v. Doe, 458 U.S. 1131 (1982).

97. See U.S. Department of State, *Biography: Vilma Martinez*, available at http://www. state.gov/r/pa/ei/biog/129351.htm (accessed Mar. 15, 2010).

98. See Paul Feldman, *Texas Case Looms over Prop. 187's Legal Future: U.S. High Court Voided That State's '75 Law on Illegal Immigrants, but Panel Has Shifted to the Right*, L.A. Times, Oct. 23, 1994, at A1. I thank María Pabón López for bringing this source to my attention.

99. Belejack, *Lesson in Equal Protection*, 13; Mary Ann Zehr, *Case Touched Many Parts of Community*, Educ. Wk., June 6, 2007, at 13; Lucy Hood, *Educating Immigrant Students*, 4 Carnegie Rep. 2 (2007) (interview with Judge William W. Justice regarding *Plyler*), available at http://carnegie.org/publications/carnegie-reporter/single/view/article/item/174/; Unmuth, *25 Years Ago*. In 2008, a special *Plyler* issue of the *Northwestern Journal of Law and Social Policy* included several articles on the case and its aftermath: http://www.law. northwestern.edu/journals/njlsp/v3/n2/. As this book's bibliography reveals, there is a very large library of scholarly and newspaper literature on this case, although surprisingly few full-length or single-authored books.

100. Martinez v. Bynum, 461 U.S. 321 (1983).

101. *Plyler*, 457 U.S. at 227 n.22.

102. League of United Latin American Citizens v. Wilson, 997 F. Supp. 1244 (C.D. Cal. 1997); see also Vanessa A. Baird, *Answering the Call of the Court: How Justices and Litigants Set the Supreme Court Agenda* 73–82 (Univ. Virginia Press, 2007) (reviewing advocacy and litigation on behalf of immigrants).

103. *Republican Party Platform of 1996*, American Presidency Project, available at http://www.presidency.ucsb.edu/ws/index.php?pid=25848. Representative Gallegly has continued his campaign, such as the bill he introduced on January 6, 2009: H.R. 126, 111th Cong. (2009). See also Stephen H. Legomsky & Cristina M. Rodriguez, *Immigration and Refugee Law and Policy* 1140–1287 (Foundation 2009); Thomas Alexander Aleinikoff, David A. Martin, Hiroshi Motomura & Maryellen Fullerton, *Immigration and Citizenship: Process and Policy* 1354–1419 (Thompson West 2008); see also 73 Interpreter Releases 1111, 1209, 1255, 1281 (1996); Rebecca A. Maynard & Daniel J. McGrath, *Family Structure, Fertility and Child Welfare*, in *The Social Benefits of Education* 125 (Jere R. Behrman & Nevzer Stacey, eds., Univ. of Michigan Press 1997). For a thorough analysis of these issues and other restrictive legislative efforts, see Kevin R. Johnson, *Public Benefits and Immigration: The Intersection of Immigration Status, Ethnicity, Gender, and Class*, 42 UCLA L. Rev. 159 (1995); Kevin R. Johnson, Raquel Aldana, Bill Ong Hing, Leticia Saucedo & Enid F. Trucios-Haynes, *Federalism and Alienage Law*, in *Understanding Immigration Law* 137–142 (LexisNexis 2009) [Ch. 4] (Public Benefits).

104. Roos later litigated the following cases: Leticia "A" v. Board of Regents of the University of California, Tentative Decision, No. 588982-5 (Cal. Super. Ct. Alameda Cty., Apr. 3, 1985); Judgment (May 7, 1985); Statement of Decision (May 30, 1985) (Leticia "A" I); Clarification (May 19, 1982) (Leticia "A" II). Peter D. Roos, *Postsecondary* Plyler (IHELG Monograph 91-7, 1991), available at http://www.law.uh.edu/ihelg/monograph/91-7.pdf. And he was involved as amicus defending the state statute in the *Day* and *Martinez* cases. See also Michael A. Olivas, *Storytelling Out of School: Undocumented College Residency, Race, and Reaction*, 22 Hastings Const. L.Q. 1019 (1995); Michael A. Olivas, *IIRIRA, the DREAM Act, and Undocumented College Student Residency*, 30 J.C. & U.L.435 (2004); María Pabón López, *Reflections on Educating Latino and Latina Undocumented Children: Beyond* Plyler v. Doe, 35 Seton Hall L. Rev. 1373 (2005); Ontiveros & Drexler, *Thirteenth Amendment*.

105. Tex. Educ. Code Ann. § 54.052 (Vernon 2006). See Clay Robison, *Budget Hits Include Judges' Pay Hike*, Hous. Chron., June 18, 2001, at 1A (describing tuition, revenue bill details). For insomniacs in the reading public, see Michael A. Olivas, *Lawmakers Gone Wild? College Residency and the Response to Professor Kobach*, 61 SMU L. Rev. 99 (2008). I was reacting to the work of Kris W. Kobach, *Immigration Nullification: In-State Tuition and Lawmakers Who Disregard the Law*, 10 N.Y.U. J. Legis. & Pub. Pol'y 473 (2006–2007). Also see Ryan Evely Gildersleeve, *Fracturing Opportunity: Mexican Migrant Students and College-Going Literacy* (Peter Lang 2010); Lisa D. Garcia & William G. Tierney, *Undocumented Immigrants in Higher Education: A Preliminary Analysis*, 113 Tchrs. Coll. Rec. (forthcoming 2011), available at http://www.tcrecord.org/PrintContent.asp?ContentID=16204; Stella M. Flores, *The First State Dream Act: In-State Resident Tuition and Immigration in Texas*, 32 Educ. Evaluation & Pol'y Analysis 435 (Dec. 2010).

106. Olivas, *Lawmakers Gone Wild?*, tbl. 2.

107. See table 2 in chapter 4. See also Immigration Policy Center, *Anti-immigrant Group Issues Deceptive Report on DREAM Act* (Dec. 2010), available at http://myemail.constant-

contact.com/Anti-Immigrant-Group-Issues-Deceptive-Report-on-DREAM-Act.html?soi
d=1101677093769&aid=02IOb7XHhEc.

108. Olivas, *Lawmakers Gone Wild*? See Johnson, Ong Hing, Saucedo & Trucios-
Haynes, *Federalism and Alienage Law*, 144–149 (Higher Education).

NOTES TO CHAPTER 3

1. Interview with Manuel H., in Michael A. Olivas, *Storytelling Out of School: Undocumented College Residency, Race, and Reaction*, 22 Hastings Const. L.Q. 1019, 1020 n.3 (1995).

2. Interview with Jose G., in *id.*, 1020 n.6.

3. National Conference of State Legislatures, *State Laws Related to Immigrants and Immigration*, July 17, 2009, available at http://www.ncsl.org/default.aspx?tabid=18030. In 2010,
forty-six state legislatures and the District of Columbia enacted 208 laws and adopted
138 resolutions for a total of 346. Ten additional bills were vetoed. (Montana, Nevada,
North Dakota or Texas were not in regular session in 2010.) National Conference of State
Legislatures, *2010 Immigration-Related Laws and Resolutions in the States (January 1–December 31, 2010)*, Jan. 5, 2011, available at http://www.ncsl.org/default.aspx?tabid=21857. In
addition, there are a number of publicly available listings of the various ordinances. Two
of the more useful and current are *Bender's Immigration Bulletin: Daily Edition*, available at
http://www.bibdaily.com, and Puerto Rican Legal Defense and Education Fund—Latino
Justice Project, available at http://prldef.org.

4. For example, see Wisconsin, 2009 Assembly Bill 75 (2009 Wisconsin Act 28); Wis.
Stat. § 36.27 (repealed 2011); Georgia Security and Immigration Compliance Act, S.B.
529 (2006) (amending Titles 13, 16, 35, 42, 43, 48, and 50 of the Official Code of Georgia
Annotated); discussions with Georgia Board Counsel, Mar. 2, 2007. For a sense of the
rapidly changing demography that has given rise to the nativist Georgia and southeastern legislation and policies, see Fran Ansley & Jon Shefner, eds., *Global Connections and
Local Receptions: New Latino Immigration to the Southeastern United States* (Univ. Tennessee Press 2009). Arizona Proposition 300, Enacting and Ordering the Submission to the
People of a Measure Relating to Public Program Eligibility (amending Sections 15-191.01,
15-232-1803, 46-801, 46-803 of the Arizona Revised Statutes and adding Section 15-1825,
Relating to Public Program Eligibility).

5. LULAC v. Wilson, 908 F. Supp. 755 (C.D. Cal. 1995); Gregorio T. by and through Jose
T. v. Wilson, 59 F.3d 1002 (9th Cir. 1995); LULAC v. Wilson, 997 F. Supp. 1244 (C.D. Cal.
1997).

6. Maricopa County undertook to prosecute undocumented persons for having con-
spired to smuggle themselves in violation of Arizona's antismuggling statute. See Ariz.
Rev. Stat. § 13-2319 (2006) ("human smuggling" statute) and Ariz. Rev. Stat. § 13-1003
(2006) (general conspiracy statute). Lindsey Collom, *54 Jailed under "Coyote" Statute*, Ariz.
Republic, Mar. 3, 2006, at 1B; Michael Kiefer, *Maricopa Court Upholds Migrant Smuggling
Law: Those Caught Can Be Charged in Conspiracy*, Ariz. Republic, June 10, 2006, at 1B;
Joseph Lelyveld, *The Border Dividing Arizona*, N.Y. Times Magazine, Oct. 15, 2006, at 40;
Matthew Benson, *[Sheriff] Arpaio to Use State Funds to Fight Smuggling*, Ariz. Republic,
Mar. 15, 2007, at B5. In the first complete trial on this issue, the superior court judge over-
turned the first jury conviction of an immigrant charged as a conspirator under the state's
smuggling law; a number of these trials are still in the pipeline. Jahna Berry, *Smuggling*

Verdict Tossed: Judge Cites Lack of Evidence, Ariz. Republic, Dec. 6, 2006, at A1 (Maricopa County Superior Court judge overturned first jury conviction of immigrant charged as conspirator under the state's smuggling law). The omnibus state legislation, S.B. 1070, has, for the most part, been put on hold while the courts sort it out. United States of America v. State of Arizona (April 11, 2011, affirming district court's preliminary injunction order enjoining these certain provisions of S.B. 1070), available at http://www.ca9.uscourts.gov/ datastore/general/2011/04/11/10-16645_opinion.pdf. See Randal C. Archibold, *Pre-emption, Not Profiling, in Challenge to Arizona*, N.Y. Times, June 8, 2010, A15. The Arizona cases have begun to generate substantial scholarly attention. See Keith Aoki & John Shuford, *Welcome to Amerizona—Immigrants Out! Assessing "Dystopian Dreams" and "Usable Futures" of Immigration Reform, and Considering Whether "Immigration Regionalism" Is an Idea Whose Time Has Come*, 38 Fordham Urb. L.J. 1 (2010).

7. Immigration Reform and Control Act (IRCA), 100 Stat. 3359 (1986); Linda S. Bosniak, *Membership, Equality and the Difference That Alienage Makes*, 69 N.Y.U. L. Rev. 1047 (1994); Kevin Johnson, *The Antiterrorism Act, the Immigration Reform Act and Ideological Regulation in the Immigration Laws: Important Lessons for Citizens and Noncitizens*, 28 St. Mary's L.J. 833 (1997).

8. I have elaborated on these issues and outlined many examples in Michael A. Olivas, *Immigration-Related State and Local Ordinances: Preemption, Prejudice, and the Proper Role for Enforcement*, 2007 U. Chi. Legal F. 27 (2007).

9. Kris W. Kobach, *The Quintessential Force Multiplier: The Inherent Authority of Local Police to Make Immigration Arrests*, 69 Alb. L. Rev. 179, 187–188 (2005). But see Huyen Pham, *The Constitutional Right Not to Cooperate? Local Sovereignty and the Federal Immigration Power*, 74 U. Cin. L. Rev. 1373 (2006); Michael Wishnie, *Laboratories of Bigotry? Devolution of the Immigration Power, Equal Protection and Federalism*, 76 N.Y.U. L. Rev. 493 (2001); Hannah Gladstein, Annie Lai, Jennifer Wagner & Michael Wishnie, *Blurring the Lines: A Profile of State and Local Police Enforcement of Immigration Law Using the National Crime Information Center Database, 2002–04* (Migration Policy Institute 2005); Alicia Triche, *Local Enforcement and Federal Preemption*, 11 Bender's Immigr. Bull. 1372 (2006) (critiquing role of local law enforcement in immigration in terms of "conflict preemption" and "field preemption" and considering the Border Protection, Antiterrorism, and Illegal Control Act of 2005 bill and Comprehensive Immigration Reform Act of 2006 bill, both introduced but not passed into law). A recent Department of Homeland Security review was generally critical of the 287(g) record. See U.S. Department of Homeland Security, Office of Inspector General, *The Performance of 287(g) Agreements* (Sept. 2010), available at http://www.dhs.gov/xoig/assets/mgmtrpts/OIG_10-124_Sep10.pdf.

10. There is a full bookcase of scholarship on this subject, but I have particularly profited from the work of Stephen Legomsky in this and other immigration areas. See, e.g., Stephen Legomsky, *Immigration Law and the Principle of Plenary Congressional Power*, 1984 Sup. Ct. Rev. 255 (1984). I have looked at these arguments in Michael A. Olivas, *Preempting Preemption: Foreign Affairs, State Rights, and Alienage Classifications*, 35 Va. J. Int'l L. 217 (1994).

11. Tex. Educ. Code Ann. § 21.031 (Vernon Supp. 1981). I have reviewed the litigation background of the case in Michael A. Olivas, *The Story of* Plyler v. Doe, *the Education of Undocumented Children, and the Polity*, in *Immigration Stories* 197 (David Martin & Peter Schuck, eds., Foundation 2005). See also María Pabón López, *Reflections on Educating*

Latino and Latina Undocumented Children: Beyond Plyler v. Doe, 35 Seton Hall L. Rev. 1373 (2005); María Pabón López & Gerardo R. López, *Persistent Inequality: Contemporary Realities in the Education of Undocumented Latina/o Students* (Routledge 2010).

12. Plyler v. Doe, 457 U.S. 202, 205 (1982).

13. *Id.* at 227 n.22.

14. Martinez v. Bynum, 461 U.S. 321 (1983). See Gadi Zohar, *Habitual Residence: An Alternative to the Common Law Concept of Domicile?*, 9 Whittier J. Child & Fam. Advoc. 169 (2009). This issue can arise in other residence-related settings, such as a policy in a wealthy California district that gave a grandfathered "legacy-credit" to families who had once had children in the prestigious schools but who no longer resided in the district. Jennifer Steinhauer, *Finances Push Beverly Hills Schools to Rescind Welcome to Neighbors*, N.Y. Times, Dec. 21, 2009, at A16.

15. Toll v. Moreno, 458 U.S. 1 (1982). Decided by the same Supreme Court, this was a higher-education case concerning residency requirements for longtime nonimmigrants and whether they could be eligible for in-state tuition. They could be and were. See Michael A. Olivas, Plyler v. Doe, Toll v. Moreno, *and Postsecondary Admissions: Undocumented Adults and "Enduring Disability,"* 15 J.L. & Educ. 19 (1986); Olivas, *Storytelling.*

16. *Plyler*, 457 U.S. at 218 n.14.

17. Examples include ballot issues in Georgia and legislation in Oklahoma. S.B. 529, Georgia Security/Immigration Compliance Act of 2006 (amending Titles 13, 16, 35, 42, 43, 48, and 50 of the Official Code of Georgia Annotated), available at http://www.legis. state.ga.us/legis/2005_06/pdf/sb529.pdf. See Laura Diamond, *470-Plus Students' Residency Unclear*, Atlanta J.-Const., Aug. 11, 2010, B1; *Georgia Urged to End Ban on Undocumented Students at Top Colleges*, Fox News Latino, Apr. 14, 2011, available at http://latino.foxnews. com/latino/news/2011/04/14/georgia-urged-end-ban-undocumented-students-colleges. Oklahoma passed the Taxpayer and Citizen Protection Act of 2007 (H.B. 1804), employment-related portions of which have thus far been invalidated by the Tenth Circuit in *Chamber of Commerce of U.S. v. Edmondson*, 594 F.3d 742 (10th Cir. 2010). See Elizabeth McCormick, *The Oklahoma Taxpayer and Citizen Protection Act: Blowing off Steam or Setting Wildfires?*, 23 Geo. Immigr. L.J. 293 (2009).

18. Among the several excellent and useful articles on this complicated matter, see Lolita K. Buckner Inniss, *California's Proposition 187—Does It Mean What It Says? Does It Say What It Means? A Textual and Constitutional Analysis*, 10 Geo. Immigr. L.J. 577 (1996); Kevin R. Johnson, *Public Benefits and Immigration: The Intersection of Immigration Status, Ethnicity, Gender, and Class*, 42 UCLA L. Rev. 1509 (1995); Ruben J. Garcia, *Critical Race Theory and Proposition 187: The Racial Politics of Immigration Law*, 17 Chicano-Latino L. Rev. 118 (1995).

19. Kevin R. Johnson, *An Essay on Immigration Politics, Popular Democracy, and California's Proposition 187: The Political Relevance and Legal Irrelevance of Race*, 70 Wash. L. Rev. 629, 672 (1995).

20. Garcia, *Critical Race Theory*, 119.

21. For these characterizations, I worked from a pamphlet distributed by the proponents of Proposition 187, but I refer to the more easily accessible version available in the Johnson article. I have carefully checked to be certain his notes accurately cited the pamphlet and ballot materials; in every instance, he was scrupulous. Johnson, *Public Benefits and Immigration*, 1561 n.241.

22. *Id.*, 1561 n.243 (emphasis omitted).

23. *Id.*, 1561 n.247 (emphasis omitted).

24. *LULAC*, 997 F. Supp. at 1261.

25. Personal Responsibility and Work Opportunity Reconciliation Act of 1996 (PRWORA), 110 Stat. 2105 (1996).

26. *LULAC*, 997 F. Supp. at 1259. See Kitty Calavita, *The New Politics of Immigration: "Balanced-Budget Conservatism" and the Symbolism of Proposition 187*, 43 Soc. Probs. 284 (1996).

27. Johnson, *Public Benefits and Immigration*, 1563 n.260 (emphasis omitted).

28. See generally López & López, *Persistent Inequality*; Buckner Inniss, *California's Proposition 187*; Johnson, *Public Benefits and Immigration*; Garcia, *Critical Race Theory*.

29. *LULAC*, 997 F. Supp. at 1259.

30. See Patrick J. McDonnell, *Davis Won't Appeal Prop. 187 Ruling, Ending Court Battles*, L.A. Times, July 29, 1999, at A1; see also Patrick J. McDonnell, *Prop. 187 Talks Offered Davis Few Choices*, L.A. Times, July 30, 1999, at A3. For a thoughtful story on current issues concerning undocumented children in California, see Teresa Watanabe, *Illegal Immigrant Youths in a Benefits Twilight Zone: State Policies toward Such Children Vary, Reflecting Sympathy for Their Situation and Disapproval of Their Parents' Behavior*, L.A. Times, Jan. 25, 2007, at B1.

31. Cal. Educ. Code § 1643. See *LULAC*, 997 F. Supp. at 1255 (citations omitted). See also Paul Feldman, *Texas Case Looms over Prop. 187's Legal Future: U.S. High Court Voided That State's '75 Law on Illegal Immigrants, but Panel Has Shifted to the Right*, L.A. Times, Oct. 23, 1994, at A1 (story of *Plyler* children in context of Proposition 187); Vanessa Baird, *Answering the Call of the Court: How Justices and Litigants Set the Supreme Court Agenda* 73–82 (Univ. Virginia Press 2007).

32. *LULAC*, 908 F. Supp. 755 (striking down state referendum prohibiting social services and benefits to undocumented residents in scheme to deter immigration); *Gregorio T.*, 59 F.3d 1002; *LULAC*, 997 F. Supp. 1244.

33. López, *Reflections*, 1395–1398; Olivas, *Story of* Plyler v. Doe, 212–213.

34. Philip G. Schrag, *A Well-Founded Fear: The Congressional Battle to Save Political Asylum in America* (Routledge 2000).

35. *Id.*, 245.

36. *Id.*, 311 n.33.

37. *Id.*, 185.

38. Interview with a senior Houston ISD official, Feb. 26, 2007. In order to gain authoritative access to this senior administrator, I agreed not to reveal the person's name.

39. See Houston Independent School District, *Alternative and Charter Listings*, available at www.houstonisd.org/HISDConnectDS/v/index.jsp?vgnextchannel=bc697438901d8 210VgnVCM10000028147fa6RCRD&vgnextfmt=alt10 (accessed Sept. 20, 2009) (listing of Houston charter schools). See also Mary Ann Zehr, *Working Immigrants Get New School Options*, Educ. Wk., Sept. 22, 2004, at 5 (various immigrant schools); Lucy Hood, *Immigrant Students, Urban High Schools: The Challenge Continues* 6–7 (Carnegie Corporation of New York 2003) (Carnegie Corporation study of immigrant education, including Houston ISD's immigrant program); Olga Byrne, *Unaccompanied Children in the United States: A Literature Review* (Vera Institute of Justice 2008).

40. Jason Spencer, *HISD Board Names [Abelardo] Saavedra as Only Finalist: He Would Be the First Hispanic to Lead City Schools*, Hous. Chron., Nov. 14, 2004, at A1.

41. Dennis J. Hutchinson, *More Substantive Equal Protection? A Note on* Plyler v. Doe, 1982 Sup. Ct. Rev. 167, 184 (1982).

42. Phillip B. Kurland & Dennis J. Hutchinson, *The Business of the Supreme Court,* [*October Term*] *1982*, 50 U. Chi. L. Rev. 628, 650 (1983).

43. Mark Tushnet, *Justice Lewis F. Powell and the Jurisprudence of Centrism*, 93 Mich. L. Rev. 1854, 1873 (1995). On the other hand, Tushnet then wrote, "On another level, the opinion had profound doctrinal significance because no one could interpret it to hold that the Supreme Court will strike down statutes that are unconstitutional when a majority of the Court thinks those statutes are unwise social policy." *Id.* In a fascinating study of Justice Brennan's notes, taken by the justice in conference over many years on the U.S. Supreme Court, Jim Newton has published a number of them online. In "Part IV: The Colleagues," he relates a story of a heated exchange between Thurgood Marshall and William Rehnquist during conferences on the *Plyler* case. See Jim Newton, *Brennan Dishes on His Colleagues*, Slate, Jan. 11, 2007.

44. Peter H. Schuck, *The Transformation of Immigration Law*, 84 Colum. L. Rev. 1, 54 (1984) (noting "epochal significance" of case for undocumented).

45. López, *Reflections*, 1405.

46. Arizona Proposition 300, Enacting and Ordering the Submission to the People of a Measure Relating to Public Program Eligibility (amending Sections 15-191.01, 15-232-1803, 46-801, 46-803 of the Arizona Revised Statutes and adding Section 15-1825, *Relating to Public Program Eligibility*). Yvonne Wingett, *Arizona's Colleges Struggle to Enforce New Tuition Statute*, Ariz. Republic, Jan. 3, 2007, at A1 (recounting implementation problems with Prop. 300); Sara Hebel, *Arizona College Officials Worry That a New Measure Approved by Voters Will Require Them to Shift Hefty Portions of Their Budgets So That They Can Play Backup for the Border Patrol*, Chron. Higher Educ., Nov. 24, 2006, at A27 (same); Mary Romero, *"Go after the Women": Mothers against Illegal Aliens' Campaign against Mexican Immigrant Women and Their Children*, 83 Ind. L.J. 1355 (2008).

47. See Immigration Policy Center, *E-Verify and Arizona: Early Experiences for Employers, Employees, and the Economy Portend a Rough Road Ahead* (Immigration Policy Center 2008), available at http://www.immigrationpolicy.org/just-facts/e-verify-and-arizona-early-experiences-portend-rough-road-ahead. For a useful analysis of these employment issues, see Leticia M. Saucedo, *Three Theories of Discrimination in the Brown Collar Workplace*, 2009 U. Chi. Legal F. 345 (2009).

48. See Ariz. Rev. Stat. § 13-2319 (2006) ("human smuggling" statute); Ariz. Rev. Stat. § 13-1003 (2006) (general conspiracy statute). In April 2011, a three-judge panel of the Ninth Circuit upheld the trial judge's injunction against many of the Arizona statute provisions. United States of America v. State of Arizona (affirming district court's preliminary injunction order enjoining these certain provisions of S.B. 1070), available at http://www.ca9.uscourts.gov/datastore/general/2011/04/11/10-16645_opinion.pdf.

49. For a survey of the employment-related immigration issues, see, e.g., Kathryne J. Couch, *This Land Is Our Land, a Local Solution to a Local Problem: State Regulation of Immigration through Business Licensing*, 21 Geo. Immigr. L.J. 641 (2007); Micah Bump, *Immigration, Technology, and the Worksite: The Challenges of Electronic Employment Verification*, 22 Geo. Immigr. L.J. 391 (2008). For particular emphasis on Arizona, see Immigration Policy Center, *E-Verify and Arizona*; McCormick, *Oklahoma Taxpayer and Citizen Protection Act*, 340–349.

50. S.B. 529 § 9 stated,

> Title 50 of the Official Code of Georgia Annotated, relating to state government, is amended by adding a new chapter at the end thereof, to be designated Chapter 36, to read as follows:
>
> (a) Except as provided in subsection (c) of this Code section or where exempted by federal law, on or after July 1, 2007, every agency or a political subdivision of this state shall verify the lawful presence in the United States of any natural person 18 years of age or older who has applied for state or local public benefits, as defined in 8 U.S.C. Section 1621, or for federal public benefits, as defined in 8 U.S.C. Section 1611, that is administered by an agency or a political subdivision of this state.
>
> (b) Verification of lawful presence under this Code section shall not be required: . . .
>
> (c) Verification of lawful presence under this Code section shall not be required:
>
> (7) For postsecondary education, whereby the Board of Regents of the University System of Georgia or the State Board of Technical and Adult Education shall set forth, or cause to be set forth, policies regarding postsecondary benefits that comply with all federal law including but not limited to public benefits as described in 8 U.S.C. Section 1611, 1621, or 1623.

Georgia Security and Immigration Compliance Act, S.B. 529 (2006).

51. S.B. 529 § 6 stated,

> Title 43 of the Official Code of Georgia Annotated, relating to professions and businesses, is amended by adding a new chapter immediately following Chapter 20 to read as follows: "This chapter shall be known and may be cited as the 'Registration of Immigration Assistance Act.' The purpose and intent of this chapter is to establish and enforce standards of ethics in the profession of immigration assistance by private individuals who are not licensed attorneys."

Georgia Security and Immigration Compliance Act, S.B. 529 (2006).

52. *Id.*

53. *Id.*

54. At the request of the Georgia Board of Regents, I submitted testimony in my personal capacity, Apr. 4, 2007, available at www.law.uh.edu/ihelg (downloadable). Undocumented students at a state college surfaced in 2010, with predictable thermodynamic reaction. See Laura Diamond, *470-Plus Students' Residency Unclear*, Atlanta J.-Const., Aug. 11, 2010, at B1. In 2011, Georgia passed legislation to prevent undocumented students from enrolling in state colleges, even as nonresidents.

See *Georgia Urged to End Ban on Undocumented Students at Top Colleges*, Fox News Latino, Apr. 14, 2011, available at http://latino.foxnews.com/latino/news/2011/04/14/georgia-urged-end-ban-undocumented-students-colleges.

55. As one example, see the Federation for American Immigration Reform website, which casts the issue as one of equity and school finance: *Breaking the Piggy Bank: How Illegal Immigration Is Sending Schools into the Red* (June 2005), available at http://www.fairus.org/site/News2?page=NewsArticle&id=17193&security=1601&news_iv_ctrl=1901. See also Kobach, *Quintessential Force Multiplier*; Kris W. Kobach, *The Senate Immigration Bill Rewards Lawbreaking: Why the DREAM Act Is a Nightmare*, Backgrounder #1960 (Heritage Foundation 2006), available at www.heritage.org/Research/Reports/2006/08/The-Senate-Immigration-Bill-Rewards-Lawbreaking-Why-the-DREAM-Act-Is-a-Nightmare.

56. This also happened in Utah, where there were unsuccessful recent efforts to repeal the provision regarding undocumented college-student tuition, enacted in 2002. Deborah Bulkeley, *Utah Measure to Repeal Tuition Break for Illegals Is Back*, Deseret Morn. News, Feb. 7, 2008, at B4; Deborah Bulkeley & Lisa Riley Roche, *Immigrant Tuition Repeal Removed from Bill*, Deseret Morn. News, Feb. 13, 2008, at B7; *A Good Session Overall*, Editorial, Deseret Morn. News, Mar. 2, 2007, A14 (reviewing repeal bill, deemed to be one that "truly would have caused harm"). On the issue of postsecondary residency tuition, there is a small shelf of articles. See, e.g., Stanley Mailman & Stephen Yale-Loehr, *College for Undocumented Immigrants After All?*, N.Y. L.J., June 25, 2001, at 3; Victor C. Romero, *Postsecondary School Education Benefits for Undocumented Immigrants: Promises and Pitfalls*, 27 N.C. J. Int'l Law & Com. Reg. 393 (2002); Victor C. Romero, *Noncitizen Students and Immigration Policy Post-9/11*, 17 Geo. Immigr. L.J. 357 (2003); Jessica Salsbury, *Evading "Residence": Higher Education, Undocumented Students, and the States*, 53 Am. U. L. Rev. 459 (2003); Daniel Walfish, Note, *Student Visas and the Illogic of the Intent Requirement*, 17 Geo. Immigr. L.J. 473 (2003) (reviewing nonimmigrant policy and procedures); Michael A. Olivas, *IIRIRA, the DREAM Act, and Undocumented College Student Residency*, 30 J.C. & U.L. 435 (2004); Kobach, *Senate Immigration Bill*; Laura J. Callahan Ragan, *Educating the Undocumented: Providing Legal Status for Undocumented Students in the United States and Italy through Higher Education*, 34 Ga. J. Int'l & Comp. L. 485 (2006); Ralph W. Kasarda, *Affirmative Action Gone Haywire: Why State Laws Granting College Tuition Preferences to Illegal Aliens Are Preempted by Federal Law*, 2 BYU Educ. & L.J. 197 (2009).

57. In 2010, 501 such students were discovered, of the 310,000 in the Georgia system. See Jack Stripling, *Georgia Bars Admission of Illegal Immigrants*, Inside Higher Ed, Oct. 14, 2010, available at http://www.insidehighered.com/news/2010/10/14/georgia. See also University System of Georgia, *Regents Adopt New Policies on Undocumented Students*, press release, Oct. 13, 2010, available at http://www.usg.edu/news/release/regents_adopt_new_policies_on_undocumented_students/. Arizona had for many years allowed undocumented college students to establish residency, following a settlement reached with MALDEF in 1987, following the *Judith A v. Arizona Board of Regents* case. See Olivas, *Storytelling*, 1022 n.19 (reviewing previous Arizona postsecondary litigation). See also Rachel L. Swarns, *In Georgia, Newest Immigrants Unsettle an Old Sense of Place*, N.Y. Times, Aug. 4, 2006, at A1; Wingett, *Arizona's Colleges*, A1; Eric Swedlund, *In-state Tuition Safeguard a Concern: AZ Schools to Verify That Illegal Entrants Pay Top Rate*, Ariz. Daily Star, Mar. 9, 2007, at A1, A4.

58. Immigration Policy Institute, *E-Verify and Arizona*. See also Fernanda Santos, *Demand for English Lessons Outstrips Supply*, N.Y. Times, Feb. 27, 2007, at A1 (report on oversubscribed adult English-language classes across United States); Nina Rabin, Mary Carol Combs & Norma Gonzalez, *Understanding* Plyler's *Legacy: Voices from Border Schools*, 37 J.L. & Educ. 15 (2008).

59. Eric Rich, *Immigration Enforcement's Shift in the Workplace: Case of Md. Restaurateurs Reflects Use of Criminal Investigations, Rather Than Fines, against Employers*, Wash. Post, Apr. 16, 2006, at C6 (analyzing Immigration and Customs Enforcement policies). The employment-related portions of the Oklahoma Taxpayer and Citizen Protection Act of 2007 (H.B. 1804) have been invalidated by the Tenth Circuit in *Chamber of Commerce of U.S. v. Edmondson*, 594 F.3d 742 (10th Cir. 2010). See McCormick, *Blowing off Steam*.

60. *Plyler*, 457 U.S. at 252 (Burger, J., dissenting).

61. See Federation for American Immigration Reform, *Birthright Citizenship* (updated Aug. 2010), available at http://www.fairus.org/site/News2?news_iv_ctrl=1010&cmd=artic les&page=NewsArticle&security=1601&id=16535&start=3 (criticizing birthright citizenship). Assertions by nativists include the false claim that undocumented mothers, in order to gain U.S. citizenship, "give birth to hundreds of thousands of babies annually—'anchor babies'—who are granted instant U.S. citizenship plus generous welfare benefits." Daniel Sheehy, *Fighting Immigration Anarchy* 15 (Rooftop 2009). By U.S. immigration and citizenship law, no citizen can convey parental-derivative citizenship until he or she reaches the age of twenty-one.

62. In the authoritative *New York Times Style Manual*, the newspaper admonishes reporters that "*illegal immigrant* is the preferred term, rather than the sinister-sounding *illegal alien*. Do not use the euphemism *undocumented*." Allan M. Siegal & William G. Connolly, *The New York Times Manual of Style and Usage* 168 (Three Rivers 1999).

63. See generally Olivas, *Story of* Plyler v. Doe, 197 (reviewing details of litigation).

64. The Federal Judicial Center website provides the basics on Judge Pfaelzer: *Biographical Directory of Federal Judges: Pfaelzer, Mariana R.*, available at http://www.fjc.gov/servlet/nGetInfo?jid=1876&cid=999&ctype=na&instate=na (accessed Sept. 9, 2009).

65. Clay Robison, *Budget Hits Include Judges' Pay Hike*, Hous. Chron., June 18, 2001, at 1A (describing 2001 session tuition, revenue bill details of original tuition legislation). In January 2007, Governor Perry (reelected for his second full term) indicated that he would not support any bills that overturned this legislation, including the revised version, S.B. 158. Matthew Tresaugue & R. G. Radcliffe, *Illegal Immigrants May See Tuition Hike: Legislation Would End Texas' Pioneering Law Granting In-State Rate, Financial Aid*, Hous. Chron., Jan. 11, 2007, at B1; Clay Robison & R. G. Ratcliffe, *Perry to Stick by Law Giving Tuition Breaks to Illegal Immigrants: He Also Predicts Legislation against Repeat Predators of Children Will Be Strengthened*, Hous. Chron., Jan. 12, 2007, at B4. The Texas Office of Controller of Public Accounts released a major report concerning the costs and benefits of the undocumented to the Texas economy: *Undocumented Immigrants in Texas: A Financial Analysis of the Impact to the State Budget and Economy* (Dec. 2006), available at http://www.cpa.state.tx.us/specialrpt/undocumented/undocumented.pdf ("This is the first time any state has done a comprehensive financial analysis of the impact of undocumented immigrants on a state's budget and economy, looking at gross state product, revenues generated, taxes paid and the cost of state services. The absence of the estimated 1.4 million undocumented immigrants in Texas in fiscal 2005 would have been a loss to our gross state product of

$17.7 billion. Undocumented immigrants produced $1.58 billion in state revenues, which exceeded the $1.16 billion in state services they received. However, local governments bore the burden of $1.44 billion in uncompensated health care costs and local law enforcement costs not paid for by the state."). See also Susan Carroll, *In-State Rates for Illegal Immigrants Attacked*, Hous. Chron., Dec. 16, 2009, at B1 (suit filed against Texas statute); Katherine Leal Unmuth, *Number of Illegal Immigrants Getting In-State Tuition for Texas Colleges Rises*, Dall. Morn. News, Mar. 15, 2010, available at http://www.dallasnews.com/sharedcontent/dws/dn/latestnews/stories/0315dnmetimmigcount.3d35b14.html.

66. In a number of these legislative sessions, the discussions and politics have been quite fascinating. For example, on April 14, 2006, Nebraska became the tenth state to provide in-state-resident tuition to undocumented-immigrant students who have attended and graduated from its high schools. It did so in dramatic fashion, overriding Governor Dave Heineman's veto. The bill had passed by a 26–19 margin but needed thirty votes for an override; supporters managed to change exactly four votes to get the necessary thirty. Ruth Marcus, *Immigration's Scrambled Politics*, Wash. Post, Apr. 4, 2006, at A23. See also Yvonne Abraham, *Immigrant Tuition Bill Defeated*, Boston Globe, Jan. 12, 2006, at A1 (Massachusetts); Mark Spencer, *Immigrant Tuition Endorsed*, Hartford Courant, Feb. 14, 2007, at B10 (Connecticut); Dirk Perrefort, *Filibuster Blocks Tuition Bill: Proposal Would Have Allowed Illegal Immigrants to Pay In-State Rates to Connecticut Schools*, Danbury News-Times, Mar. 16, 2007, at A1 (Connecticut); Jean Hopfensperger, *Immigration Proposals Clash: The Governor and DFL Lawmakers Offered Differing Views on Issues Involving the State's Immigrants*, Minneapolis Star-Trib., Feb. 15, 2007, at 5B (Minnesota); Lisa Rein, [Maryland] *House Heats Up over Bill to Give Illegal Immigrants In-State Tuition*, Wash. Post, Mar. 28, 2007, at B2; Doug Thompson, *Panel Rejects Immigrant Tuition Bill*, Morn. News of Northwest Arkansas (Little Rock), Mar. 23, 2009 (immigrant tuition bill dies in state senate committee); Jennifer Gonzalez, *North Carolina Community Colleges to Resume Enrolling Illegal Immigrants*, Chron. Higher Educ., Sept. 18, 2009. Several Virginia colleges in the past appeared to allow undocumented students to enroll and establish in-state-residency tuition, prompting different legislative proposals in both 2008 and 2009. The legislature considered strengthening the current statute to ban the practice but also considered legislation to permit a subgroup of undocumented students who met a heightened standard to receive in-state tuition. The legislation died in 2009, and no changes were enacted. See Virginia General Assembly Legislative Information System, http://leg1.state.va.us (bill died in committee). Olympia Meola, *Colleges' Admittance of Illegals Opposed: Bill Would End Practice at Some Va. Schools of Allowing Undocumented Immigrants*, Richmond Times-Dispatch, Jan. 18, 2008, at A1; Jim Nolan, *Va. Senate Backs Bill to Restrict Tuition Benefits for Illegal Immigrants*, Richmond Times-Dispatch, Jan. 27, 2009, at A4; Jim Nolan, *What's Happening at the Legislature?*, Richmond Times-Dispatch, Jan. 28, 2009, at A6. For more detailed and recent developments in the statues, see Olivas, *IIRIRA*; Michael A. Olivas, *Lawmakers Gone Wild? College Residency and the Response to Professor Kobach*, 61 SMU L. Rev. 99 (2008); Michael A. Olivas, *The Political Economy of the DREAM Act and the Legislative Process: A Case Study of Comprehensive Immigration Reform*, 55 Wayne L. Rev. 1757 (2010). In April 2011, Maryland enacted a residency-tuition statute. Julie Bykowicz & Annie Linskey, *Lawmakers Approve Tuition Break for Illegal Immigrants, New Sales Tax on Alcohol*, Baltimore Sun, Apr. 12, 2011. Due to a ballot recission measure in 2011, the statute has not been enacted.

67. See generally Olivas, *Lawmakers Gone Wild?*

68. As an example in Virginia, see Kerry Brian Melear, *Undocumented Immigrant Access to Public Higher Education: The Virginia Response*, 194 Educ. L. Reporter 27 (2005); Nathan Cortez, *The Local Dilemma: Preemption and the Role of Federal Standards in State and Local Immigration Laws*, 47 SMU L. Rev. 61 (2008). See Day v. Sibelius, 376 F. Supp. 2d 1022 (Kan. 2005) (upholding residency requirement that allows undocumented to establish residency and denying standing to challengers). Because the trial judge removed the governor as a defendant, the case at the Tenth Circuit, which upheld the district court, was styled as Day v. Bond, 500 F.3d 1127 (10th Cir. 2007); Day v. Bond, 511 F.3d 1030 (10th Cir 2007) (denying petition for rehearing and for consideration *en banc*); 128 S. Ct. 2987 (2008) (denying *certiorari*). The California state court case is Martinez et al. v Regents of the Univ. of Cal., CV-05-2064 (Cal. Super. Ct., Oct. 6, 2006) [Order on Demurrers, Motion to Strike, and Motions by Proposed Intervenors]. This action, dismissed on October 6, 2006, was the state equivalent of the *Day v. Sibelius* federal case in Kansas, which was argued at the Tenth Circuit in September 2006. It was reversed by the California Appeals Court, and the trial court decision was affirmed in late 2010 by the California Supreme Court. 83 Cal. Rptr. 518 (Cal. App. 3 Dist. 2008). Timberly Ross, *Nebraska Judge Tosses Illegal Immigrant Tuition Suit*, CNSNews.com, Dec. 17, 2010, available at http://www.cnsnews.com/news/article/nebraska-judge-tosses-illegal-immigrant. See Kristen Miller & Celina Moreno, *Martinez v. Regents: Mis-step or Wave of the Future?* (IHELG Monograph 08-07, 2008), available at http://www.law.uh.edu/ihelg/monograph/08-07.pdf; Kasarda, *Affirmative Action Gone Haywire*. In late 2010, the California Supreme Court upheld the statute. Martinez v. U.C. Regents, 50 Cal. 4th 1277, 241 P.3d 855, 117 Cal. Rptr. 3d 359 (2010).

69. For this discussion, I rely on the excellent work of Francine J. Lipman, whose careful work in this complicated subject has made it much more understandable to civilian readers. Francine J. Lipman, *The Taxation of Undocumented Immigrants: Separate, Unequal, and without Representation*, 9 Harv. Latino L. Rev. 19 (2006); Francine J. Lipman, *Bearing Witness to Economic Injustices of Undocumented Immigrant Families: A New Class of "Undeserving Poor,"* 7 Nev. L.J. 736 (2007).

70. Lipman, *Taxation*, 20. There is a growing technical and policy literature on the issue of the taxation of undocumented persons. See, e.g., Paula N. Singer & Linda Dodd-Major, *Identification Numbers and U.S. Government Compliance Initiatives*, 104 Tax Notes 1429 (Sept. 20, 2004); Staff of Joint Commission on Taxation, *Present Law and Background Relating to Individual Taxpayer Identification Numbers* 3 (Mar. 5, 2004) (The Internal Revenue Code "does not contain special rules regarding the treatment of illegal aliens, or the tax identification number requirements with respect to illegal aliens."); Lipman, *Taxation*; Cynthia Blum, *Rethinking Tax Compliance of Unauthorized Workers after Immigration Reform*, 21 Geo. Immigr. L.J. 595 (2007); John Coyle, *The Legality of Banking the Undocumented*, 22 Geo. Immigr. L.J. 21 (2007). Michael A. Olivas, *Undocumented College Students, Taxation, and Financial Aid: A Technical Note*, 32 Rev. Higher Educ. 407 (2009). See also Miriam Jordan, *Mortgage Prospects Dim for Illegal Immigrants*, Wall St. J., Oct. 22, 2008, at A3 (IRS does not issue Social Security numbers to unauthorized immigrants; it issues ITINs, which enable them to open bank accounts and report their income to the government for tax purposes).

71. Lipman, *Taxation*.

72. *Id.*, 20–21.

73. *Id.*, 19 (title of article).

74. *Id.*, 22 (section title of article).

75. For an illustrative report on the issue of identity theft and the undocumented, see Julia Preston, *Illegal Worker, Troubled Citizen and Stolen Name*, N.Y. Times, Mar. 22, 2007, at A1 (recounting examples of identity theft and use of SSNs and credit documents by undocumented workers). Such fraud has serious consequences, both in the civil system and in the immigration regime. See, e.g., Hernandez v. State, 639 S.E.2d 473 (Ga. 2007) (Georgia Supreme Court decision on identity theft and fraudulent use of SSNs). Such immigration fraud is not exclusive to the undocumented. For an example of a Georgia college immigration official who trafficked in student visas, see United States v. Evans, 188 Fed. App'x 878 (11th Cir. 2006) (not chosen for publication in West's *Federal Reporter*).

76. That this is so is best evidenced by the extensive research literature on the subject. See, as just two examples, Hazel G. Beh, *Student versus University: The University's Implied Obligation of Good Faith and Fair Dealing*, 59 Md. L. Rev. 183 (2000); Kerry Brian Melear, *The Contractual Relationship between Student and Institution: Discipline, Academic, and Consumer Contexts*, 30 J.C. & U.L. 175 (2003). For an illustrative report on the issue of identity theft and the undocumented, see Preston, *Illegal Worker*. The National School Boards Association and the National Education Association teamed up to review a number of these problems and issued a joint report in fall 2009. National School Boards Association & National Education Association, *Legal Issues for School Districts Related to the Education of Undocumented Children* (National School Board Association 2009).

77. See, e.g., Commonwealth of Virginia, Department of Education, *Enrollment Requirements*, available at http://www.pen.k12.va.us (memo concerning 2003 Virginia General Assembly amendment of § 22.1-260 of the Code of Virginia, which requires that parents provide school divisions with an SSN for each student at the time of enrollment in school, amended to permit another identifying number or waiver of the requirement if a parent is unwilling to present an SSN for the child). See generally López & López, *Persistent Inequality*, 39–40.

78. As two examples, state educators in Missouri and Illinois have published such information on websites: Missouri Department of Elementary and Secondary Education, *Guidelines Regarding the Use of Social Security Numbers and the Attendance at School of Undocumented Students*, http://www.dese.mo.gov/schoollaw/freqaskques/undocumentedstudents.htm (accessed Apr. 24, 2011). For a national registry of such legislation concerning SSN penalties, see National Conference of State Legislatures, *Enacted Social Security Numbers Legislation—2010 Session*, available at http://www.ncsl.org/default.aspx?tabid=20634 (accessed Apr. 24, 2011) (listing state legislation enacted or introduced in 2010 to penalize persons who use false SSNs for governmental transactions). See also Jaclyn Brickman, *Educating Undocumented Children in the United States: Codification of* Plyler v. Doe *through Federal Legislation*, 20 Geo. Immigr. L.J. 385 (2006).

79. See, e.g., Illinois State Board of Education, *Immigrant Students' Rights*, available at http://www.isbe.state.il.us (accessed Sept. 21, 2009) (Illinois homeless-child policies FAQ). See generally López & López, *Persistent Inequality*, 128–131.

80. See María Pabón López, *More Than a License to Drive: State Restrictions on the Use of Driver's Licenses*, 29 S. Ill. U. L.J. 89 (2004) (reviewing license issues and identification problems).

81. See, e.g., Edward Hegstrom & Elena Vega, *One Nation, Two Worlds: Creating an American Life*, Hous. Chron., Dec. 6, 2005, at A1 (reviewing barriers to undocumented workers, including identification and tax identification); Tim Walker, *Caught in the Crossfire: Schools in Oklahoma Grapple with New Laws Targeting Illegal Immigration*, NEA Today (Jan. 2008), available at http://www.nea.org/home/7855.htm. In 2010, restrictionist legislation was introduced in the Oklahoma legislature to require public reporting of undocumented schoolchildren enrollments in the state's K–12 schools. Michael McNutt, *Bill Seeks Non-U.S. Students' Details*, Oklahoman, Feb. 25, 2010, at A3; Randy Krehbiel, *Hispanics Decry House Bill*, Tulsa World, Mar. 16, 2010, at A9. See generally Kevin R. Johnson, Raquel Aldana, Bill Ong Hing, Leticia Saucedo & Enid F. Trucios-Haynes, *Federalism and Alienage Law*, in *Understanding Immigration Law* 137–142 (LexisNexis 2009) [Ch. 4] (Public Benefits); David B. Thronson, *Entering the Mainstream: Making Children Matter in Immigration Law*, 38 Fordham Urb. L.J.393, 403–407 (2010) (outlining consequences of citizen deported with undocumented parents). See also Jacqueline Bhabha, *"Not a Sack of Potatoes": Moving and Removing Children across Borders*, 15 B.U. Pub. Int. L.J. 197, 198–199 (2006).

82. Joel R. v. Manheim Middle Sch. Dist., 686 N.E.2d 650 (1997).

83. *Id.* at 653.

84. See, for example, the useful manual on these issues: Dan H. Berger & Scott M. Borene, eds., *Immigration Options for Academics and Researchers* (American Immigration Lawyers Association 2005) (describing complex immigration provisions for students and academic employees).

85. Murillo v. Musegades, 809 F. Supp. 487 (W.D. Tex. 1992) (enjoining immigration officers from searching El Paso high school students on mere suspicion of immigration compliance and Mexican appearance).

86. *Id.* at 501.

87. Discussions with El Paso attorney Albert Armendariz, Jr., counsel for students and Bowie administrators, Mar. 20, 2007.

88. Amy Miller, *APS Safe for Migrant Students*, Albuq. J., June 2, 2006, at A1.

89. Amy Miller, *Migrants Are Safe at APS*, Albuq. J., June 15, 2006, at C1.

90. The students scattered, but the one still in school in 2007 was paroled into the United States to allow him to complete his studies. Discussions with MALDEF attorneys, Mar. 16, 2007.

91. Miller, *Migrants Are Safe*, C1.

92. *Berry Right to Temper Sanctuary City Rhetoric*, Editorial, Albuq. J., Dec. 21, 2009, available at http://www.abqjournal.com/opinion/editorials/2122195927860pinioneditori als12-21-09.htm.

93. The judge pointed to a "gentleman's agreement" previously in place that had been observed in the breach. *Murillo*, 809 F. Supp. at 496. In addition, "Although he has heard about the injunction or opinion issued in *Mendoza v. INS*, 559 F. Supp. 842, 850 (W.D. Tex. 1982), El Paso Border Patrol Sector Chief Dale Musegades has not read the injunction or opinion. Defendant Musegades has done nothing to implement or monitor compliance with the terms of the injunction." *Id.* at 495.

94. Discussions with MALDEF lawyers, Mar. 16, 2007. See generally López & López, *Persistent Inequality*, 124–127.

95. *Murillo*, 809 F. Supp. at 501 (striking down Border Patrol profiling practices). For a small sampler of the extensive literature about border enforcement with Mexico, see David Spener, *Clandestine Crossings: Migrants and Coyotes on the Texas-Mexico Border* (Cornell Univ. Press 2009); Roxanne L. Doty, *The Law into Their Own Hands: Immigration and the Politics of Exceptionalism* (Univ. Arizona Press 2009); César Cuauhtémoc García Hernández, *La Migra in the Mirror: Immigration Enforcement and Racial Profiling on the Texas Border*, 23 Notre Dame J.L. Ethics & Pub. Pol'y 167 (2009).

96. She was the dependent of a tourist (B-2), who overstayed. Rosalind Rossi, *Schools Slammed for Barring Child*, Chi. Sun-Times, Feb. 24, 2006, at A8. See also Sam Dillon, *In Schools across U.S., the Melting Pot Overflows*, N.Y. Times, Aug. 27, 2006, at YT-1; Nina Bernstein, *On Lucille Avenue, the Immigration Debate*, N.Y. Times, June 26, 2006, at A1; Jennifer Radcliffe, *1982 Ruling a Catalyst in Immigration Debate*, Hous. Chron., May 21, 2006, at B1. As with most of the issues in this field, there are competing values here. To my way of thinking, how someone becomes undocumented plays a large role in arguing the equities of his or her situation. In this calculus, a child brought surreptitiously or legally by adults does not have dirty hands; an adult who falls out of status is a different matter, with fewer equitable arguments. Courts and critics do not always acknowledge this distinction, or they do so but argue that it makes no difference. See, e.g., Dan Stein, *Why Illegal Immigrants Should Not Receive In-State Tuition Subsidies*, Univ. Bus. (Apr. 2002), at 64 (arguing that according resident status or allowing undocumented students to enroll only encourages lawbreaking). But see Michael A Olivas, *A Rebuttal to FAIR*, Univ. Bus. (June 2002), at 72 (making dirty-hands distinctions).

97. Eric Herman, *Schools Cry "Uncle,"* Chi. Sun-Times, Feb. 25, 2006, at A3; Colleen Mastony & Diane Redo, *Elmwood Park Schools Give In: To Keep State Funds, District Drops Fight on Immigrant Student*, Chi. Trib., Feb. 25, 2006, at News-1; Colleen Mastony & Diane Redo, *Barred Teen Pleased as Lawsuit Is Dropped: Elmwood Park District Reluctantly Ends Fight*, Chi. Trib., Feb. 28, 2006, at Metro-1. In a different suburb of Chicago, Mt. Pleasant, a school administrator required a number of Latino students to sign a pledge that they would not use Spanish in school and that doing so would be treated as "bullying" and a violation of the district's antibullying policy. Jeff Long, *"Bully" Contract Leads to Apology: District 26 Denies Spanish Speakers Were Targeted*, Chi. Trib., Dec. 13, 2006, at Metro-1.

98. Burgos v. Illinois Dep't of Children and Family Servs., No. 75 C 7934 (N.D. Ill.) (case settled). discussions with Ricardo Meza, MALDEF, Mar. 17, 2007 (on file with author).

99. Discussions with MALDEF attorneys, Mar. 22, 2010. In 2009–2010, a number of school districts began strict enforcement of laws and policies, resulting in regular press stories on undocumented schoolchildren. See, e.g., Melissa del Bosque, *Child X-ing: Del Rio's Controversial Crackdown on Border-Crossing Students*, Texas Observer, Dec. 11, 2009, at 8–9, 11–13 (Texas border controls); A. G. Sulzberger, *Growing Anti-immigrant Sentiments in an Unlikely State*, N.Y. Times, Oct. 3, 2010, at A16 (concerning Nebraska); Kirk Semple, *Immigration Agency's Tactic Spurs Alarm*, N.Y. Times, Sept. 18, 2010, at A15; Nina Bernstein, *No Visa, No School, Many New York Districts Say*, N.Y. Times, July 22, 2010, at A16 (access to New York student files); Sandra Baltazar Martínez, *Arizona Teen Pursues Education in Friendlier State*, Santa Fe New Mexican, Sept. 7, 2010, available at http://www.santafenewmexican.com/PrintStory/Illegal-immigration—Arizona-teen-pursues-college-

dream-in-frie (New Mexico, Arizona); Claudia Núñez, *California Border Schools to Ask Students for Papers*, New Am. Media, Aug. 27, 2010, available at http://newamericamedia.org/2010/08/california-border-schools-to-ask-students-for-papers.php (California border enforcement).

100. Pub. L. No. 104-208, 116 Stat. 3009 (1996).

101. INA§ 214 (1)(1)(A), 8 U.S.C. § 1184(1), as enacted by IIRIRA § 625(a)(1).

102. This was the argument advanced by Elmwood Park school officials, who essentially argued that being in lapsed B-2 (visitor) status was a "helicopter parent" situation. Mastony & Redo, *Barred Teen Pleased*. In fact, "helicoptering" is placing minor children in F-1 status as if they were enrolled students on their own, rather than dependent on their parents' legal or illegal status and domicile. Interior states have periodically ratcheted up the attention paid to district residency, depending on local politics. See, e.g., Michelle Roberts, *District Gives Pop Quiz on Residency*, Virginian-Pilot, Sept. 22, 2009, at A3; Bernstein, *No Visa, No School*; Cindy Gonzalez, *Fairbury Next in Immigration Battle*, Omaha World-Herald, Sept. 1, 2010, available at http://www.omaha.com/article/20100901/NEWS01/709019918#fairbury-next-in-immigration-battle.

103. KTBC television station, *Email Warns of Illegal Immigration Crackdowns in Classrooms*, Texas Civil Rights Project Newsclip, Apr. 4, 2006, available at http://www.texas-civilrightsproject.org/newspub/clip_060426_email_warns.html. Discussion with James Harrington, Texas Civil Rights Project lawyer, Mar. 20, 2009.

104. KTBC, *Email*.

105. In 2006, an E-2 (the dependent of a nonimmigrant treaty investor) was precluded from securing an F-1 visa to attend college in the United States. See Kelly Griffith, *E-2 Kids Hoping for a Dream*, Orlando Sentinel, Sept. 10, 2006, at J1. Although the article does not say so, the likely culprit was the requirement that such applicants for student visas not have an "intending immigrant" intent; that is, they must not appear to be intending to remain in the United States after their studies are completed, or else the consular official will, with virtually unreviewable discretion, refuse admission into the country. See Walfish, *Student Visas*.

106. *LULAC*, 908 F. Supp. 755.

107. Schrag, *Well-Founded Fear*, 141–143 (summarizing Gallegly Amendment dynamics).

108. *Id.*, 311 n.31 (citing opposition by senior Republicans and Catholic bishops).

109. "More than 5,400 students benefited from the tuition law last spring [fall 2006], up from 393 in 2001, according to the Texas Higher Education Coordinating Board." Tresaugue & Radcliffe, *Illegal Immigrants May See Tuition Hike*, B1; Robison & Ratcliffe, *Perry to Stick by Law*, B4. My own regular discussions with the Coordinating Board staff have suggested that nearly ten thousand different students have employed this provision since it was enacted. See also Olivas, *IIRIRA*. The most current available state data are compiled by the National Immigration Law Center, at www.nilc.org, which usefully tracks DREAM Act issues: *DREAM Act*, available at http://www.nilc.org/immlawpolicy/DREAM/index.htm (accessed Apr. 24, 2011). See generally Sara Hebel, *States Take Diverging Approaches on Tuition Rates for Illegal Immigrants*, Chron. Higher Educ., Nov. 30, 2001, at A22. Virginia was sued by the undocumented to secure resident-tuition eligibility. Doe 1 v. Merten, 219 F.R.D. 387 (E.D. Va. 2004) (procedural); Equal Access Educ. v. Merten, 305 F. Supp. 2d 585 (E.D. Va. 2004) (procedural); Equal Access Educ. v. Merten, 325 F. Supp. 2d 655 (E.D. Va. 2004) (merits of the case, upholding statute denying alien residency). See Cortez, *Local*

Dilemma. In Kansas, the opposite occurred, when restrictionist lawyers sued to strike down the state law that allowed resident tuition. Kan. Stat. Ann. § 76-731a (2004); Day v. Sebelius, 376 F. Supp. 2d 1022 (D. Kan. 2005) (upholding statute). In the interests of full disclosure: I served as the Kansas expert witness in this litigation.

110. Cheryl Smith, *Immigrants Tell Country to "Listen Up,"* Austin Chron., May 4, 2007, available at http://www.austinchronicle.com/gyrobase/Issue/ story?oid=oid:471800; discussions with James Harrington, Austin attorney, Sept. 10, 2009; Raam Wong, *ICE Picks Up Dad at School: District, City Officials Upset with Timing, Location of Arrest,* Albuq. J., Mar. 29, 2007, at A1; Niraj Warikoo, *Immigration Agents Improperly Targeted Detroit School Parents, Feds Admit,* Detroit Free Press, April 7, 2011, available at http://www.freep.com/article/20110407/NEWS01/110407041/ Immigration-agents-improperly-targeted-Detroit-school-parents-feds-admit.

111. As of 2011, the matter was still under review in the Northern District of Illinois, Docket No. 1:75-cv-03974, ecf.ilnd.uscourts.gov; discussions with MALDEF staff, Apr. 7, 2011.

112. *Id.*; discussions with MALDEF-Chicago attorney, May 12, 2009.

113. Isaura Santiago-Santiago, Aspira v. Board of Education *Revisited,* 95 Am. J. Educ. 149 (1986); Luis O. Reyes, *The ASPIRA Consent Decree: A Thirtieth-Anniversary Retrospective of Bilingual Education in New York City,* 76 Harv. Educ. Rev. 369 (Fall 2006).

114. On the subject of mayors' controls over public schooling in their cities, see *From the Editors: Mayoral Takeovers in Education: A Recipe for Progress or Peril?,* 76 Harv. Educ. Rev.141 (Summer 2006).

115. American Civil Rights Found. v. Los Angeles Unified Sch. Dist., Nos. BC-341341, BC-341363 (Cal. Super. Ct.). Discussions with MALDEF attorneys, Mar. 2, 2007 (on file with author). See also Pacific Legal Foundation, *PLF and American Civil Rights Foundation File Two Lawsuits against Los Angeles Unified School District for Violating Prop. 209,* available at http://www.pacificlegal.org/page.aspx?pid=272 (accessed Apr. 24. 2001) ("preference" suits brought against LAUSD).

116. Consortium for Adequate School Funding in Georgia, Inc. v. State of Georgia, CV-91004 (denying the State's motion for summary judgment). See Georgia School Funding Association website, www.casfg.org.

117. I have found that the most comprehensive sources of information on these cases are the individual websites of the many groups that undertake such litigation, on both sides. Several of these have quite detailed information and post briefs, pleadings, and other legal materials in the cases. A sampler of these includes NAACP Legal Defense Fund, www. naacpldf.org; Southern Poverty Law Center, www.splcenter.org; Pacific Legal Foundation, www.pacificlegal.org; MALDEF, www.maldef.org; Center for Individual Rights, www.cir-usa.org; PRLDEF, www.prldef.org; ACLU, www.aclu.org; and National Access Network, www.schoolfunding.info.

118. For two such examples of undocumented high schoolers, both prompted by robotics competitions, see Peter Carlson, *Stinky the Robot, Four Kids and a Brief Whiff of Success,* Wash. Post, Mar. 29, 2005, at C1 (undocumented Mexican students); Mel Melendez, *Doors Finally Open for 4 Phoenix Migrant Youths a Year after Beating MIT in Robotics Competition,* Ariz. Republic, Apr. 23, 2005, at 1A; Daniel Gonzalez, *"Wilson Four" Deportation Case Settled: Panel Says Students Wrongly Targeted,* Ariz. Republic, Dec. 12, 2006, at 10A (Board of Immigration Appeals agrees children may remain in United States after being wrongly

targeted). One of these students resurfaced in 2010, having self-deported to Mexico and returned legally to Arizona, having been assisted by Senator Richard Durbin (D-IL), one of the longtime proponents of the DREAM Act legislation. Richard Ruelas, *The Hard Way Home*, Ariz. Republic, Aug. 31, 2010, at D1, available at http://www.azcentral.com/php-bin/clicktrack/email.php/9541294.

119. Nina Bernstein, *Student's Prize Is a Trip into Immigration Limbo*, N.Y. Times, Apr. 26, 2006, at A1 (Senegalese student); Nina Bernstein, *Senegalese Teenager Wins Right to Study in the U.S.*, N.Y. Times, July 29, 2006, at A13; Miriam Jordan, *Princeton's 2006 Salutatorian Heads to Oxford, Still an Illegal Immigrant*, Wall St. J., Sept. 14, 2006, at B1; Maria Sacchetti, *Illegal Immigrant Students Tell of Lost Opportunities*, Boston Globe, Nov. 26, 2010, available at http://www.boston.com/news/local/massachusetts/articles/2010/11/26/illegal_immigrant_students_tell_of_lost_opportunities/?page=full; Melissa Ludwig, *DREAM Act Hunger Strike Spreads in Texas*, San Antonio Express-News, Nov. 24, 2010, at B8, available at http://www.mysanantonio.com/news/dream_act_hunger_strike_spreads_110273704.html?showFullArticle=y; Maggie Jones, *Coming Out Illegal*, N.Y. Times Magazine, Oct. 24, 2010, at MM36–39; Anonymous, *I'm an Illegal Immigrant at Harvard*, Daily Beast (blog), Nov. 27, 2010, available at http://www.thedailybeast.com/blogs-and-stories/2010-11-27/dream-act-im-an-illegal-immigrant-at-harvard; Jessica Kwong, *Student Freed as Feinstein Steps In*, S.F. Chron., Nov. 20, 2010, at C1; Hector Tobar, *Law Grad's Legal Quandary*, L.A. Times, Nov. 26 2010, A2, available at http://www.latimes.com/news/local/la-me-tobar-20101126,0,1358739.column; Reeve Hamilton, *Undocumented Students Stump for the DREAM Act*, Texas Trib., Nov. 11, 2010, available at http://www.texastribune.org/immigration-in-texas/immigration/undocumented-students-stump-for-the-dream-act/; Diana Marcum, *He's the Cal State Fresno Student Body President—and an Illegal Immigrant*, L.A. Times, Nov. 18, 2010, available at http://www.latimes.com/news/local/la-me-1118-illegal-immigrant-presiden20101118,0,5635027.story; Jesse Ricke, *Student Organization Rallies for DREAM Act in Times Square*, Brooklyn Progressive Examiner, Nov. 29, 2010, available at http://www.examiner.com/progressive-in-new-york/student-organization-rallies-for-dream-act-times-square; Melissa Ludwig, *15 DREAM Act Demonstrators Arrested*, San Antonio Express-News, Nov. 30, 2010, at A1, available at http://www.mysanantonio.com/news/police_respond_to_dream_act_rally_111008674.html?showFullArticle=y; Richard Ruelas, *Dream Act Students Risk Deportation to Win Support*, Ariz. Republic, Nov. 16, 2010, at D1, available at http://www.azcentral.com/php-bin/clicktrack/email.php/9541290; Diana Marcum, *Standing Up for a Dream*, L.A. Times, Nov. 28, 2010, at A1, available at http://www.latimes.com/news/local/la-me-dream-act-20101128,0,5057601.story; E. J. Montini, *Dream Act Kids Facing a Political Nightmare*, Ariz. Republic, Nov. 24, 2010, at B1, available at http://www.azcentral.com/phpbin/clicktrack/email.php/9542002.

120. The news media carried a number of stories and editorials, largely in support of the legislation proposed to be taken up in the lame-duck session of Congress, to no avail, as the political bickering again stalled the enactment. Even Republicans who had voted for the cloture motion in 2007 refused to do so in either of the 2010 actions. Shankar Vedantam, *Undocumented Youths Chasing a Dream*, Wash. Post, Nov. 28, 2010, at C1; David M. Herszenhorn, *Reid to Push to Allow End of "Don't Ask, Don't Tell,"* N.Y. Times, Nov. 18, 2010, at A23, available at http://www.nytimes.com/2010/11/18/us/politics/18gays.html?nl=todaysheadlines&emc=a24; *A Worthy Immigration Bill: The Dream Act Rewards Military Service and Student Achievement*, Wall St. J., Nov. 27, 2010, at A16, available at

http://online.wsj.com/article/SB10001424052748703572404575635202343271966.html?KE
YWORDS=aworthyimmigrationbill; Immigration Policy Center, *Dispelling DREAM Act
Myths*, Nov. 23, 2010, available at http://www.immigrationpolicy.org/just-facts/dispelling-
dream-act-myths; Scott Wong, *Democratic Senator Reid Moves Forward with Dream Act*,
Politico, Nov. 30, 2010, available at http://www.politico.com/news/stories/1110/45761.
html#ixzz16qY5uwVG; *Dreaming of Reform*, Editorial, N.Y. Times, Nov. 30, 2010, at A30;
Daniel Rubin, *More Courage from a Dreamer on Immigration*, Phil. Inq., Apr. 11, 2011, B1;
Juan E. Gastelum, *How Immigration Activists Are Fighting Deportation Policy with Social
Media*, Mashable.com, Apr. 19, 2011, available at http://mashable.com/2011/04/19/immi-
gration-activism-social-media/; Julia Preston, *Latinos and Democrats Press Obama to Curb
Deportations*, N.Y. Times, Apr. 21, 2011, at A18.

121. "Today, Mr. Plyler is happy the school district didn't win. That's a different view
from the one he expressed after the high court's ruling, when he called illegal immigrant
children a 'burden.' . . . 'It would have been one of the worst things to happen in education—they'd cost more not being educated,' the retired superintendent said. 'Right after
we let those youngsters in, I was pleased. Then more and more came, and now we have
schools with a lot of Hispanics all over the district.'" Katherine Leal Unmuth, *25 Years Ago,
Tyler Case Opened Schools to Illegal Migrants*, Dall. Morn. News, June 11, 2007, at A1. But
this is an ongoing case of whack-a-mole, where for every converted school official, there
is a new agnostic, especially along the border. Roberts, *District Gives Pop Quiz* (recounting new policies in Del Rio, Texas, school); Roberto G. Gonzales, *On the Wrong Side of the
Tracks: Understanding the Effects of School Structure and Social Capital in the Educational
Pursuits of Undocumented Immigrant Students*, 85 Peabody J. Educ. 469 (2010); Bernstein,
No Visa, No School; Melissa del Bosque, *Children of the Exodus: What Becomes of Kids Who
Are Deported without Their Families?*, Texas Observer, Nov. 4, 2010, available at: http://
www.texasobserver.org/cover-story/children-of-the-exodus.

122. Stephanie Sandoval, *Funding Intact for Youth Group*, Dall. Morn. News, Sept. 21,
2006, at 1B.

123. Ralph Blumenthal, *Texas Lawmakers Put New Focus on Illegal Immigration*, N.Y.
Times, Nov. 16, 2006, at A22. By January 2007, there were three federal suits and a state
suit in this case, and a temporary restraining order was issued. Thomas Korosec, *Leasing
Rule Sent to Voters for OK: Councilman Says Farmers Branch May Set Precedent on Illegal
Residents*, Hous. Chron., Jan. 23, 2007, at B1; Gretel C. Kovach, *Dallas Suburb Amends
Its Ban on Renting to Illegal Immigrants*, N.Y. Times, Jan. 25, 2007, at A22 (city council
voted to revise policy; revised policy "allows landlords to rent to families with a head
of household or a spouse who has legal residency or citizenship, and it exempts minors
from mandatory document checks"); Stephanie Sandoval, *Restraining Order Issued against
Rental Ordinance*, Dall. Morn. News, Sept. 13, 2008, at B1. In March 2010, four years after
the statute was first enacted, the federal judge permanently enjoined the city from implementing the ordinance, finding that it violated the supremacy clause and was preempted
by federal law. Villas at Parkside Partners v. City of Farmers Branch, Texas, 701 F. Supp. 2d
835 (2010). Dianne Solis, *Judge Rejects Rental Ban*, Dall. Morn. News, Mar. 25, 2010, at B1
(details about permanent injunction in Farmers Branch case).

124. *Martinez*, 461 U.S. 321.

125. *Id.* at 322–323. This issue waxes and wanes along the border, often depending
on school overcrowding, border transience, political and electoral politics, and col-

lateral issues such as drug-related violence. See, e.g., Faye Bowers, *In Growing Cities, a Loss of Students: Schools Aren't Sure Why Enrollment Is Down,* Christian Science Monitor, Sept. 24, 2007, available at http://www.csmonitor.com/2007/0924/p02s01-ussc. html; Randy Dotinga & Mary Know Merrill, *Schools Crack Down on Students Living in Mexico,* Santa Fe New Mexican, May 27, 2008, at C6; del Bosque, *Child X-ing,* 8; Michelle Roberts, *Superintendent Tells Mexican Residents Attending U.S. Schools: Prove Texas Residency or Leave,* Chi. Trib., Sept. 21, 2009, available at http://abcnews.go.com/US/wirestory?id=8637664&page=3; NSBA & NEA, *Legal Issues for School Districts*; Doty, *Law into Their Own Hands.* See *In the Child's Best Interest? The Consequences of Losing a Lawful Immigrant Parent to Deportation* (International Human Rights Law Clinic, University of California, Berkeley, School of Law; Warren Institute on Race, Ethnicity and Diversity, University of California, Berkeley, School of Law; Immigration Law Clinic; University of California, Davis, School of Law, Mar. 2010); Mary Ann Zehr, *With Immigrants, Districts Balance Safety, Legalities,* Educ. Wk., Sept. 12, 2007, at 1–15; Wong, *ICE Picks Up Dad* (Santa Fe, NM); Bowers, *In Growing Cities*; Howard Fischer, *Sheriff: Schools Should Question Students' Citizen Status,* Yuma (AZ) Sun, Apr. 28, 2009, available at 2009 WLNR 7985977; Juan Carlos Rodriguez, *Family Came to N.M. to Escape Immigration Law,* Albuq. J., Aug. 30, 2010, at A1 (following AZ legislation); Núñez, *California Border Schools.* These issues, as is evident, are not limited to the border states. Legislation proposed in Oklahoma would require schools to identify the immigration status of all students in each school district. See McNutt, *Bill Seeks.*

Districts along the border: Romero, *"Go after the Women"*; García Hernández, *La Migra in the Mirror.*

Districts away from the border: Roberts, *District Gives Pop Quiz*; McNutt, *Bill Seeks*; Randy Krehbiel, *Tulsa Hispanic Leaders Oppose School Bill,* Tulsa World, Mar. 15, 2010, available at http://www.tulsaworld.com/news/article.aspx?subjectid=19&articl eid=20100315_12_0_Abillp998569; Niraj Warikoo, *Immigration Agents Improperly Targeted Detroit School Parents, Feds Admit,* Detroit Free Press, Apr. 7, 2011, available at http://www.freep.com/article/20110407/NEWS01/110407041/Immigration-agents-improperly-targeted-Detroit-school-parents-feds-admit; Jonathan Oosting, *U.S. Immigration Agents Accused of "Stalking" Parents Dropping Off Kids at Detroit School,* MLive.com, Apr. 7, 2011, available at http://www.mlive.com/news/detroit/index.ssf/2011/04/federal_immigration_agents_acc.html.

126. These issues have surfaced over the years and have been addressed by many private studies. On my bookshelf, some of the more worn and well used have included Joan McCarty First, *New Voices: Immigrant Students in U.S. Public Schools* (National Coalition of Advocates for Students 1988); Laurie Olsen, *Crossing the Schoolhouse Border: Immigrant Students and the California Public Schools* (California Tomorrow 1988); and John Willshire Carrera, *Immigrant Students: Their Legal Right of Access to Public Schools* (National Coalition of Advocates for Students 1989); Brian Fry, *Nativism and Immigration: Regulating the American Dream* (LFB 2006); National Education Association, Office of General Counsel, *Immigration Status and the Right to a Free Public Education,* available at http://www.nea.org/assets/img/pubToday/0801/ImmigrationStatusandRights.pdf.

127. *Joel R.,* 686 N.E.2d at 656–657.

128. *Plyler,* 457 U.S. at 227 n.22.

129. Jorge Ruiz-de-Velasco, Michael E. Fix & Beatriz Chu Clewell, *Overlooked and Underserved: Immigrant Students in U.S. Secondary Schools* (Urban Institute 2000), available at http://www.urban.org/publications/310022.html.

130. Zehr, *Working Immigrants*; Mike Snyder, *HISD's ESL Enrollment Belies Census Numbers on Immigrants*, Hous. Chron., Apr. 5, 2007, at B1.

131. López, *Reflections*, 1398–1406. For the effect of disasters, such as the cataclysmic New Orleans flooding, on Latino children, see Augustina H. Reyes, *The Right to an Education for Homeless Students: The Children of Katrina*, in *Children, Law, and Disasters: What Have We Learned from the Hurricanes of 2005?* 261–312 (Laura Oren, Ellen Marrus & H. Davidson, eds., American Bar Association and the Center for Children, Law and Policy 2009); Kevin Sieff, *No Way Out: Will the Border Patrol Use Hurricane Evacuations to Snag Undocumented Immigrants?*, Texas Observer, Aug. 7, 2009, available at http://www.texasobserver.org/features/no-way-out.

132. Olivas, *Storytelling*, 1080–1081 (recounting experiences recruiting migrant students).

133. Barbara Ferry, *"Out of the Shadows," Immigrant Women Shed Fears to Lead Push for Rights in Santa Fe*, Santa Fe New Mexican, June 12, 2006, at A1 (recounting stories by undocumented women); Dan McKay, *Sanctuary Policy Change Delayed*, Albuq. J., Dec. 17, 2009, at A1 (Albuquerque policies); Ryan Evely Gildersleeve, *Fracturing Opportunity: Mexican Migrant Students and College-Going Literacy* (Peter Lang 2010). See, e.g., Ruiz-de-Velasco, Fix & Clewell, *Overlooked and Underserved* (noting hardships faced by undocumented students); NSBA & NEA, *Legal Issues for School Districts*; Jeffrey S. Passel, *Unauthorized Migrants: Numbers and Characteristics; Background Briefing Prepared for Task Force on Immigration and America's Future* (Pew Hispanic Center 2005); Kirk Semple, *Immigration Agency's Tactic Spurs Alarm*, N.Y. Times, Sept. 18, 2010, at A15; National Education Association, *Immigration Status*.

134. For evidence of this troubling phenomenon, see Cecilia Menjívar, *Liminal Legality: Salvadoran and Guatemalan Immigrants' Lives in the United States*, 111 Am. J. of Soc. 999 (2006); Matthew J. Lindsay, *Immigration as Invasion: Sovereignty, Security, and the Origins of the Federal Immigration Power*, 45 Harv. C.R.-C.L. L. Rev. 1 (2010); Jorge M. Chavez & Doris Marie Provine, *Race and the Response of State Legislatures to Unauthorized Immigrants*, 623 Annals Am. Acad. Pol. & Soc. Sci. 78 (2009), available at http://ann.sagepub.com/cgi/content/abstract/623/1/78.

NOTES TO CHAPTER 4

1. Daniel Gonzalez, *"Wilson Four" Deportation Case Settled: Panel Says Students Wrongly Targeted*, Ariz. Republic, Dec. 12, 2006, at 10. As recently as 2010, these students were in the local news. See Richard Ruelas, *The Hard Way Home*, Ariz. Republic, Aug. 31, 2010, at D1, available at http://www.azcentral.com/php-bin/clicktrack/email.php/9541294. For developments in Arizona, see Keith Aoki & John Shuford, *Welcome to Amerizona—Immigrants Out! Assessing "Dystopian Dreams" and "Usable Futures" of Immigration Reform, and Considering Whether "Immigration Regionalism" Is an Idea Whose Time Has Come*, 38 Fordham Urb. L.J. 1 (2010).

2. A 2006 MPI study estimated that approximately fifty thousand undocumented college students were enrolled, including full-time and part-time students. Jeanne Batalova & Michael Fix, *New Estimates of Unauthorized Youth Eligible for Legal Status under the*

DREAM Act 4 (Migration Policy Institute 2006), available at http://www.migrationpolicy. org/pubs/Backgrounder1_Dream_Act.pdf. These data do not include persons who might be eligible for the act's military options for legalization. Additional studies or data include Elizabeth Redden, *Data on the Undocumented*, Inside Higher Ed, Mar. 17, 2009, available at http://www.insidehighered.com/news/2009/03/17/undocumented; Jeffrey S. Passel & D'Vera Cohn, *A Portrait of Unauthorized Immigrants in the United States* iv (Pew Hispanic Center 2009) ("[A]mong unauthorized immigrants ages 18 to 24 who have graduated from high school, half (49%) are in college or have attended college. The comparable figure for U.S.-born residents is 71%."); Dawn Konet, *Unauthorized Youths and Higher Education: The Ongoing Debate* (Migration Policy Institute 2007); Raphael Lewis, *In-State Tuition Not a Draw for Many Immigrants*, Boston Globe, Nov. 9, 2005, at A1 (report on individual state enrollments).

3. See generally Michael A. Olivas, *Immigration-Related State and Local Ordinances: Preemption, Prejudice, and the Proper Role for Enforcement*, 2007 U. Chi. Legal F. 27 (2007); Amy Thompson, *A Child Alone and without Papers* (Center for Public Policy Priorities 2008), available at http://www.cppp.org/repatriation; María Pabón López & Gerardo R. López, *Persistent Inequality: Contemporary Realities in the Education of Undocumented Latina/o Students* 55–89 (Routledge 2010); Ajay Chaudry, Randolph Capps, Juan Pedroza, Rosa Maria Castaneda, Robert Santos & Molly M. Scott, *Facing Our Future: Children in the Aftermath of Immigration Enforcement* (Urban Institute 2010), available at http://www. urban.org/publications/412020.html.

4. Plyler v. Doe, 457 U.S. 202 (1982). Michael A. Olivas, *The Story of* Plyler v. Doe, *the Education of Undocumented Children, and the Polity*, in *Immigration Stories* 197 (David Martin & Peter Schuck, eds., Foundation 2005); see also María Pabón López, *Reflections on Educating Latino and Latina Undocumented Children: Beyond* Plyler v. Doe, 35 Seton Hall L. Rev. 1373 (2005); Jaclyn Brickman, Note, *Educating Undocumented Children in the United States: Codification of* Plyler v. Doe *through Federal Legislation*, 20 Geo. Immigr. L.J. 385 (2006). Historically, Texas is widely considered to have been the state most restrictive and nativist toward its Mexican-origin population. See, e.g., Cynthia E. Orozco, *No Mexicans, Women, or Dogs Allowed: The Rise of the Mexican American Civil Rights Movement* (Univ. Texas Press 2009). But on the issue of undocumented college students, Texas has been in the vanguard for according residency.

5. See, e.g., Paula R. v. Goldstein, 297 A.D.2d 905, 2002 WL 2025999 (N.Y.A.D. 1 Dept.) [Unreported Disposition]; *Law Lowers Tuition for Immigrants*, Albany Times Union, Aug. 10, 2002, at B4; see also Laura S. Yates, Plyler v. Doe *and the Rights of Undocumented Immigrants to Higher Education: Should Undocumented Students be Eligible for In-State College Tuition Rates?*, 82 Wash. U. L.Q. 585, 609 (2004) ("More recently, California and New York courts have confronted the question of whether a state can deny in-state tuition benefits to undocumented immigrants."). In a series of articles, I have tracked these developments through 2004. See generally Michael A. Olivas, *Storytelling Out of School: Undocumented College Residency, Race, and Reaction*, 22 Hastings Const. L.Q. 1019 (1995); Michael A. Olivas, *IIRIRA, the DREAM Act, and Undocumented College Student Residency*, 30 J.C. & U.L. 435 (2004). I have continued to analyze these developments and have detailed regular changes on a website: http://www.law.uh.edu/ihelg. See also Michael A. Olivas, *Lawmakers Gone Wild? College Residency and the Response to Professor Kobach*, 61 SMU L. Rev. 99 (2008); Kevin R. Johnson, Raquel Aldana, Bill Ong Hing, Leticia Saucedo &

Enid F. Trucios-Haynes, *Federalism and Alienage Law*, in *Understanding Immigration Law* 144–149 (LexisNexis 2009) [Ch. 4] (Higher Education); Stella M. Flores, *State Dream Acts: The Effect of In-State Resident Tuition Policies and Undocumented Latino Students*, 33 Rev. Higher Educ. 239 (2010); Kevin J. Dougherty, H. Kenny Nienhusser & Blanca E. Vega, *Undocumented Immigrants and State Higher Education Policy: The Contrasting Politics of In-State Tuition Eligibility in Texas and Arizona* (IHELG Monograph 09-11, 2009), available at http://www.law.uh.edu/ihelg/monograph/09-11.pdf. For an example of the issue in comparative context, see Bertelsmann Stiftung & Migration Policy Institute, eds., *Migration, Public Opinion and Politics* (Transatlantic Council on Migration 2009); Marie-Theresa Hernandez, *The French Banlieue Riots of 2005 and Their Impact on US Immigration Policy: A Transatlantic Study*, 7 Atlantic Stud. 79 (2010).

6. National Academies, *Policy Implications of International Graduate Students and Post-doctoral Scholars in the United States* (National Academies Press 2005). See also Michael A. Olivas, *The Political Economy of Immigration, Intellectual Property, and Racial Harassment: Case Studies of the Implementation of Legal Change on Campus*, 63 J. Higher Educ. 570, 573–577 (1992); Victor C. Romero, *Postsecondary School Education Benefits for Undocumented Immigrants: Promises and Pitfalls*, 27 N.C. J. Int'l Law & Com. Reg. 393 (2002); Victor C. Romero, *Noncitizen Students and Immigration Policy Post-9/11*, 17 Geo. Immigr. L.J. 357 (2003); Carl Krueger, *In-State Tuition for Undocumented Immigrants* (Education Commission of the States 2005); Aimee Chin & Chinhui Juhn, *Does Reducing College Costs Improve Educational Outcomes for Undocumented Immigrants?* (Rice University Baker Institute 2007), available at http://bakerinstitute.org/Program_View.cfm?PID=58; Neeraj Kaushal, *In-State Tuition for the Undocumented: Education Effects on Mexican Young Adults*, 27 J. Pol'y Analysis & Mgmt. 771 (2008). See generally Karen Engle, *The Political Economy of State and Local Immigration Regulation: Comments on Olivas and Hollifield, Hunt & Tichenor*, 61 SMU L. Rev. 159 (2008); S. Karthick Ramakrishnan & Tom (Tak) Wong, *Immigration Policies Go Local: The Varying Responses of Local Governments to Undocumented Immigration* 22 (Warren Institute on Race, Ethnicity, and Diversity 2007), available at http://www.law.berkeley.edu/centers/ewi/Ramakrishnan&Wongpaperfinal.pdf; López & López, *Persistent Inequality*, 55–89 (undocumented college applicants and students); Lisa D. Garcia & William G. Tierney, *Undocumented Immigrants in Higher Education: A Preliminary Analysis*, 113 Tchrs. Coll. Rec. (forthcoming 2011), available at http://www.tcrecord.org/PrintContent.asp?ContentID=16204; Stella M. Flores, *The First State Dream Act: In-State Resident Tuition and Immigration in Texas*, 32 Educ. Evaluation & Pol'y Analysis 435 (Dec. 2010).

7. See LULAC v. Wilson, 997 F. Supp. 1244, 1261 (C.D. Cal. 1997) (striking down virtually all of Proposition 187). See generally Kevin R. Johnson, *An Essay on Immigration Politics, Popular Democracy, and California's Proposition 187: The Political Relevance and Legal Irrelevance of Race*, 70 Wash. L. Rev. 629 (1995); Ruben J. Garcia, *Critical Race Theory and Proposition 187: The Racial Politics of Immigration Law*, 17 Chicano-Latino L. Rev. 118 (1995).

8. The full text of Proposition 187 appears in LULAC v. Wilson, 908 F. Supp. 755, app. 787–791 (C.D. Cal. 1995). There is an extensive literature on the events leading to and from this ballot initiative. See generally Evangeline G. Abriel, *Rethinking Preemption for Purposes of Aliens and Public Benefits*, 42 UCLA L. Rev. 1597 (1995); Linda S. Bosniak, *Opposing Prop. 187: Undocumented Immigrants and the National Imagination*, 28 Conn. L.

Rev. 555 (1996); Richard A. Boswell, *Restrictions on Non-citizens' Access to Public Benefits: Flawed Premise, Unnecessary Response*, 42 UCLA L. Rev. 1475 (1995); Lolita K. Buckner Inniss, *California's Proposition 187—Does It Mean What It Says? Does It Say What It Means? A Textual and Constitutional Analysis*, 10 Geo. Immigr. L.J. 577 (1996); Johnson, *Essay on Immigration Politics*; Kevin R. Johnson, *Public Benefits and Immigration: The Intersection of Immigration Status, Ethnicity, Gender, and Class*, 42 UCLA L. Rev. 1509 (1995); Stephen H. Legomsky, *Immigration, Federalism, and the Welfare State*, 42 UCLA L. Rev. 1453 (1995); Hiroshi Motomura, *Immigration and Alienage, Federalism and Proposition 187*, 35 Va. J. Int'l L. 201 (1994); Gerald L. Neuman, *Aliens as Outlaws: Government Services, Proposition 187, and the Structure of Equal Protection Doctrine*, 42 UCLA L. Rev. 1425 (1995); Michael A. Olivas, *Preempting Preemption: Foreign Affairs, State Rights, and Alienage Classifications*, 35 Va. J. Int'l L. 217 (1994); Peter L. Reich, *Environmental Metaphor in the Alien Benefits Debate*, 42 UCLA L. Rev. 1577 (1995); Peter H. Schuck, *The Message of Proposition 187*, 26 Pac. L.J. 989 (1995). Some of the fuller studies include, e.g., Vanessa A. Baird, *Answering the Call of the Court, How Justices and Litigants Set the Supreme Court Agenda* 73–82 (Univ. Virginia Press 2007); Robin Dale Jacobson, *The New Nativism: Proposition 187 and the Debate over Immigration* (Univ. Minnesota Press 2008); Frederick J. Boehmke, *The Initiative Process and the Dynamics of State Interest Group Populations*, 8 St. Pol. & Pol'y Q. 362 (2008).

9. *LULAC*, 908 F. Supp. 755; *LULAC*, 997 F. Supp. 1244. For a review of the residency issues leading up to this time, and the result of *LULAC*, see Olivas, *Storytelling*; Gary Libman, *Losing Out on a Dream?*, L.A. Times, Jan. 23, 1992, at E3 ("The [*Bradford*] decision will affect only about 100 UC students but about 14,000 at state community colleges, officials estimate."); Larry Gordon, *Immigrants Face Cal State Fee Hike*, L.A. Times, Sept. 9, 1992, at A3 (decision "could affect 800 of the 361,000 Cal State students"). At the time, California public-college students totaled over 2 million, including over 1.5 million in the community colleges.

10. Chiles v. United States, 69 F.3d 1094 (11th Cir. 1995) (Florida); Padavan v. United States, 82 F.3d 23 (2d Cir. 1996) (New York); New Jersey v. United States, 91 F.3d 463 (3d Cir. 1996) (New Jersey); Arizona v. United States, 104 F.3d 1095 (9th Cir. 1997) (Arizona); California v. United States, 104 F.3d 1086 (9th Cir. 1997) (California); Texas v. United States, 106 F.3d 661 (5th Cir. 1997) (Texas). Notwithstanding these cases, which all the states lost, it was a complex issue. For example, in 1993, Texas did not even spend all its federal dollars allocated for immigrant-program support and returned ninety million dollars unspent to the government. See James Cullen, Editorial, *Blame the Newcomers*, Texas Observer, Aug. 19, 1994, at 2–3.

11. Olivas, *Plyler v. Doe, the Education*, 212–213. For an authoritative review of the 1996 legislative histories and restrictionist efforts leading to the Personal Responsibility and Work Opportunity Reconciliation Act of 1996 and Illegal Immigration Reform and Immigrant Responsibility Act of 1996, written by an observer-participant, see Philip G. Schrag, *A Well-Founded Fear: The Congressional Battle to Save Political Asylum in America* 141–144, 178–182, 244–245 (Routledge 2000). While *Plyler* provided constitutional protection to the undocumented children from state laws, the case would not apply in similar fashion to congressional legislation. For other thoughtful studies of *Plyler* and the issues of federal preemption, see generally Peter H. Schuck, *The Transformation of Immigration Law*, 84 Colum. L. Rev. 1 (1984); Stephen H. Legomsky, *Fear and Loathing in Congress and*

the Courts: Immigration and Judicial Review, 78 Tex. L. Rev. 1615 (2000); Gerald L. Neuman, *Jurisdiction and the Rule of Law after the 1996 Immigration Act,* 113 Harv. L. Rev. 1963 (2000).

12. Personal Responsibility and Work Opportunity Reconciliation Act of 1996, Pub. L. No. 104-193, 110 Stat. 2105 (1996) (codified as amended in scattered sections of 2, 5, 7, 8, 10, 11, 13, 15, 20, 21, 25, 26, 28, 29, 31, 42 U.S.C.) [hereinafter PRWORA]; Illegal Immigration Reform and Immigrant Responsibility Act of 1996, Pub. L. No. 104-208, 110 Stat. 3009 (1996) (codified as amended in scattered sections of 8, 18 U.S.C.) [hereinafter IIRIRA].

13. Provisions codified at 8 U.S.C. §§ 1621, 1623 (2000).

14. *LULAC,* 997 F. Supp. at 1253.

15. Patrick J. McDonnell, *Davis Won't Appeal Prop. 187 Ruling, Ending Court Battles,* L.A. Times, July 29, 1999, at A1. See also Patrick J. McDonnell, *Prop. 187 Talks Offered Davis Few Choices,* L.A. Times, July 30, 1999, at A3.

16. Tex. Educ. Code § 54.052 (Vernon 2003). See generally Sara Hebel, *States Take Diverging Approaches on Tuition Rates for Illegal Immigrants,* Chron. Higher Educ., Nov. 30, 2001, at A22. Additional litigation was undertaken in the area of immigrant higher education, both to widen state veteran benefits and, in suits by restrictionist lawyers, to enjoin the state from undertaking the tuition residency provisions; the case is pending in summer 2011. Matthew B. Allen, *The Unconstitutional Denial of a Texas Veterans Benefit,* 46 Hous. L. Rev. 1607 (2010); Susan Carroll, *In-State Rates for Illegal Immigrants Attacked,* Hous. Chron., Dec. 16, 2009, at B1; Dougherty, Nienhusser & Vega, *Undocumented Immigrants*; Flores, *First State Dream Act.*

17. See Kevin R. Johnson, *Sept. 11 and Mexican Immigrants: Collateral Damage Comes Home,* 52 DePaul L. Rev. 849, 852–865 (2003); Olivas, *IIRIRA,* 457–463; Michael A. Olivas, *What the "War on Terror" Has Meant for U.S. Colleges and Universities,* in *Doctoral Education and the Faculty of the Future* 249–258 (Ronald G. Ehrenberg & Charlotte V. Kuh, eds., Cornell Univ. Press 2009). For a study of the larger issue of terrorism, see Louis Fisher, *The Constitution and 9/11: Recurring Threats to America's Freedoms* (Univ. Press Kansas 2008).

18. S.C. Code Ann. § 59-103-5 (2008). See *Strong Illegal Immigration Bill Biggest Legislative Achievement,* Charleston (SC) Post & Courier, June 7, 2008, at A10. The state's regulatory interpretation of the law is at http://www.law.uh.edu/ihelg. See Table 1.

19. See, e.g., J. Austin Smithson, Comment, *Educate the Exile: Creating a Double Standard in Education for* Plyler *Students Who Want to Sit for the Bar Exam,* 11 Scholar 87 (2008); Susan Carroll, *Immigrant Spends Life Looking over Her Shoulder,* Hous. Chron., Nov. 28, 2009, at B1 (undocumented schoolteacher). This is also an issue with immigrants throughout the regime of legal immigration. See, e.g., Jeanne Batalova & B. Lindsay Lowell, *Immigrant Professionals in the United States,* 44 Soc'y 26 (2007).

20. The total college enrollment in the United States in 2007 was over eighteen million students. See U.S. Department of Education, National Center for Education Statistics, *Digest of Education Statistics* (2008), available at http://nces.ed.gov/fastFacts/display. asp?id=98.

21. Jody Feder, *Unauthorized Alien Students, Higher Education, and In-State Tuition Rates: A Legal Analysis* 6 (Congressional Research Service 2010).

22. Letter from Jim Pendergraph, Executive Director, Office of State and Local Coordination, U.S. Immigration and Customs Enforcement, to Thomas J. Ziko, Special Deputy

Attorney General, N.C. Dep't of Justice (July 28, 2008), available at http://www.nacua. org/documents/AdmissionUndocAlien072008.pdf; Institute for Higher Education Law and Governance website, http://www.law.uh.edu/ihelg. In March 2010, North Carolina reversed course and allowed the students to enroll, but as nonresidents. Mark Johnson, *N.C. Community College Board Votes to Allow Illegal Immigrants*, Charlotte Observer, Mar. 19, 2010, available at http://www.charlotteobserver.com/2010/03/19/1324052/nc-commu-nity-college-board-votes.html.

23. Day v. Sebelius, 376 F. Supp. 2d 1022, 1039–1040 (D. Kan. 2005) (denying standing to challengers, upholding residency requirement that allows undocumented aliens to establish residency). See also Gary Reich & Alvar Ayala Mendoza, *"Educating Kids" versus "Coddling Criminals": Framing the Debate over In-State Tuition for Undocumented Students in Kansas*, 8 St. Pol. & Pol'y Q. 177 (2008).

24. *Day*, 376 F. Supp. 2d 1022. There was also an unsuccessful attempt in 2006 to repeal the statute. Chris Moon, *Immigrant Tuition Vote Typifies Fragile Statehouse Ties*, Topeka Capital-J., Feb. 17, 2006, at A1.

25. Because the trial judge removed the governor as a defendant, the case at the Tenth Circuit was styled as *Day v. Bond*, 500 F.3d 1127, 1136–1140 (10th Cir. 2007) (upholding trial court).

26. *Id.*, cert. denied, 128 S. Ct. 2987 (2008). Approximately a year later, the same attorneys brought a case in Nebraska to overturn its state residency plan. In late 2010, *Mannschreck v. Clare*, the Kris W. Kobach challenge to Nebraska's residency statute, was dismissed on standing grounds. Kevin Abourezk, *Judge Tosses Suit on Tuition to Illegal Immigrants: Plaintiffs Likely to Refile Suit*, Lincoln J.-Star, Dec. 18, 2010, A1; Timberly Ross, *Nebraska Judge Tosses Illegal Immigrant Tuition Suit*, Wash. Post, Dec. 17, 2010, available at http://www.washingtonpost.com/wpdyn/content/article/2010/12/17/AR2010121704097. html?referrer=emailarticle.

27. Martinez v. Regents of the Univ. of Cal., CV-05-2064, 2006 WL 2974303 (Cal. Super. Ct. Oct. 4, 2006) (Order on Demurrers, Motion to Strike, and Motions by Proposed Intervenors) (dismissing challenge to state residency statute), rev'd, 83 Cal. Rptr. 3d 518, superseded by 198 P.3d 1 (Cal. 2008) (granting respondents' petition for review). See Ralph W. Kasarda, *Affirmative Action Gone Haywire: Why State Laws Granting College Tuition Preferences to Illegal Aliens Are Preempted by Federal Law*, 2 BYU Educ. & L.J. 197 (2009); Kristen Miller & Celina Moreno, Martinez v. Regents: *Mis-step or Wave of the Future?* (IHELG Monograph 08-07, 2008), available at http://www.law.uh.edu/ihelg/monograph/08-07.pdf.

28. Martinez v. Regents of the Univ. of Cal., 87 Cal. Rptr. 3d 198, 198 P.3d 1 (2008).

29. In November 2010, the California Supreme Court ruled for the defendants. Maura Dolan & Larry Gordon, *In-State Tuition Benefit Upheld*, L.A. Times, Nov. 16, 2010, at A1, available at http://www.latimes.com/news/local/la-me-illegal-students-20101116,0,2917015. story; David Moltz, *Big Win for Undocumented Students*, Inside Higher Ed, Nov. 16, 2010, available at http://www.insidehighered.com/news/2010/11/16/california. Martinez v. U.C. Regents, 50 Cal. 4th 1277, 241 P.3d 855, 117 Cal. Rptr. 3d 359 (2010).

30. The decision has been entered into the official San Francisco, California, Superior Court site, which is hard to find and harder to use: http://www.sftc.org/Scripts/Magic94/mgrqispi94.dll?APPNAME=IJS&PRGNAME= ROA&ARGUMENTS=-ACPF06506755 (note the buttons at the top and toggle the pages after you click "enter"). A consent

decree was entered by that court on April 19, 2007. Student Advocates for Higher Educ. v. Trustees, Cal. St. Univ., No. CPF-06-506755 (Cal. Super. Ct. Apr. 19, 2007), available at http://www.sftc.org; see also Cal. Educ. Code § 68040 (West 2003); Cal. Code Regs. tit. V, § 41904 (2007). It was a challenge to Cal. Educ. Code § 68040; Cal. Code Regs. tit. V, § 41904, and the state constitution (postsecondary-residency and financial-aid provisions). Full disclosure: I am a member of the board of the Mexican American Legal Defense and Educational Fund, which was a party to this challenge, and participated in the litigation and settlement discussions.

31. *Student Advocates*, No. CPF-06-506755. In Virginia, citizen applicants of undocumented parents were the subject of an attorney general memo; the memo advised its client colleges to deal with these students on a case-by-case basis for residency-tuition purposes. See Ronald Forebrand, *Re: Domicile Matter*, Va. Atty. Gen. Memo, Mar. 6, 2008, available at http://www.law.uh.edu/ihelg. See also Susan Kinzie, *The University of Uncertainty: Va. Children of Illegal Immigrants Lack In-State Status*, Wash. Post, Mar. 14, 2008, at B1; Susan Kinzie, *U-VA Accepts Residency Claim*, Wash. Post, Mar. 24, 2008, at B5. Colorado AGO 07-03 can be found at http://extras.mnginteractive.com/live/media/site3 6/2007/0814/20070814_084925_Tuition.pdf. See generally Allison Sherry, *Tuition Tussle Takes Shape*, Denver Post, Aug. 15, 2007, at A1.

32. 147 Cong. Rec. 8581 (2001) (statement of Sen. Orrin Hatch). S. 1291, 107th Cong. (2001) (as introduced in the Senate); S. 1291, 107th Cong. (2001) (as reported in the Senate); Student Adjustment Act, H.R. 1918, 107th Cong. (2001) (as introduced in the House). All House and Senate bills can be searched online through the THOMAS system, available at http://thomas.loc.gov. DREAM Act of 2003, S. 1545, 108th Cong. (2003) (as introduced in the Senate); DREAM Act of 2003, S. 1545, 108th Cong. (2003) (as reported in the Senate); Student Adjustment Act, H.R. 1684, 108th Cong. (2003) (as introduced in the House); S. Rep. No. 108-224 (2004) (as reported by S. Comm. on the Judiciary) (regarding the proposed amendment of the Illegal Immigration Reform Act of 1996); DREAM Act of 2005, S. 2075, 109th Cong. (2005) (as introduced in the Senate); American Dream Act of 2006, H.R. 5131, 109th Cong. (2006) (as introduced in the Hose); Comprehensive Immigration Reform Act of 2006, S. 2611, 109th Cong. (2006) (as placed on calendar in the Senate).

33. Comprehensive Immigration Reform Act of 2007, S. 1348, 110th Cong. (2007) (as placed on calendar in the Senate); S. 774, 110th Cong. (2007) ("A bill to amend the Illegal Immigration Reform and Immigrant Responsibility Act of 1996 to permit States to determine State residency for higher education purposes and to authorize the cancellation of removal and adjustment of status of certain alien students who are long-term United States residents and who entered the United States as children, and for other purposes"); H.R. 1221, 110th Cong. (2007) (as introduced in the House) ("To provide for cancellation of removal and adjustment of status for certain long-term residents who entered the United States as children"); H.R. 1275, 110th Cong. (2007) (as introduced in the House) ("To amend the Illegal Immigration Reform and Immigrant Responsibility Act of 1996 to permit States to determine State residency for higher education purposes and to authorize the cancellation of removal and adjustment of status of certain alien students who are long-term United States residents and who entered the United States as children, and for other purposes"); S. 2205, 110th Cong. (2007) (as placed on calendar in the Senate) ("A bill to authorize the cancellation of removal and adjustment of status of certain alien

students who are long-term United States residents and who entered the United States as children, and for other purposes," voted on, 44–52, on October 24, 2007); Department of Defense Authorization Bill, S. 2919, 110th Cong. (2007).

34. *The Future of Undocumented Immigrant Students: Hearing on Comprehensive Immigration Reform before the H. Subcomm. on Immigration, Citizenship, Refugees, Border Security & Int'l Law*, 110th Cong. (2007) (transcript, votes, and committee transcript excerpts), available at http://judiciary.house.gov/hearings/May2007/hear_051807.html.

35. Security through Regularized Immigration and a Vibrant Economy (STRIVE) Act of 2007, H.R. 1645, 110th Cong. (2007); 2007 STRIVE hearing, available at http://judiciary.house.gov/hearings/September2007/hear_090607_2.html (taped remarks), http://judiciary.house.gov/hearings/printers/110th/37603.PDF (report). Details of the 2007 vote can be found at http://www.senate.gov/legislative/LIS/roll_call_lists/roll_call_vote_cfm.cfm?congress=110&session=1&vote=00394 (Vote No. 394, Motion to Invoke Cloture on the Motion to Proceed to Consider S. 2205, Oct. 24, 2007). The details of the 2010 actions were well chronicled. See, e.g., David M. Herszenhorn, *Move to End "Don't Ask, Don't Tell" Stalls in Senate*, N.Y. Times, Sept. 22, 2010, at A1; Kelly Field, *The Dream Act Is Dead, at Least for Now*, Chron. Higher Educ., Sept. 22, 2010, available at http://chronicle.com/article/The-Dream-Act-Is-Dead-at/124560/?sid=at&utm_source=at&utm_medium=en; David M. Herszenhorn, *Passion and Politics on Immigration Act*, N.Y. Times, Sept. 22, 2010, at A18; Shankar Vedantam, *Senate to Look at Dream Act for Illegal Immigrants*, Wash. Post, Sept. 21, 2010, at A2; David M. Herszenhorn, *Republicans Threaten to Bring Senate to Halt over Tax Dispute*, N.Y. Times, Dec. 2, 2010, at A24. The most enigmatic vote against the legislation was that of Senator Orrin Hatch (R-UT), who had been a staunch and early supporter; party blood runs thicker than legislative water. Roxana Orellana, *DREAM Act Supporter Jailed for Refusing to Leave Federal Building*, Salt Lake Trib., Dec. 1, 2010, at A1.

36. U.S. Department of Education, *Eligibility for Title IV Program Assistance for Victims of Human Trafficking*, Student Aid on the Web (DCL ID: GEN-06-09), May 2006, available at http://ifap.ed.gov/dpcletters/GEN0609.html. In addition, the Department of Education provides information for trafficking victims and case managers regarding applying for federal financial aid: U.S. Department of Education, *FAQs—New Process Benefits Victims of Human Trafficking Seeking College Aid*, Student Aid on the Web, May 11, 2006, available at http://studentaid.ed.gov/PORTALSWebApp/students/english/TraffickingFaqs.jsp.

37. Pendergraph to Ziko, July 28, 2008; Institute for Higher Education Law and Governance website, http://www.law.uh.edu/ihelg.

38. See, e.g., Kris W. Kobach, *Immigration Nullification: In-State Tuition and Lawmakers Who Disregard the Law*, 10 N.Y.U. J. Legis. & Pub. Pol'y 473, 477, 517, 521 (2006–2007). But see Olivas, *Lawmakers Gone Wild?*, 99–132. See also Kris W. Kobach, *The Senate Immigration Bill Rewards Lawbreaking: Why the DREAM Act Is a Nightmare*, Backgrounder #1960 (Heritage Foundation 2006), available at http://www.heritage.org/Research/Reports/2006/08/The-Senate-Immigration-Bill-Rewards-Lawbreaking-Why-the-DREAM-Act-Is-a-Nightmare. Kobach apparently suffers from recurring dreams—he also characterized the 2007 comprehensive immigration-reform proposals as a "nightmare." Kris W. Kobach, *The Senate Immigration Bill: A National Security Nightmare*, WebMemo #1513 (Heritage Foundation 2007), available at http://www.heritage.org/Research//Reports/2007/06/The-Senate-Immigration-Bill-A-National-Security-Nightmare. In

2010, he filed suit in Nebraska state court to overturn the legislation (*Mannschreck v. University of Nebraska*). See Don Walton, *It's All about "Rule of Law": Kansas Law Prof. Argues Nebraska Tuition Statute Violates Federal Law*, Lincoln J.-Star, Feb. 22, 2010, at B1; Julia Preston, *A Professor Fights Illegal Immigration One Court at a Time*, N.Y. Times, July 21, 2009, at A10; Margery A. Beck, *Lawsuit Targets Nebraska's Immigrant-Tuition Law*, Lincoln J.-Star, Jan. 25, 2010, available at http://www.journalstar.com/news/state-and-regional/nebraska/article_c6ed17f0-09e5-11df-b231-001cc4c002e0.html; Martha Stoddard, *In-State Tuition Repeal Unlikely*, Omaha World-Herald, Feb. 2, 2010, available at http://www.omaha.com/article/20100202/NEWS01/702029941; JoAnne Young, *Senators Hear Arguments on Repealing Nebraska Dream Act*, Lincoln J.-Star, Feb. 2, 2010, at A1. In late 2010, the *Mannschreck* case was dismissed. Abourezk, *Judge Tosses Suit on Tuition to Illegal Immigrants*.

39. Andorra Bruno, *Unauthorized Alien Students: Issues and "DREAM Act" Legislation*, Report RL33863 (Congressional Research Service 2008); Feder, *Unauthorized Alien Students*.

40. Batalova & Fix, *New Estimates*; National Immigration Law Center, *Basic Facts about In-State Tuition for Undocumented Immigrant Students* (National Immigration Law Center 2006); Elizabeth Redden, *A Message to Prospective Undocumented Students*, Inside Higher Ed, Oct. 16, 2008, available at http://www.insidehighered.com/news/2008/10/16/vassar (NACAC, Vassar open to students); American Association of Collegiate Registrars and Admission Officers, *Undocumented Students in the U.S.: Admission and Verification* (AACRAO 2009), available at http://www.aacrao.org/pro_development/surveys/undocu-mented_results.pdf.

41. Roberto G. Gonzales, *Young Lives on Hold: The College Dreams of Undocumented Students* (College Board 2009), available at http://professionals.collegeboard.com/profdownload/young-lives-on-hold-college-board.pdf; Megan Eckstein, *College Board Announces Support for Immigration Bill*, Chron. Higher Educ., Apr. 22, 2009, available at http://chronicle.com/article/College-Board-Announces/47203; Megan Eckstein, *In-State Tuition for Undocumented Students: Not Quite Yet*, Chron. Higher Educ., May 8, 2009, at A19; Anastasia R. Mann, *Garden State Dreams: In-State Tuition for Undocumented Kids* (New Jersey Policy Perspective 2010), available at http://www.njpp.org/assets/reports/budget-fiscal/2-rpt tuition.pdf.

42. For several careful studies of the various legislative developments, see generally Maria Arhancet, *Current Developments in the Legislative Branch: Platforms of Presidential Candidates Regarding Immigration Reform*, 21 Geo. Immigr. L.J. 507 (2007); Keun Dong Kim, *Current Developments in the Legislative Branch: Comprehensive Immigration Reform Nixed*, 21 Geo. Immigr. L.J. 685 (2007); Jeffrey N. Poulin, *Current Developments in the Legislative Branch: The Piecemeal Approach Falls Short of Achieving the DREAM of Immigration Reform*, 22 Geo. Immigr. L.J. 353 (2008).

The national press has kept up a substantial drumbeat, much of it remarkably positive. See, e.g., Miriam Jordan, *Illegal at Princeton*, Wall St. J., Apr. 15, 2006, at A1; Joseph Berger, *Debates Persist over Subsidies for Immigrant College Students*, N.Y. Times, Dec. 12, 2007, at A31; Michael Luo, *Romney's Words Testify to Threat from Huckabee*, N.Y. Times, Dec. 2, 2007, at YT 29; Feder, *Unauthorized Alien Students*; Eddy Ramirez, *The Crash Course in Citizenship*, U.S. News & World Report, Aug. 18, 2008, at 46; Mary Beth Marklein, *Illegal Immigrants Face Threat of No College*, USA Today, July 7, 2008, at A1; Elizabeth Redden, *For the Undocu-*

mented: To Admit or Not to Admit, Inside Higher Ed, Aug. 18, 2008, available at http://www.insidehighered.com/news/2008/08/18/immigrants; Kathleen Mangan, *Most Colleges Knowingly Admit Illegal Immigrants as Students, Survey Finds*, Chron. Higher Educ., Mar. 17, 2009, available at http://chronicle.com/news/index.php?id=6139&utm_source=pm&utm_medium=en; AACRAO, *Undocumented Students*; Martin Ricard, *Students Stage Mock Graduation to Advocate for Undocumented*, Wash. Post, June 24, 2009, at B2. In 2010, the drumbeat increased. See, e.g., Melissa Ludwig, *DREAM Act Hunger Strike Spreads in Texas*, San Antonio Express-News, Nov. 24, 2010, at B8, available at http://www.mysanantonio.com/news/dream_act_hunger_strike_spreads_110273704.html?showFullArticle=y; Maggie Jones, *Coming Out Illegal*, N.Y. Times Magazine, Oct. 24, 2010, at MM36–39; Anonymous, *I'm an Illegal Immigrant at Harvard*, Daily Beast (blog), Nov. 27, 2010, available at http://www.thedailybeast.com/blogs-and-stories/2010-11-27/dream-act-im-an-illegal-immigrant-at-harvard; Jessica Kwong, *Student Freed as Feinstein Steps In*, S.F. Chron., Nov. 20, 2010, at C1; Hector Tobar, *Law Grad's Legal Quandary*, L.A. Times, Nov. 26 2010, at A2, available at: http://www.latimes.com/news/local/la-me-tobar-20101126,0,1358739.column; Reeve Hamilton, *Undocumented Students Stump for the DREAM Act*, Texas Trib., Nov. 11, 2010, available at: http://www.texastribune.org/immigration-in-texas/immigration/undocumented-students-stump-for-the-dream-act/; Diana Marcum, *He's the Cal State Fresno Student Body President—and an Illegal Immigrant*, L.A. Times, Nov. 18, 2010, available at http://www.latimes.com/news/local/la-me-1118-illegal-immigrant-presiden20101118,0,5635027.story; Jesse Ricke, *Student Organization Rallies for DREAM Act in Times Square*, Brooklyn Progressive Examiner, Nov. 29, 2010, available at http://www.examiner.com/progressive-in-new-york/student-organization-rallies-for-dream-act-times-square; Melissa Ludwig, *15 DREAM Act Demonstrators Arrested*, San Antonio Express-News, Nov. 30, 2010, at A1, available at http://www.mysanantonio.com/news/police_respond_to_dream_act_rally_111008674.html?showFullArticle=y; Richard Ruelas, *Dream Act Students Risk Deportation to Win Support*, Ariz. Republic, Nov. 16, 2010, at D1, available at http://www.azcentral.com/php-bin/clicktrack/email.php/9541290; Diana Marcum, *Standing Up for a Dream*, L.A. Times, Nov. 28 2010, at A1, available at http://www.latimes.com/news/local/la-me-dream-act-20101128,0,5057601.story; E. J. Montini, *Dream Act Kids Facing a Political Nightmare*, Ariz. Republic, Nov. 24, 2010, at B1, available at http://www.azcentral.com/php-bin/clicktrack/email.php/9542002; Maria Sacchetti, *Illegal Immigrant Students Tell of Lost Opportunities*, Boston Globe, Nov. 26, 2010, available at http://www.boston.com/news/local/massachusetts/articles/2010/11/26/illegal_immigrant_students_tell_of_lost_opportunities/?page=full; Daniel Rubin, *More Courage from a Dreamer on Immigration*, Phila. Inq., Apr. 11, 2011, B1.

43. The National Conference of State Legislatures compiles legislative data on a variety of subjects, including state-level enactments of immigration laws, which showed in the last six months of 2010 that all but a handful of states passed such laws, most restrictionist. See National Conference of State Legislatures, *State Laws Related to Immigrants and Immigration*, Apr. 24, 2011, available at http://www.ncsl.org/default.aspx?tabid=21857. See also Jorge M. Chavez & Doris Marie Provine, *Race and the Response of State Legislatures to Unauthorized Immigrants*, 623 Annals Am. Acad. Pol. & Soc. Sci. 78 (2009), available at http://ann.sagepub.com/cgi/content/abstract/623/1/78 (analyzing NCSL data).

44. National Conference of State Legislatures, *Immigration Reform—Official Policy*, available at http://www.ncsl.org/default.aspx?tabid=18094 (accessed Mar. 17, 2010) (NCSL policy on preemption). For example, compare Peter J. Spiro, *The States and Immigra-*

tion in an Era of Demi-sovereignties, 35 Va. J. Int'l L. 121 (1994), with Olivas, *Preempting Preemption*.

45. Benjamin Márquez & John F. Witte, *Immigration Reform: Strategies for Legislative Action*, 7 Forum 1 (2009), available at http://www.bepress.com/cgi/viewcontent. cgi?article=1324&context=forum. See also Ryan Lizza, *Return of the Nativist*, New Yorker, Dec. 17, 2007, at 46 (reviewing political views on immigration).

46. Marquez & Witte, *Immigration Reform*, 24–25.

47. *Id.*, 5–8.

48. *Id.*, 8.

49. *Plyler*, 457 U.S. 202. Olivas, *Story of* Plyler v. Doe, 197; López & López, *Persistent Inequality*.

50. Dolan & Gordon, *In-State Tuition Benefit Upheld*; Moltz, *Big Win*. Additional state court litigation on residency statutes ended with a win for the State in *Mannschreck v. Board of Regents of the University of Nebraska, et al.* [challenging Neb. Rev. Stat. 85-502 (5) and (8) (Reissue 2008)] and continues in 2011 in *IRCOT v Texas*, 706 F. Supp. 2d 760 (S.D. Tex. 2010) (challenging Texas residency statutes). Abourezk, *Judge Tosses Suit on Tuition to Illegal Immigrants*.

51. Marquez & Witte, *Immigration Reform*, 25.

52. Table 2 details the various permutations of the bills introduced. See generally Olivas, *IIRIRA*, 461–462; Bruno, *Unauthorized Alien Students*; Ruth Ellen Wasem, *Immigration Reform: Brief Synthesis of Issue*, Report RS2257 (Congressional Research Service 2007); Laurence M. Krutchik, Comment, *Down but Not Out: A Comparison of Previous Attempts at Immigration Reform and the Resulting Implemented Changes*, 32 Nova L. Rev. 455, 468–479, 479–481 (2008).

53. The several bills summarized in table 2 were introduced during this period, including stand-alone bills and bills attached to larger statutory schemes. See generally American Association of State Colleges and Universities, *Access for All? Debating In-State Tuition for Undocumented Alien Students* (American Association of State Colleges and Universities 2005), available at www.aascu.org/policy/special_report/access_for_all.htm; National Immigration Law Center, *DREAM Act: Basic Information* (National Immigration Law Center 2005), available at http://www.nilc.org/immlawpolicy/DREAM/dream_basic_info_0406.pdf; Julia Preston, *Latinos and Democrats Press Obama to Curb Deportations*, NY Times, Apr. 21, 2011, A18.

54. For details of the military immigration issues, see generally Margaret D. Stock, *The DREAM Act: Tapping an Overlooked Pool of Home-Grown Talent to Meet Military Enlistment Needs*, 6 Engage 99, 99–103 (2005), available at http://hq.democracyinaction.org/dia/organizations/NILC/images/Stock_on_DREAM_Act.pdf; Julia Preston, *U.S. Military Will Offer Path to Citizenship*, N.Y. Times, Feb. 15, 2009, at A1; Margaret D. Stock & Kristan K. Exner, *Immigration Issues Relating to Military Service: Practical Problems and Solutions*, in *Immigration and Nationality Law Handbook, 2009–10*, 921 (Rizwan Hassan ed., American Immigration Lawyers Association 2009); Susan E. Timmons & Margaret D. Stock, *Immigration Issues Faced by U.S. Servicemembers: Challenges and Solutions*, 43 Clearinghouse Rev.: J. Poverty L.& Pol'y 270–276 (Sept.–Oct. 2009); Francine J. Lipman, *Saving Private Ryan's Tax Refund: Poverty Relief for All Working Poor Military Families*, 9 A.B.A. Sect. Tax'n News Q. 9 (Winter 2010).

55. See notes 32 and 34 (introduction of bills), note 33 (DREAM Act hearings), and note 35 (STRIVE Act hearings).

56. Details of the vote can be found at http://www.senate.gov/legislative/LIS/roll_call_lists/roll_call_vote_cfm.cfm?congress=110&session=1&vote=00394. (Vote No. 394, Motion to Invoke Cloture on the Motion to Proceed to Consider S. 2205, Oct. 24, 2007).

57. McCain's absence was widely regarded as strategic, as he was in the thick of a Republican primary fight. See, e.g., Stephen Dinan, *McCain Caters to GOP Voters*, Wash. Times, Oct. 31, 2007, at A1 (stating, "Sen. John McCain has quietly been piling up flip-flops," citing previous DREAM Act support). See also Michael Luo, *McCain Says Immigration Reform Should Be Top Priority*, The Caucus (blog), N.Y. Times, May 22, 2008, available at http://thecaucus.blogs.nytimes.com. Senator Kennedy, recovering from surgery at the time of the cloture vote, died from a brain tumor on August 25, 2009, at the age of seventy-seven. *Edward M. Kennedy*, N.Y. Times, Sept. 3, 2009, available at http://topics.nytimes.com/top/reference/timestopics/people/k/edward_m_kennedy/index.html?scp=1-spot&sq=edward%20kennedy&st=cse.

58. See, e.g., Chris Dodd, *Dodd to Sponsor Rare Private Bill Preventing Haitian Girl's Deportation*, press release (July 16, 2004), available at http://dodd.senate.gov/?q=node/3270/print&pr=press/Releases/04/0716.htm (sponsoring 2004 private relief bill for undocumented Haitian college student and urging passage of DREAM Act); Julia Preston, *Measure Would Offer Legal Status to Illegal Immigrant Students*, N.Y. Times, Sept. 20, 2007, at A1 (Sen. Dodd securing private relief legislation for undocumented college student).

59. Senator Specter's 2007 vote regarding the DREAM Act is available at http://www.govtrack.us/congress/vote.xpd?vote=s2007-394 (accessed Feb. 23, 2011).

60. White House, "Statement of Administration Policy on DREAM Act," available at http://dreamact.info/forum/archive/index.php?t-6594.html (archived copy of White House statement opposing DREAM Act, Oct. 24, 2007, http://www.whitehouse.gov/omb/legislative/sap/110-1/s2205sap-s.pdf). See also, Julia Preston, *Bill for Immigrant Students Fails Test Vote in Senate*, N.Y. Times, Oct. 25, 2007, at A1 (discussing White House opposition).

61. Carl Hulse & Adam Nagourney, *Specter Switches Parties*, N.Y. Times, Apr. 28, 2009, at A1. Of course, these political alliances are fleeting and malleable. See, e.g., Carl Hulse, *Democrats Gain as Stevens Loses His Senate Race*, N.Y. Times, Nov. 19, 2008, at A1 (politics of Sen. Joe Lieberman's switch from Democrat to Independent); Katharine Q. Seelye, *Specter Feels Squeeze from New Friends and Old*, N.Y. Times, Jan. 27, 2010, at A12.

62. James C. McKinley, Jr., *Governor's Race Exposes Republican Rift in Texas*, N.Y. Times, Aug. 15, 2009, at A11 (discussing differences between Perry and Hutchison); Robert Draper, *It's Just a Texas-Governor Thing*, N.Y. Times Magazine, Dec. 6, 2009, at 30–35; James C. McKinley, Jr., *A Texas Senator, Now a Challenger Lagging in Polls*, N.Y. Times, Feb. 21, 2010, at A14.

63. Discussions with staff attorneys, National Immigration Law Center, Mexican American Legal Defense and Educational Fund, Sept. 27, 2007 (on file with author). See also Julia Preston, *Measure on Legal Status for Immigrant Students Blocked*, N.Y. Times, Sept. 28, 2007, at A1; Elizabeth Redden, *DREAM Act Vote on Tap*, Inside Higher Ed, Oct. 24, 2007, available at http://insidehighered.com/news/2007/10/24/dream.

64. Barbara Sinclair, *Question: What's Wrong with Congress? Answer: It's a Democratic Legislature*, 89 B.U. L. Rev. 387, 396 (2009) (citations omitted). See generally Barbara Sinclair, *Party Wars: Polarization and the Politics of National Policy Making* (Univ. Oklahoma

Press, 2006). See also Preston, *Measure Would Offer*; Preston, *Bill for Immigrant Students*; Julia Preston, *Illegal Immigrant Students Publicly Take Up a Cause*, N.Y. Times, Dec. 11, 2009, at A25.

65. Sara Hebel, *Candidates Grapple with How to Expand Access to College*, Chron. Higher Educ., Sept. 14, 2007, at A17; Berger, *Debates Persist*.

66. See Matthew Spalding, *Getting Reform Right: The White House's Immigration Initiative*, WebMemo #1585 (Heritage Foundation 2007), available at http://www.heritage.org/Research/Reports/2007/08/Getting-Reform-Right-The-White-Houses-Immigration-Initiative; Preston, *Bill for Immigrant Students*; Kobach, *Immigration Nullification*; Kasarda, *Affirmative Action Gone Haywire*. I do not suggest that all conservative views are of one reductive accord, on this topic or any other. Some of the more libertarian views, for example, advocate for more open borders, legalization, and increased immigration for both higher-end and lower-skill jobs. See, e.g., Daniel Griswold, *Comprehensive Immigration Reform: Finally Getting It Right*, Free Trade Bulletin No. 29, 1 (Cato Institute, Center for Trade Policy Studies 2007).

67. Olivas, *IIRIRA*, 436. See also Leonard M. Baynes, *Racial Profiling, September 11, and the Media: A Critical Race Theory Analysis*, 2 Va. Sports & Ent. L.J. 1, 17–21 (2002) (detailing accounts of several hijackers). The student visas of two of the hijackers were actually approved exactly six months after they took over the planes. See generally Laura Khatcheressian, *FERPA and the Immigration and Naturalization Service: A Guide for University Counsel on Federal Rules for Collecting, Maintaining and Releasing Information about Foreign Students*, 29 J.C. & U.L. 457, 466–467 (2003).

68. See, e.g., Fareed Zakaria, *The Post-American World* (Norton 2008); Richard Florida, *How the Crash Will Reshape America*, Atlantic Monthly (Mar. 2009), at 44; Andrew Ross Sorkin, *Too Big to Fail: The Inside Story of How Wall Street and Washington Fought to Save the Financial System from Crisis—and Themselves* (Viking 2009); John Cassidy, *How Markets Fail: The Logic of Economic Calamities* (Farrar, Straus and Giroux 2009). See Gregory Koger, *Making Change: A Six-Month Review*, Forum (July 2009), available at http://www.bepress.com/forum/vol7/iss3/art8 (reviewing first six months of Obama's legislative agenda). See also John M. Broder, *Obama Hobbled in Fight against Global Warming*, N.Y. Times, Nov. 16, 2009, at A1.

69. See Daniel J. Tichenor, *Navigating an American Minefield: The Politics of Illegal Immigration*, Forum (July 2009), available at http://www.bepress.com/forum/vol7/iss3/art1; Eckstein, *In-State Tuition*. By early 2010, these efforts were stalled in Congress, but in March 2010, President Obama successfully steered his health-reform proposals through Congress, with provisions for student-loan reform tacked on. David M. Herszenhorn & Robert Pear, *Democrats Put Lower Priority on Health Bill*, N.Y. Times, Jan. 27, 2010, at A27; Paul Kane & Shailagh Murray, *Democrats Confused about Road Forward*, Wash. Post, Jan. 29, 2010, at A1; Carl Hulse & Sheryl Gay Stolberg, *His Health Bill Stalled, Obama Juggles an Altered Agenda*, N.Y. Times, Jan. 29, 2010, at A1; Julia Preston, *Obama Links Immigration Overhaul in 2010 to G.O.P. Backing*, N.Y. Times, Mar. 12, 2010, at A12; David M. Herszenhorn & Tamar Levin, *Student Loan Overhaul Approved by Congress*, N.Y. Times, Mar. 26, 2010, at A16; Julia Preston, *In Shadow of Health Care Vote, Immigrant Advocates Keep Pushing for Change*, N.Y. Times, Mar. 21, 2010, at A12.

70. Kelly Field, *Deal Is Reached on Immigration Bill Affecting Students, Says Senate Leader*, Chron. Higher Educ., Nov. 24, 2008, available at http://chronicle.com/article/

Deal-Is-Reached-on-Immigrat/42007. Senator Reid's views are set out on his website and in remarks he made at a national Latino organization in 2008: Harry Reid, *Issues: Immigration*, Harry Reid's Senate website, http://reid.senate.gov/issues/immigration.cfm (accessed Apr. 20, 2011); Harry Reid, *Reid Remarks at NALEO National Conference*, press release, June 26, 2008, available at http://reid.senate.gov/newsroom/pr_070308_NALEO.cfm. In addition, on June 24, 2009, at Georgetown University Law Center, Senator Reid's chief immigration staff counsel addressed a group of immigration professionals and outlined the senator's plans and legislative strategies. For a webcast recording of her remarks, see Serena Hoy, *Remarks at the 6th Annual Immigration Law and Policy Conference at Georgetown University Law Center*, June 26, 2008, available at http://www.law.georgetown.edu/webcast/eventDetail.cfm?eventID=863.

71. The comprehensive reform effort that Napolitano was addressing was to be undertaken in spring 2010. Center for American Progress, *We Can Fix This: Homeland Security Secretary Janet Napolitano Speaks on Immigration Reform*, press release, Nov. 13, 2009, available at http://www.americanprogress.org/issues/2009/11/napolitano_event.html (JN conference remarks). See also Lee Hockstader, *Immigration Awaits Its Turn*, Wash. Post, Sept. 13, 2009, at A23; Julia Preston, *White House Plan on Immigration Includes Legal Status*, N.Y. Times, Nov. 14, 2009, at A10; Spencer S. Hsu, *Obama Presses Congress to Rework Immigration Laws*, Wash. Post, Nov. 14, 2009, at A16; Libby Nelson, *Undocumented College Students Could Become Citizens Faster under New House Proposal*, Chron. Higher Educ., Dec. 15, 2009, available at http://chronicle.com/article/Undocumented-College-Students/49496.

72. See Herszenhorn & Pear, *Democrats Put Lower Priority*; Kane & Murray, *Democrats Confused*; Hulse & Stolberg, *His Health Bill Stalled*. See also Sewell Chan, *Dodd Calls Obama Plan Too Grand*, N.Y. Times, Feb. 3, 2010, at B1 (banking and financial-institution reform bogged down); Preston, *Obama Links*. Robert Pear & David M. Herszenhorn, *House Approves Health Overhaul, Sending Landmark Bill to Obama*, N.Y. Times, Mar. 22, 2010, at A1; Peter Nicholas, *Immigration Plan Offered to Obama*, L.A. Times, Mar. 12, 2010, at AA1 (three-page blueprint for a bipartisan agreement to overhaul immigration system, but proposal is threatened by health-care politics); Herszenhorn & Levin, *Student Loan Overhaul*. As health-care debates wound down, Senators Schumer (D-NY) and Lindsey Graham (R-SC) moved immigration proposals forward. Charles E. Schumer & Lindsey O. Graham, *The Right Way to Mend Immigration*, Wash. Post, Mar. 19, 2010, at A23, available at http://www.washingtonpost.com/wp-dyn/content/article/2010/03/17/AR2010031703115.html?referrer=emailarticle.

73. Senator Schumer delivered his comprehensive remarks as the keynote speaker at the GULC conference and posted the remarks on his official website: Charles E. Schumer, *Schumer Announces Principles for Comprehensive Immigration Reform Bill in Works in Senate*, press release, June 24, 2009, available at http://schumer.senate.gov/new_website/record_print.cfm?id=314990 (website); http://www.law.georgetown.edu/webcast/eventDetail.cfm?eventID=866 (GULC webcast).

74. Details of the vote can be found at http://www.senate.gov/legislative/LIS/roll_call_lists/roll_call_vote_cfm.cfm?congress=110&session=1&vote=00394 (DREAM Act vote, 110th Congress, 1st session, to Invoke Cloture on the Motion to Proceed to Consider S. 2205, Oct. 24, 2007). See also Schumer & Graham, *Right Way to Mend Immigration*; Julia Preston, *2 Senators Offer Immigration Overhaul*, N.Y. Times, Mar. 19, 2010, at A11.

75. Justice Sonia Sotomayor was confirmed to the U.S. Supreme Court on August 6, 2009, with a 68–31 vote. See Charlie Savage, *Senate Confirms Sotomayor for the Supreme Court*, N.Y. Times, Aug. 7, 2009, at A1. Almost a year later, on August 5, 2010, Solicitor General Elena Kagan was confirmed to the Court, following a 63–37 vote: Supreme Court of the United States, *Biographies of Current Justices of the Supreme Court: Elena Kagan*, available at http://www.supremecourt.gov/about/biographies.aspx (accessed Apr. 24, 2011).

76. Koger, *Making Change*, 11. For a useful study of how the political and media cycles of the U.S. presidency have evolved, see Jeffrey E. Cohen, *The Presidency in the Era of 24-Hour News* (Princeton Univ. Press 2008).

77. Julia Preston, *Congress Quarrels on Covering Immigrants*, N.Y. Times, Nov. 4, 2009, at A1. A week after Representative Wilson shouted out in the chambers, he was admonished by the House, by a vote of 240–179: "[The House d]eclares that the House of Representatives disapproves of the behavior of the Representative from South Carolina, Mr. Wilson, during the joint session of Congress held on September 9, 2009." H.R. Res. 744, 111th Cong. (2009) (as passed by Senate, Sept. 15, 2009), available at http://thomas.loc.gov/cgi-bin/bdquery/z?d111:H.RES.744. On the issue of immigrant health care, see Randy Capps, Marc R. Rosenblum & Michael Fix, *Immigrants and Health Care Reform: What's Really at Stake?* (Migration Policy Institute 2009); Kevin Sack, *The Breaking Point: Hospital Falters as Refuge for Illegal Immigrants*, N.Y. Times, Nov. 21, 2009, at A1.

78. There is a lifetime of reading on the subject of nativism, restrictionism, and the racist roots of immigration. See generally Mae Ngai, *The Strange Career of the Illegal Alien: Immigration Restriction and Deportation Policy in the United States, 1921–1965*, 21 Law & Hist. Rev. 69 (2003); Daniel J. Tichenor, *Dividing Lines: The Politics of Immigration Control in America* (Princeton Univ. Press 2002); Carolyn Wong, *Lobbying for Inclusion: Rights Politics and the Making of Immigration Policy* (Stanford Univ. Press 2006); Kevin R. Johnson, *Opening the Floodgates: Why America Needs to Rethink Its Borders and Immigration Laws* (NYU Press 2007); David Bacon, *Illegal People: How Globalization Creates Migration and Criminalizes Immigrants* (Beacon 2008); Leo R. Chavez, *The Latino Threat: Constructing Immigrants, Citizens, and the Nation* (Stanford Univ. Press 2008); Laura E. Gómez, *What's Race Got to Do with It? Press Coverage of the Latino Electorate in the 2008 Presidential Primary Season*, 24 St. John's J. Legal Comment. 425 (2009).

79. "While . . . only a few states have changed their practice post-IIRIRA and enacted statutes to allow the undocumented to attend college as resident students, the major receiver states have done so, and it is likely that political pressure will continue to fill in the spots on the map, at least the spots where the undocumented are likely to enroll. In addition, the unlikely scenario of a major conservative Republican U.S. Senator from Utah (Sen. Orrin Hatch) taking on this issue after September 11 has rendered it more likely that federal action will occur, and not only accord these students federal protection, but a limited amnesty of one form or another." Olivas, *IIRIRA*, 456–457 (citations omitted).

80. Reich & Ayala Mendoza, *"Educating Kids,"* 192–194.

81. For an excellent and comprehensive analysis of the complicated Oklahoma legislative history of enactment and rescission, see Elizabeth McCormick, *The Oklahoma Taxpayer and Citizen Protection Act: Blowing off Steam or Setting Wildfires?*, 23 Geo. Immigr. L.J. 293 (2009). For the history of litigation and legislative developments in Nebraska and

Texas, where similar restrictionist repeal efforts were undertaken in 2010, see Young, *Senators Hear Arguments*; *Texas Group Sues to Block In-State Tuition for Undocumented Students*, The Ticker (blog), Chron. Higher Educ., Dec. 15, 2009, available at http://chronicle.com/blogPost/Texas-Group-Sues-to-Block/9223/?sid=pm&utm_source=pm&utm_medium=en. Also see *Mannschreck*; *IRCOT*, 706 F. Supp. 2d 760; Abourezk, *Judge Tosses Suit on Tuition to Illegal Immigrants*.

82. In fall 2009, the chief House proponent of the DREAM Act and immigration reform introduced his "Core Principles," as his Senate counterpart Charles Schumer did. David Montgomery, *No Turning Back, Rep. Luis Gutierrez Is Making Immigration Reform a Personal Cause*, Wash. Post, May 8, 2009, at C1. See also Hockstader, *Immigration Awaits Its Turn*; Muszaffar Chishi & Claire Bergeron, *New Immigration Bill Edges Comprehensive Reform Back on the Legislative Agenda* (Migration Policy Institute, Jan. 2010), available at http://www.migrationinformation.org/USfocus/display.cfm?id=769. See also Kane & Murray, *Democrats Confused*; Hulse & Stolberg, *His Health Bill Stalled*; Chan, *Dodd Calls* (complexities of financial regulation). See also Center for American Progress, *We Can Fix This*; Preston, *Congress Quarrels*; Preston, *White House Plan*; Hsu, *Obama Presses Congress*.

83. Immigration Policy Center, *Breaking Down the Problems: What's Wrong with Our Immigration System?* 3 (Immigration Policy Center, 2009), available at www.immigrationpolicy.org/sites/default/files/docs/Problem_Paper_FINAL_102109_0.pdf.

84. There had been language regarding the DREAM Act in the Department of Defense legislative plans, such as their "Strategic Goals" in December 2009 ("as well as the DREAM initiative"); see, e.g., Jim Garamone, *DREAM Act Would Expand Recruiting Pool*, Am. Forces Pr. Serv., Dec. 2, 2010, available at http://www.defense.gov/news/newsarticle.aspx?id=61928. Announcements of the change of mind by Senator Reid was first a small trickle: see his interview with the Spanish-language *La Opinion*, picked up by *Roll Call* on July 21, 2010: John Stanton, *Reid May Push DREAM Act in Lieu of Immigration Reform*, Roll Call, July 21, 2010, available at http://www.rollcall.com/news/48542-1.html. Senator Reid made some comments on the issue at the Netroots Nation Conference in Las Vegas: Harry Reid, *Remarks at the Netroots Nation Conference in Las Vegas*, July 24, 2010, available at http://www.youtube.com/watch?v=8e0QXsh24Ac. Julia Preston of the *New York Times* reported on the developing policy of withholding of removal for DREAM Act students who came to Department of Justice attention: Julia Preston, *Administration Spares Students in Deportations*, N.Y. Times, Aug. 9, 2010, at A1. The trade press began to pick up the chatter as well: *Senate Leader Will Press for Passage of "Dream Act" This Year*, The Ticker (blog), Chron. Higher Educ., Sept. 14, 2010, available at http://chronicle.com/blogPost/Senate-Leader-Will-Press-fo/26922/; *Senate Democrats Renew DREAM Act Push*, Inside Higher Ed, Sept. 15, 2010, available at http://www.insidehighered.com/news/2010/09/15/qt#238171. And Senator John McCain, who took a walk on the 2007 DREAM Act vote, even though he had been an earlier supporter, was quoted in Josh Rogin, *McCain and Graham Lash Out at Levin over Defense Bill*, The Cable (blog), Foreign Policy, Sept. 14, 2010, available at http://thecable.foreignpolicy.com/posts/2010/09/14/mccain_and_graham_lash_out_at_levin_over_defense_bill. The *New York Times* had two stories that suggested McCain's stance was a political ploy: David M. Herszenhorn, *Democrats Use Power of Majority to Pursue Agenda*, N.Y. Times, Sept. 17, 2010, at A17; Julia Preston, *Democrats Reach Out to Hispanics on Immigration Bill*, N.Y. Times, Sept. 17, 2010, at A15. See also David M. Herszenhorn, *Move to End "Don't Ask, Don't Tell" Stalls in Senate*, N.Y. Times, Sept. 22,

2010, at A1; Carl Hulse & Adam Nagourney, *Obama's Afghanistan Decision Is Straining Ties with Democrats*, N.Y. Times, Dec. 4, 2009, at A20; John M. Broder & Elisabeth Rosenthal, *Obama Has Goal to Wrest a Deal in Climate Talks*, N.Y. Times, Dec. 18, 2009, at A1; Chan, *Dodd Calls*, B9 (complexities of financial regulation); Mark A. Rothstein, *Health Insurance Reforms: Unintended Consequences* (Hastings Center Bioethics Forum, forthcoming 2010), available at http://ssrn.com/abstract=1551397; Preston, *Obama Links*; Immigration Policy Center, *DHS Progress Report: The Challenge of Reform* (Immigration Policy Center, Mar. 2, 2010), available at http://immigrationpolicy.org/special-reports/dhs-progress-report-challenge-reform. In March 2010, Congress acted on health-care and student-loan legislation, which cleared the decks somewhat. Pear & Herszenhorn, *House Approves*; Nicholas, *Immigration Plan Offered*; Herszenhorn & Levin, *Student Loan Overhaul*.

85. Scott Wong, *Democratic Senator Reid Moves Forward with Dream Act*, Politico, Nov. 30, 2010, available at http://www.politico.com/news/stories/1110/45761.html#ixzz16qY5uwVG. See, e.g., Laura Diamond, *Collegiate Ban Proposed: Plans Target Students Unable to Prove Legal U.S. Residency*, Atlanta J.-Const., Sept. 22, 2010, at A1; Katherine Mangan, *Illegal Voices: 4 Undocumented Students Describe Uncertain Futures*, Chron. Higher Educ., Sept. 24, 2010, at B17–19, available at http://chronicle.com/article/Illegal-Voices-Undocumented/124441; H. Kenny Nienhusser & Kevin J. Dougherty, *Implementation of College In-State Tuition for Undocumented Immigrants in New York* (SUNY, New York Latino Research and Resources Network, Spring 2010); Richard Morgan, *Ole Miss Student Faces Deportation for Revealing Illegal Status: Family Secret Threatens Daughter*, Memphis Commercial Appeal, Sept. 16, 2010, available at http://www.commercialappeal.com/news/2010/sep/16/family-secret-threatens-daughter/; Preston, *Administration Spares Students*; Nina Bernstein, *Border Sweeps in North Reach Miles into U.S.*, N.Y. Times, Aug. 30, 2010, at A1; Kelly Heyboer, *Rutgers University Students Protest Illegal Immigrant Tuition during President's Fundraising Speech*, Newark Star-Ledger, Sept. 25, 2010, available at http://www.nj.com/news/index.ssf/2010/09/rutgers_students_question_ille.html; Miriam Jordan, *A Route to Citizenship in Defense Bill: Legislation Offers Illegal Residents Chance to Become Americans through Military Service or College; Foes Call It Amnesty*, Wall St. J., Sept. 18, 2010, at A5; Shankar Vedantam, *Undocumented Youths Chasing a Dream*, Wash. Post, Nov. 28, 2010, at C1; Julia Preston, *After False Dawn, Anxiety for Students Who Are Illegal Immigrants*, N.Y. Times, Feb. 9, 2011, at A15; Julia Preston, *Latinos and Democrats Press Obama to Curb Deportations*, N.Y. Times, Apr. 21, 2011, at A18; Michael Winerip, *Dreaming of Having an American Life in Full*, N.Y. Times, Feb. 21, 2011, at A10; Richard Fausset, *Young Migrants Protest Uncertain Fate*, L.A. Times, Apr. 10, 2011, at A18.

86. Who would have guessed that by this time Don't Ask, Don't Tell (DADT) would be improbably repealed by Congress, as it was in December 2010? Garamone, *DREAM Act Would Expand Recruiting Pool* (2010 Department of Defense testimony in support of legislation); Carl Hulse, *Senate Ends Military Ban on Gays Serving Openly*, N.Y. Times, Dec. 19, 2010, A1. In July 2011, President Obama certified the repeal.

87. See generally Tamar Lewin, *A Crown Jewel of Education Struggles with Cuts in California*, N.Y. Times, Nov. 20, 2009, at A1; Tamar Lewin & Rebecca Cathcart, *Students Protest Decision to Raise Tuition in California*, N.Y. Times, Nov. 20, A25; Larry Gordon & Amina Khan, *Regents OK Hike in UC Fees*, L.A. Times, Nov. 20, 2009, at A3; Carla Rivera, *Budget Cuts Hit Broad Swath of Cal State*, L.A. Times, Nov. 29, 2009, at A1.

88. Bob Egelko, *Fight over Illegals' Tuition Reaches High Court*, S.F. Chron., Oct. 6, 2010, at C1; Kyle William Colvin, Comment, *In-State Tuition and Illegal Immigrants: An Analysis of Martinez v. Regents of the University of California*, 2010 BYU Educ. & L.J. 391 (2010); Mary Ann Zehr, *Undocumented Students Get a Break in California*, Educ. Wk., Nov. 17, 2010, available at http://blogs.edweek.org/edweek/learning-thelanguage/2010/11/undocumented_students_get_a_br.html.

89. And they also have gone on to graduate school. In one fascinating case, in which a Princeton honors graduate was awarded a Marshall Scholarship to study in England, it turned out the Dominican student was undocumented. His case drew national attention. See, e.g., Jordan, *Illegal at Princeton*. The Princeton student went off to Oxford on a two-year scholarship. He applied for a temporary visa to visit his family in the United States. As part of the visa process, he applied for a waiver under INA § 212(d) (3); these were both denied in November 2006. That same month, Princeton filed an H-1B petition on his behalf. He reapplied for the 212(d) (3) waiver that would allow him to return to the United States on term breaks from Oxford to work for Princeton. In April 2007, he received that waiver, overcoming his "unlawful presence" problem. After completing his graduate degree, he renewed his visa and worked temporarily at Princeton on an H-1B. In 2008, he successfully changed status to F-1 so that he could start a Ph.D. program in classics at an elite West Coast institution, where he is enrolled as of 2009–2010. Email from Dan-el Padilla Peralta to Michael A. Olivas (Nov. 23, 2009) (on file with author). See also Carroll, *Immigrant Spends Life* (Houston-area undocumented teacher). The Princeton student was not the only undocumented student to be outed by public achievements, as when one wins a national award that bring press coverage. For two such examples of achieving undocumented high schoolers, both prompted by robotics competitions, see Peter Carlson, *Stinky the Robot, Four Kids and a Brief Whiff of Success*, Wash. Post, Mar. 29, 2005, at C1 (reporting on undocumented Mexican students' science project); Mel Melendez, *Doors Finally Open for 4 Phoenix Migrant Youths a Year after Beating MIT in Robotics Competition*, Ariz. Republic, Apr. 23, 2005, at 1A (same); Nina Bernstein, *Student's Prize Is a Trip Into Immigration Limbo*, N.Y. Times, Apr. 26, 2006, at A1 (reporting Senegalese student science project reveals illegal status); Nina Bernstein, *Senegalese Teenager in Deportation Fight Wins Right to Study in the U.S.*, N.Y. Times, July 29, 2006, at B2 (same); Karina Bland, *District Backs Aid for Kids of Migrants: Phoenix Union Board Votes to Lend Support to Federal DREAM Act*, Ariz. Republic, Jan. 13, 2007, at 3. See also Preston, *Illegal Immigrant Students*; Julia Preston, *To Overhaul Immigration, Advocates Alter Tactics*, N.Y. Times, Jan. 2, 2010, at A11. He was not even the only undocumented student to surface at Princeton and achieve. See Joseph Berger, *An Undocumented Princetonian: Illegal at 13, Ivy League at 18, and Then . . . Caught*, N.Y. Times, Jan. 3, 2010, at ED-28 (undocumented Princeton graduate and, after he gained status, heart surgeon). As recently as summer 2011 the Obama administration indicated that it will not deport undocumented college students, although their fate is unclear, absent the passage of a legalization provision: Julia Preston, *Students Spell Out Messages on Their Immigration Frustration*, N.Y. Times, Sept. 21, 2010, at A14; Herszenhorn, *Passion and Politics*; Morgan, *Ole Miss Student*; Preston, *Administration Spares Students*; Bernstein, *Border Sweeps*; Jones, *Coming Out Illegal*; Anonymous, *I'm an Illegal Immigrant*; Kwong, *Student Freed*; Tobar, *Law Grad's Legal Quandary* (UCLA law graduate sitting for California state bar exam); Fausset, *Young Migrants Protest Uncertain Fate*; Preston, *Latinos and Democrats Press Obama*

to Curb Deportations; Juan E. Gastelum, *How Immigration Activists Are Fighting Deportation Policy with Social Media*, Mashable.com, Apr. 19, 2011, available at http://mashable.com/2011/04/19/immigration-activism-social-media/.

NOTES TO CHAPTER 5

1. Peter Carlson, *Stinky the Robot, Four Kids and a Brief Whiff of Success*, Wash. Post, Mar. 29, 2005, at C1.

2. Ohio Rev. Code Ann. § 3333.31 (Anderson 1994) ("Rules for determining residence"); Ohio Admin. Code § 3333-1-10 (1994) ("Ohio student residency for state subsidy and tuition surcharge purposes").

3. Ohio Rev. Code Ann. § 3333.18 (Anderson 1994) (durational requirements). I came to know the Ohio Board of Regents as well, and wrote my 1977 Ph.D. dissertation on the history of the agency. In my defense, everyone needs a dissertation topic. See Michael A. Olivas, *A Legislative History of the Ohio Board of Regents*, 19 Cap. U. L. Rev. 81 (1990).

4. I have chaired the University of Houston's Residency Appeals Committee since its inception in 1987 and as a consultant to its University of Wisconsin counterpart during my year there as a visiting professor of law, 1989–1990. Each institution considers hundreds of appeals each year. I have served as a witness or consultant to plaintiffs or advocates filing briefs in the *Leticia "A"* cases, *Bradford* cases, *Alarcon* case, and *Martinez* cases. I served as the State's expert witness, defending the Kansas statute in the *Day v. Sebelius* and *Day v. Bond* cases. As of this writing, I am a consultant to public college counsel in cases pending or recently completed in 2011 in Texas and Nebraska.

5. Smith v. Board of Regents of the Univ. of Houston Sys., 874 S.W.2d 706 (Tex. App. 1994).

6. See, e.g., Michael A. Olivas, *Undocumented College Students, Taxation, and Financial Aid: A Technical Note*, 32 Rev. Higher Educ. 407 (2009) (reviewing technical issues in admissions and financial aid).

7. Testimony of Dr. Leo Chavez, anthropology professor at UC-Irvine, in Leticia "A" I, No. 588982-4, transcript at 26–34; and Leticia "A" II, No. 588982-4, slip op. at 2–4 (children are brought to United States without any plans for them to enroll in college).

8. Ralph W. Kasarda, *Affirmative Action Gone Haywire: Why State Laws Granting College Tuition Preferences to Illegal Aliens Are Preempted by Federal Law*, 2 BYU Educ. & L.J., 197, 199, 202, 244 (2009) (citations omitted).

9. Kris W. Kobach, *Immigration Nullification: In-State Tuition and Lawmakers Who Disregard the Law*, 10 N.Y.U. J. Legis. & Pub. Pol'y 473, 517 (2006–2007).

10. *Id.*, 517.

11. Kris W. Kobach, *The Senate Immigration Bill Rewards Lawbreaking: Why the DREAM Act Is a Nightmare*, Backgrounder #1960 (Heritage Foundation 2006), available at www.heritage.org/Research/Reports/2006/08/The-Senate-Immigration-Bill-Rewards-Lawbreaking-Why-the-DREAM-Act-Is-a-Nightmare.

12. Michael Luo, *Romney's Words Testify to Threat from Huckabee*, N.Y. Times, Dec. 2, 2007, at YT-29. By no means do I suggest that historical inquiry into the origins and meaning of the Fourteenth Amendment is inappropriate or a shibboleth. Serious scholars must follow their leads, wherever the research leads, as in the case of Peter H. Schuck & Rogers M. Smith, *Citizenship without Consent: Illegal Aliens in the American Polity* (Yale

Univ. Press 1985); Rogers M. Smith, *The Second Founding: Birthright Citizenship and the Fourteenth Amendment in 1868 and 2008*, 11 U. Pa. J. Const. L. 1329 (2009); and Ayelet Shachar, *The Birthright Lottery: Citizenship and Global Inequality* (Harvard Univ. Press 2009).

13. For examples of scholarship documenting public reaction and the scapegoating phenomenon, see Thomas Muller, *Immigrants and the American City* (NYU Press 1993); Alan Dowty, *Closed Borders: The Contemporary Assault on Freedom of Movement* (Yale Univ. Press 1987); Rita J. Simon, *Public Opinion and the Immigrant: Print Media Coverage, 1880–1980* (Lexington Books 1985) (reviewing negative media coverage of immigrants in newspapers and magazines); Kevin R. Johnson, *The "Huddled Masses" Myth: Immigration and Civil Rights* (Temple Univ. Press 2004); Kevin R. Johnson, *Opening the Floodgates: Why America Needs to Rethink Its Borders and Immigration Laws* (NYU Press 2007); Miriam J. Wells, *The Grassroots Reconfiguration of U.S. Immigration Policy*, 38 Int'l Migration Rev. 1308 (2004); and Kerry Abrams, *The Hidden Dimension of Nineteenth-Century Immigration Law*, 62 Vand. L. Rev. 1353 (2009). For a useful study of this phenomenon in a comparative setting, see Catherine Dauvergne, *Making People Illegal: What Globalization Means for Migration and Law* (Cambridge Univ. Press 2008).

14. For a precise summary of objections to immigration reform and legalization, see Kris W. Kobach, *Immigration, Amnesty, and the Rule of Law*, 36 Hofstra L. Rev. 1323 (2008).

15. For a representative example of such a belief system, including the use of the ugly term "anchor baby" to suggest that U.S.-born children can readily convey citizenship status to parents, see the Federation for American Immigration Reform screed *Birthright Citizenship* (updated Aug. 2010), available at http://www.fairus.org/site/News2?news_iv_ctrl=1010&cmd=articles&page=NewsArticle&security=1601&id=16535&start=3. Back on earth, where U.S. immigration laws apply, INA Sec. 101 (b)(2) requires that any sponsoring citizen son or daughter must be at least twenty-one years of age to sponsor his or her parent. One scholar has put it in inaccurate and dyspeptic fashion: "Perhaps even more importantly if the deported parents opt to take the American-citizen child with them, the child can return to this country for permanent residence at any time. The child can then, upon becoming an adult, serve as what is known in immigration law as an 'anchor child,' the basis for a claim that his or her parents be admitted and granted permanent resident status. The parents will then ordinarily be admitted without regard to quota limitations." Lino A. Graglia, *Birthright Citizenship for Children of Illegal Aliens: An Irrational Public Policy*, 14 Tex. Rev. L. & Pol. 1, 3 (2009).

16. See, e.g., Michael A. Olivas, *Immigration-Related State Statutes and Local Ordinances: Preemption, Prejudice, and the Proper Role for Enforcement*, 2007 Univ. Chi. Legal F. 27 (2007); Jill Esbenshade, *Division and Dislocation: Regulating Immigration through Local Housing Ordinances* (American Immigration Law Foundation 2007); Hiroshi Motomura, *Immigration Outside the Law*, 108 Colum. L. Rev. 2038, 2047–2069 (2008) (discussing state and local ordinances); Clare Huntington, *The Constitutional Dimension of Immigration Federalism*, 61 Vand. L. Rev. 787 (2008).

It is also true that immigration has always been a complex transaction and dangerous sojourn and was always controlled by local forces, especially as the country was being formed and borders had not been fully established. See, as excellent examples of this history, Gerald L. Neuman, *The Lost Century of American Immigration Law (1776–1875)*, 93 Colum. L. Rev. 1833 (1993); Aristide R. Zolberg, *A Nation by Design: Immigration*

Policy in the Fashioning of America 74–76 (Harvard Univ. Press 2006); Laura E. Gómez, *Manifest Destinies: The Making of the Mexican American Race* (NYU Press 2007); Matthew J. Lindsay, *Immigration as Invasion: Sovereignty, Security, and the Origins of the Federal Immigration Power*, 45 Harv. C.R.-C.L. L. Rev. 1 (2010). In difficult economic times, the scapegoating is even easier to reach, lower-hanging fruit for elected officials. See generally Kevin R. Johnson, *Hurricane Katrina: Lessons about Immigrants in the Administrative State*, 45 Hous. L. Rev. 11, 58–64 (2008) (describing Hurricane Katrina rebuilding politics and New Orleans mayor having "expressed fear about the future prospects of his city: 'How do I ensure that New Orleans is not overrun by Mexican workers?'").

17. Of all the facets of this complex issue, the economics—more properly, the voodoo economics—of undocumented immigration are the most notable. For an example of the more thoughtful governmental reports, see Texas Comptroller of Public Accounts, *Undocumented Immigrants in Texas: A Financial Analysis of the Impact to the State Budget and Economy* (Dec. 2006), available at http://www.cpa.state.tx.us/specialrpt/undocumented/undocumented.pdf. Among the more measured academic efforts, see Howard F. Chang, *The Disadvantages of Immigration Restriction as a Policy to Improve Income Distribution*, 61 SMU L. Rev. 23, 25 (2008).

18. For an excellent analysis of this phenomenon in historical perspective, see Rita Simon, *Public Opinion and the Immigrant: Print Media Coverage, 1880–1980* (Lexington Books 1985). See also Maria L. Ontiveros, *To Help Those Most in Need: Undocumented Workers' Rights and Remedies under Title VII*, 20 N.Y.U. Rev. L. & Soc. Change 607 (1993–1994); Lesley Williams Reid, Harold E. Weiss, Robert M. Adelman & Charles Jaret, *The Immigration Crime Relationship: Evidence across U.S. Metro Areas*, 34 Soc. Sci. Res. 757 (2005); Rubén G. Rumbaut & Walter A. Ewing, *The Myth of Immigrant Criminality and the Paradox of Assimilation: Incarceration Rates among Native and Foreign-Born Men* (Immigration Policy Center 2007).

19. There is a long history of the poor schooling available to Latino children. As just a sampler of this genre, see Carlos K. Blanton, *"They Cannot Master Abstractions, but They Can Often Be Made Efficient Workers": Race and Class in the Intelligence Testing of Mexican Americans and African Americans in Texas during the 1920s*, 81 Soc. Sci. Q. 1014 (2000); Marc S. Rodriguez, *A Movement Made of "Young Mexican Americans Seeking Change": Critical Citizenship, Migration and the Chicano Movement in Texas and Wisconsin, 1960–1975*, 34 W. Hist. Q. 275 (2003); Richard R. Valencia, *Chicano Students and the Courts* (NYU Press 2008).

Latino students show poor educational achievement at virtually every level. See generally M. Beatriz Arias, *The Context of Education for Hispanic Students: An Overview*, 95 Am. J. Educ. 26 (1986); Michael A. Olivas, ed., *Latino College Students* (Teachers College Press 1986); Veronica Vélez, Lindsay Perez Huber, Corina Benavides Lopez, Ariana de la Luz & Daniel G. Solórzano, *Battling for Human Rights and Social Justice: A Latina/o Critical Race Analysis of Latina/o Student Youth Activism in the Wake of 2006 Anti-immigrant Sentiment*, 7 Soc. Just. 7 (2008); Lindsay Perez Huber, Corina Benavides Lopez, Maria C. Malagon, Veronica Vélez & Daniel G. Solórzano, *Getting beyond the "Symptom," Acknowledging the "Disease": Theorizing Racist Nativism*, 11 Contemp. Just. Rev. 39 (2008). For a useful compendium of such data, see Rick Fry & Felisa Gonzales, *One-in-Five and Growing Fast: A Profile of Hispanic Public School Students* (Pew Hispanic Center, 2008), available at http://pewhispanic.org/files/reports/92.pdf.

20. Leisy Abrego, *Legitimacy, Social Identity, and the Mobilization of Law: The Effects of Assembly Bill 540 on Undocumented Students in California*, 33 Law & Soc. Inquiry 709, 731 (2008) (citations omitted).

21. See generally Laurel S. Terry, *The Bologna Process and Its Implications for U.S. Legal Education*, 57 J. Legal Educ. 237 (2007); Meng Lu, *Not Part of the Family: U.S. Immigration Policy and Foreign Students*, 34 T. Marshall L. Rev. 343 (2009); Michael A. Olivas, *What the "War on Terror" Has Meant for U.S. Colleges and Universities*, in *Doctoral Education and the Faculty of the Future* 249–258 (Ronald G. Ehrenberg & Charlotte V. Kuh, eds., Cornell Univ. Press 2009); Pew Hispanic Center, *Statistical Portrait of the Foreign-Born Population in the United States, 2007* (Pew Hispanic Center, Mar. 2009), available at http://pewhispanic.org/factsheets/factsheet.php?FactsheetID=45; Michael G. Finn, *Stay Rates of Foreign Doctorate Recipients from U.S. Universities, 2007* (Oak Ridge Institute for Science and Education 2010). For a fascinating comparative study of the interaction between U.S and French events, see Marie-Theresa Hernandez, *The French Banlieue Riots of 2005 and Their Impact on US Immigration Policy: A Transatlantic Study*, 7 Atlantic Stud. 79 (2010).

22. For a sharp exchange on Zozobra and its meanings, see Michael A. Olivas, *Torching Zozobra: The Problem with Linda Chavez*, 2 Reconstruction 48 (1993) (review of Linda Chavez, *Out of the Barrio: Toward a New Politics of Hispanic Assimilation* (Basic Books 1991)); Linda Chavez, *A Response to Olivas*, 2 Reconstruction 182 (1993); Michael A. Olivas, *A Reply to Chavez*, 2 Reconstruction 184 (1993). Phil Parker & Mark Oswald, *Annual Event Not Shuster's Idea, Foundation Says*, Albuq. J., Aug. 27, 2009, at A1.

23. This period, approximately 130 years ago, is widely regarded as the most overtly racist period of U.S. immigration policy. In addition to the petty harassments directed at Chinese workers, a more substantial federal legislative onus was directed at all Asians: the "Chinese Exclusion" case. Chae Chan Ping v. United States, 130 U.S. 581 (1889). See Louis Henkin, *The Constitution and United States Sovereignty: A Century of Chinese Exclusion and Its Progeny*, 100 Harv. L. Rev. 853 (1987); Hiroshi Motomura, *Immigration Law after a Century of Plenary Power: Phantom Constitutional Norms and Statutory Interpretation*, 100 Yale L.J. 545, 550–554 (1990); Michael A. Olivas, *The Chronicles, My Grandfather's Stories, and Immigration Law: The Slave Traders Chronicle as Racial History*, 34 St. Louis Univ. L.J. 425, 434–435 (1990); Frank H. Wu, *Yellow: Race in America beyond Black and White* (Basic Books 2002); Gabriel J. Chin, *Regulating Race: Asian Exclusion and the Administrative State*, 37 Harv. C.R.-C.L. L. Rev. 1 (2002); Gabriel J. Chin, ed., *United States Commission on Civil Rights: Reports on Asian Pacific Americans* (Fred B. Rothman 2005). An additional feature from these times that has resurfaced is the questioning of birthright citizenship, which has been resolved by longstanding decisions by the U.S. Supreme Court from this period, which determined that the principle of jus soli confers full citizenship and nationality on children born within the United States territory. United States v. Wong Kim Ark, 169 U.S. 649, 693 (1898). This view is not universally held by scholars, but no Supreme Court has reversed or retreated from this view. See, for example, Schuck & Smith, *Citizenship without Consent*. But see Gerald L. Neuman, Wong Wing v. United States: *The Bill of Rights Protects Illegal Aliens*, in *Immigration Stories* 31–50 (David A. Martin & Peter H. Schuck, eds., Foundation 2005); Lindsay, *Immigration as Invasion*.

24. Kevin R. Johnson, *It's the Economy, Stupid: The Hijacking of the Debate over Immigration Reform by Monsters, Ghosts, and Goblins (or the War on Drugs, War on Terror, Narcoterrorists, Etc.)*, 13 Chapman L. Rev. 583 (2010). See also Jennifer M. Chacon, *Whose*

Community Shield? Examining the Removal of the "Criminal Street Gang Member," 2007
Univ. Chi. Legal F. 317 (2007) (noting the demonization of gangs and prisoners).

25. See, e.g., Leticia M. Saucedo, *National Origin, Immigrants, and the Workplace: The Employment Cases in Latinos and the Law and the Advocates' Perspective*, 12 Harv. Latino L. Rev. 53 (2009); Elizabeth McCormick, *The Oklahoma Taxpayer and Citizen Protection Act: Blowing off Steam or Setting Wildfires?*, 23 Geo. Immigr. L.J. 293 (2009) (reviewing employment and other immigration restrictions in Oklahoma).

26. The first person arrested in Georgia when a township enacted a comprehensive immigration ban in 1999 was a Spanish-language Christian minister, who was prosecuted under the English-only provisions for posting signs for church services in the language of his congregation. Carlos Guevara v City of Norcross, 52 F. App'x 486 (11th Cir. 2002) (affirming, without opinion, N.D. Ga., No. 00-00190-CV-CAP-1) (involving a city ordinance restricting the use of a language other than English for any displayed sign serving a nonresidential purpose; dismissal of criminal charges against Spanish-language minister for posting signs in Spanish announcing religious services). While this was a MALDEF case, I was not on the board at the time the action was undertaken. See generally Lisa R. Pruitt, *Latina/os, Locality, and Law in the Rural South*, 12 Harv. Latino L. Rev. 135 (2009); Karla Mari McKanders, *The Constitutionality of State and Local Laws Targeting Immigrants*, 31 U. Ark. Little Rock L. Rev. 579 (2009) (reviewing local and state immigration regulation in the South); Fran Ansley & Jon Shefner, eds., *Global Connections and Local Receptions: New Latino Immigration to the Southeastern United States* (Univ. Tennessee Press 2009).

27. Lozano v. City of Hazleton, Pennsylvania, 496 F. Supp. 2d 477 (M.D. Pa. 2007). The Third Circuit upheld the trial court opinion and struck down the ordinance in September 2010. In 2011, the U.S. Supreme Court remanded this case in light of its decision in the Arizona S.B. 1070 case. In this important case, the circuit court drew on implicit preemption grounds, and even referred to undocumented college students, who had not been specifically singled out by the proposed and doomed ordinance: "Merely because an immigrant may have a present status does not mean that this status is correct, unchangeable, or may cause the federal government to exercise its discretion to remove the immigrant. Stitched into the fabric of Hazleton's housing provisions, then, is either a lack of understanding or a refusal to recognize the complexities of federal immigration law. Hazleton would effectively remove from its City an alien college student the federal government has purposefully declined to initiate removal proceedings against. So too would Hazleton remove an alien battered spouse, currently unlawfully present, but eligible for adjustment of status to lawful permanent resident under the special protections Congress has afforded to battered spouses and children." See also Karla Mari McKanders, *Welcome to Hazleton! "Illegal" Immigrants Beware: Local Immigration Ordinances and What the Federal Government Must Do about It*, 39 Loy. U. Chi. L.J. 1 (2007); Stephanie Sandoval, *Restraining Order Issued against Rental Ordinance*, Dall. Morn. News, Sept. 13, 2008, at B1 ("So far, the third time is not the charm for Farmers Branch. U.S. District Judge Jane Boyle issued a temporary restraining order Friday barring the city from implementing its latest ordinance aimed at halting housing rentals to illegal immigrants."). The Texas ordinance was permanently enjoined in March 2010. Villas at Parkside Partners v. City of Farmers Branch, Texas, 701 F. Supp. 2d 835 (2010). Dianne Solis, *Judge Rejects Rental Ban*, Dall. Morn. News, Mar. 25, 2010, at B1 (details about permanent injunction in Farmers Branch case).

28. Linda Greenhouse, *What Would Justice Powell Do? The "Alien Children" Case and the Meaning of Equal Protection*, 25 Const. Comment. 29, 32–33, 33–34 (2008). For another useful account of Justice Powell's jurisprudence, see Anders Walker, *Diversity's Strange Career: Recovering the Racial Pluralism of Lewis F. Powell, Jr.*, 50 Santa Clara L. Rev. 647 (2010).

29. Peter H. Schuck, *The Transformation of Immigration Law*, 84 Colum. L. Rev. 1, 82–83 (1984).

30. Brown v. Board of Education, 347 U.S. 483, 489–490 (1954).

31. Authoritative scholarship on the Treaty of Guadalupe Hidalgo includes work by Guadalupe Luna, *On the Complexities of Race: The Treaty of Guadalupe Hidalgo and Dred Scott v. Sandford*, 53 U. Miami L. Rev. 691 (1999), and *En el Nombre de Dios Todo-Poderoso: The Treaty of Guadalupe Hidalgo and Narrativos Legales*, 5 Sw. J.L. & Trade Americas 45 (1998); and by Christopher D. Cameron, *One Hundred Fifty Years of Solitude: Reflections on the End of the History Academy's Dominance of Scholarship on the Treaty of Guadalupe Hidalgo*, 5 Sw. J.L. & Trade Americas 83 (1998)

32. Mae M. Ngai, *Impossible Subjects: Illegal Aliens and the Making of Modern America* (Princeton Univ. Press 2004). See also Peter Schrag, *The Unwanted: Immigration and Nativism in America* (Immigration Policy Center, Sept. 13, 2010).

33. Chevron, U.S.A., Inc. v. Natural Res. Def. Council, Inc., 467 U.S. 837 (1984).

34. Johnson, *Hurricane Katrina*, 20.

35. Schuck, *Transformation*, 16–19.

36. INS v. Chadha, 103 S. Ct. 2764, 2779 (1983). See generally Motomura, *Immigration Law*.

37. Sandoval, *Restraining Order Issued*. In March 2010, four years after the statute was first enacted, the federal judge permanently enjoined the city from implementing the ordinance, finding that it violated the supremacy clause and was preempted by federal law. 701 F. Supp. 2d 835 (2010). Solis, *Judge Rejects Rental Ban* (details about TROs and permanent injunction in Farmers Branch case).

38. See, e.g., Ansley & Shefner, *Global Connections*.

39. David B. Thronson, *Entering the Mainstream: Making Children Matter in Immigration Law*, 38 Fordham Urb. L.J. 393, 403–407 (2010) (outlining consequences of citizen deported with undocumented parents). See also Jacqueline Bhabha, *"Not a Sack of Potatoes": Moving and Removing Children across Borders*, 15 B.U. Pub. Int. L.J. 197, 198–199 (2006).

Bibliography

Abourezk, Kevin. "Judge tosses suit on tuition to illegal immigrants: Plaintiffs likely to refile suit." *Lincoln Journal Star*, December 18, 2010, A1.

Abraham, Yvonne. "Immigrant tuition bill defeated." *Boston Globe*, January 12, 2006, A1.

Abrams, Kerry. "The hidden dimension of nineteenth-century immigration law." *Vanderbilt Law Review* 62 (2009).

Abrego, Leisy. "Legitimacy, social identity, and the mobilization of law: The effects of Assembly Bill 540 on undocumented students in California." *Law and Social Inquiry* 33 (2008).

Abriel, Evangeline G. "Rethinking preemption for purposes of aliens and public benefits." *UCLA Law Review* 42 (1995).

Aleinikoff, Thomas Alexander, David A. Martin, Hiroshi Motomura, and Maryellen Fullerton. *Immigration and citizenship: Process and policy.* 6th ed. St. Paul, MN: Thompson West, 2008.

Allen, Matthew B. "The unconstitutional denial of a Texas veterans benefit." *Houston Law Review* 46 (2010).

Allsup, Carl. *The American G.I. Forum: Origins and evolution.* Austin: University of Texas Press, 1982.

American Association of Collegiate Registrars and Admission Officers (AACRAO). *Undocumented students in the U.S.: Admission and verification.* Washington, DC: AACRAO, 2009. Available at http://www.aacrao.org/pro_development/surveys/undocumented_results.pdf.

American Association of State Colleges and Universities. *Access for all? Debating in-state tuition for undocumented alien students.* Washington, DC: American Association of State Colleges and Universities, 2005. Available at www.aascu.org/policy/special_report/access_for_all.htm.

Anonymous. "I'm an illegal immigrant at Harvard." *Daily Beast* (blog), November 27, 2010. Available at http://www.thedailybeast.com/blogs-and-stories/2010-11-27/dream-act-im-an-illegal-immigrant-at-harvard.

Ansley, Fran, and Jon Shefner, eds. *Global connections and local receptions: New Latino immigration to the southeastern United States.* Knoxville: University of Tennessee Press, 2009.

Aoki, Keith, and John Shuford. "Welcome to Amerizona—Immigrants Out! Assessing 'Dystopian Dreams' and 'Usable Futures' of Immigration Reform, and Considering Whether 'Immigration Regionalism' Is an Idea Whose Time Has Come." *Fordham Urban Law Journal* 38 (2010).

Archibold, Randal C. "Pre-emption, Not Profiling, in Challenge to Arizona." *New York Times*, June 8, 2010, A15.

Arhancet, Maria. "Current developments in the legislative branch: Platforms of presidential candidates regarding immigration reform." *Georgetown Immigration Law Journal* 21 (2007).

Arias, M. Beatriz. "The context of education for Hispanic students: An overview." *American Journal of Education* 95 (1986).

Arriola, Christopher. "Knocking on the schoolhouse door: *Mendez v. Westminster*, equal protection, public education, and Mexican Americans in the 1940's." *La Raza Law Journal* 8 (1995).

Bacon, David. *Illegal people: How globalization creates migration and criminalizes immigrants*. Boston: Beacon, 2008.

Baird, Vanessa A. *Answering the call of the court: How justices and litigants set the Supreme Court agenda*. Charlottesville: University of Virginia Press, 2007.

Balkin, Jack M., ed. *What Brown v. Board of Education should have said*. New York: NYU Press, 2001.

Barrera, Lisa Lizette. "Minorities and the University of Texas Law School (1950–1980)." *Texas Hispanic Journal of Law and Policy* 4 (1998).

Batalova, Jeanne, and Michael Fix. *New estimates of unauthorized youth eligible for legal status under the DREAM Act*. Washington, DC: Migration Policy Institute, 2006. Available at http://www.migrationpolicy.org/pubs/Backgrounder1_Dream_Act.pdf.

Batalova, Jeanne, and B. Lindsay Lowell. "Immigrant professionals in the United States." *Society* 44 (2007).

Baynes, Leonard M. "Racial profiling, September 11, and the media: A critical race theory analysis." *Virginia Sports and Entertainment Law Journal* 2 (2002).

Beck, Margery A. "Lawsuit targets Nebraska's immigrant-tuition law." *Lincoln Journal-Star*, January 25, 2010. Available at http://www.journalstar.com/news/state-and-regional/nebraska/article_c6ed17f0-09e5-11df-b231-001cc4c002e0.html.

Beh, Hazel G. "Student versus university: The university's implied obligation of good faith and fair dealing." *Maryland Law Review* 59 (2000).

Belejack, Barbara. "A lesson in equal protection: The Texas cases that opened the schoolhouse door to undocumented immigrant children." *Texas Observer*, July 13, 2007, 14–21.

Bender, Steven W. *Greasers and gringos: Latinos, law, and the American imagination*. New York: NYU Press, 2003.

Benson, Matthew. "[Sheriff] Arpaio to use state funds to fight smuggling." *Arizona Republic*, March 15, 2007, B5.

Berger Dan H., and Scott M. Borene, eds. *Immigration options for academics and researchers*. Washington, DC: American Immigration Lawyers Association, 2005.

Berger, Joseph. "Debates persist over subsidies for immigrant college students." *New York Times*, December 12, 2007, A31.

———. "An undocumented Princetonian: Illegal at 13, Ivy League at 18, and then . . . caught. *New York Times*, January 3, 2010, ED-28.

Bernstein, Nina. "Border sweeps in north reach miles into U.S." *New York Times*, August 30, 2010, A1.

———. "No visa, no school, many New York districts say." *New York Times*, July 22, 2010, A16.

———. "On Lucille Avenue, the immigration debate." *New York Times*, June 26, 2006, A1.

———. "Senegalese teenager wins right to study in the U.S." *New York Times*, July 29, 2006, A13.

———. "Student's prize is a trip into immigration limbo." *New York Times*, April 26, 2006, A1.

Berry, Jahna. "Smuggling verdict tossed: Judge cites lack of evidence." *Arizona Republic*, December 6, 2006, A1.

"Berry right to temper sanctuary city rhetoric." Editorial. *Albuquerque Journal*, December 21, 2009. Available at http://www.abqjournal.com/opinion/editorials/2122195927860pin ioneditorials12-21-09.htm.

Bertelsmann Stiftung and Migration Policy Institute, eds. *Migration, public opinion and politics*. Gütersloh, Germany: Transatlantic Council on Migration, 2009.

Bhabha, Jacqueline. "'Not a sack of potatoes': Moving and removing children across borders." *Boston University Public Interest Law Journal* 15 (2006).

Bland, Karina. "District backs aid for kids of migrants: Phoenix union board votes to lend support to federal DREAM Act." *Arizona Republic*, January 13, 2007, 3.

Blanton, Carlos K. "From intellectual deficiency to cultural deficiency: Mexican Americans, testing, and public school policy in the American Southwest, 1920–1940." *Pacific Historical Review* 72 (2003).

———. "'They cannot master abstractions, but they can often be made efficient workers': Race and class in the intelligence testing of Mexican Americans and African Americans in Texas during the 1920s." *Social Science Quarterly* 81 (2000).

Blum, Cynthia. "Rethinking tax compliance of unauthorized workers after immigration reform." *Georgetown Immigration Law Journal* 21 (2007).

Blumenthal, Ralph. "Texas lawmakers put new focus on illegal immigration." *New York Times*, November 16, 2006, A22.

Boehmke, Frederick J. "The initiative process and the dynamics of state interest group populations." *State Politics and Policy Quarterly* 8 (2008).

Bosniak, Linda S. "Membership, equality, and the difference that alienage makes." *New York University Law Review* 69 (1994).

———. "Opposing Prop. 187: Undocumented immigrants and the national imagination." *Connecticut Law Review* 28 (1996).

Boswell, Richard A. "Restrictions on non-citizens' access to public benefits: Flawed premise, unnecessary response." *UCLA Law Review* 42 (1995).

Bowers, Faye. "In growing cities, a loss of students; Schools aren't sure why enrollment is down." *Christian Science Monitor*, September 24, 2007. Available at http://www.csmonitor.com/2007/0924/p02s01-ussc.html.

Brickman, Jaclyn. "Educating undocumented children in the United States: Codification of *Plyler v. Doe* through federal legislation." *Georgetown Immigration Law Journal* 20 (2006).

Brimelow, Peter. *Alien nation: Common sense about America's immigration disaster*. New York: HarperPerennial, 1995.

Broder, John M. "Obama hobbled in fight against global warming." *New York Times*, November 16, 2009, A1.

Broder, John M., and Elisabeth Rosenthal. "Obama has goal to wrest a deal in climate talks." *New York Times*, December 18, 2009, A1.

Bruno, Andorra. *Unauthorized alien students: Issues and "DREAM Act" legislation.* Report RL33863. Washington, DC: Congressional Research Service, U.S. Library of Congress, 2008.

Buckner Inniss, Lolita K. "California's Proposition 187—Does it mean what it says? Does it say what it means? A textual and constitutional analysis." *Georgetown Immigration Law Journal* 10 (1996).

Bulkeley, Deborah. "Utah measure to repeal tuition break for illegals is back." *Deseret Morning News,* February 7, 2008, B4.

Bulkeley, Deborah, and Lisa Riley Roche. "Immigrant tuition repeal removed from bill." *Deseret Morning News,* February 13, 2008, B7.

Bump, Micah. "Immigration, technology, and the worksite: The challenges of electronic employment verification." *Georgetown Immigration Law Journal* 22 (2008).

Bykowicz, Julie, and Annie Linskey. "Lawmakers approve tuition break for illegal immigrants, new sales tax on alcohol." *Baltimore Sun,* April 12, 2011. Available at http://www.baltimoresun.com/news/maryland/politics/bs-md-sine-die-20110411,0,762321.story.

Byrne, Olga. *Unaccompanied children in the United States: A literature review.* New York: Vera Institute of Justice, 2008.

Calavita, Kitty. "The new politics of immigration: 'Balanced-budget conservatism' and the symbolism of Proposition 187." *Social Problems* 43 (1996).

Callahan Ragan, Laura J. "Educating the undocumented: Providing legal status for undocumented students in the United States and Italy through higher education." *Georgia Journal of International and Comparative Law* 34 (2006).

Cameron, Christopher D. "One hundred fifty years of solitude: Reflections on the end of the history academy's dominance of scholarship on the Treaty of Guadalupe Hidalgo." *Southwestern Journal of Law and Trade in the Americas* 5 (1998).

Capps, Randy, Marc R. Rosenblum, and Michael Fix. *Immigrants and health care reform: What's really at stake?* Washington, DC: Migration Policy Institute, 2009.

Carlson, Peter. "Stinky the robot, four kids and a brief whiff of success." *Washington Post,* March 29, 2005, C1.

Carrera, John Willshire. *Immigrant students: Their legal right of access to public schools.* Boston: National Coalition of Advocates for Students, 1989.

Carroll, Susan. "Immigrant spends life looking over her shoulder." *Houston Chronicle,* November 28, 2009, B1.

———. "In-state rates for illegal immigrants attacked." *Houston Chronicle,* December 16, 2009, B1.

Casey, Theresa Mesa, and Pedro Hernández, eds. *Research guide to the records of MALDEF (Mexican American Legal Defense and Educational Fund) and PRLDEF (Puerto Rican Legal Defense and Education Fund).* Stanford: Stanford University Libraries, 1996.

Cassidy, John. *How markets fail: The logic of economic calamities.* New York: Farrar, Straus and Giroux, 2009.

Castillo, Leonel. "Foreword." *Houston Journal of International Law* 5 (1983).

Center for American Progress. "We can fix this: Homeland Security Secretary Janet Napolitano speaks on immigration reform." Press release. November 13, 2009. Available at http://www.americanprogress.org/issues/2009/11/napolitano_event.html.

Chacon, Jennifer M. "Whose community shield? Examining the removal of the 'criminal street gang member.'" *University of Chicago Legal Forum,* 2007.

Chan, Sewell. "Dodd calls Obama plan too grand." *New York Times*, February 3, 2010, B1.

Chang, Howard F. "The disadvantages of immigration restriction as a policy to improve income distribution." *SMU Law Review* 61 (2008).

Chaudry, Ajay, Randolph Capps, Juan Pedroza, Rosa Maria Castaneda, Robert Santos, and Molly M. Scott. *Facing our future: Children in the aftermath of immigration enforcement.* Washington DC: Urban Institute, 2010. Available at http://www.urban.org/publications/412020.html.

Chavez, Jorge M., and Doris Marie Provine. "Race and the response of state legislatures to unauthorized immigrants." *Annals of the American Academy of Political and Social Science* 623 (2009). Available at http://ann.sagepub.com/cgi/content/abstract/623/1/78.

Chavez, Leo R. *The Latino threat: Constructing immigrants, citizens, and the nation.* Stanford: Stanford University Press, 2008.

Chavez, Linda. *Out of the barrio: Toward a new politics of Hispanic assimilation.* New York: Basic Books, 1991.

———. "A response to Olivas." *Reconstruction* 2 (1993).

Chin, Aimee, and Chinhui Juhn. *Does reducing college costs improve educational outcomes for undocumented immigrants?* Houston: Rice University Baker Institute, 2007. Available at http://bakerinstitute.org/Program_View.cfm?PID=58.

Chin, Gabriel J. "Regulating race: Asian exclusion and the administrative state." *Harvard Civil Rights–Civil Liberties Law Review* 37 (2002).

———, ed. *United States Commission on Civil Rights: Reports on Asian Pacific Americans.* Washington, DC: Fred B. Rothman, 2005.

Chishi, Muszaffar, and Claire Bergeron. *New immigration bill edges comprehensive reform back on the legislative agenda.* Washington, DC: Migration Policy Institute, January 2010. Available at http://www.migrationinformation.org/USfocus/display.cfm?id=769.

Cohen, Jeffrey E. *The presidency in the era of 24-hour news.* Princeton: Princeton University Press, 2008.

Collom, Lindsey. "54 jailed under 'coyote' statute." *Arizona Republic*, March 3, 2006, 1B.

Colvin, Kyle William. Comment. "In-state tuition and illegal immigrants: An analysis of *Martinez v. Regents of the University of California*." *BYU Education and Law Journal*, 2010.

Commonwealth of Virginia, Department of Education. "Enrollment requirements." Available at http://www.pen.k12.va.us.

Cortez, Nathan. "The local dilemma: Preemption and the role of federal standards in state and local immigration laws." *SMU Law Review* 47 (2008).

Cottrol, Robert J., Raymond T. Diamond, and Leland B. Ware. *Brown v. Board of Education: Caste, culture, and the Constitution.* Lawrence: University Press of Kansas, 2003.

Couch, Kathryne J. "This land is our land, a local solution to a local problem: State regulation of immigration through business licensing." *Georgetown Immigration Law Journal* 21 (2007).

Coyle, John. "The legality of banking the undocumented." *Georgetown Immigration Law Journal* 22 (2007).

Crenshaw, Kimberlé Williams. "Race, reform, and retrenchment: Transformation and legitimation in antidiscrimination law." *Harvard Law Review* 101 (1988).

Cullen, James. Editorial. "Blame the newcomers." *Texas Observer*, August 19, 1994, 2–3.

Dauvergne, Catherine. *Making people illegal: What globalization means for migration and law.* Cambridge: Cambridge University Press, 2008.

del Bosque, Melissa. "Children of the exodus: What becomes of kids who are deported without their families?" *Texas Observer*, November 4, 2010. Available at http://www.texasobserver.org/cover-story/children-of-the-exodus.

———. "Child x-ing: Del Rio's controversial crackdown on border-crossing students." *Texas Observer*, December 11, 2009, 8–9, 11–13.

De León, Arnoldo. *They called them greasers: Anglo attitudes toward Mexicans in Texas, 1821–1900*. Austin: University of Texas Press, 1983.

Delgado, Richard, and Victoria Palacios. "Mexican Americans as a legally cognizable class under Rule 23 and the Equal Protection Clause." *Notre Dame Lawyer* 50 (1975).

Delgado, Richard, and Jean Stefancic. "The social construction of *Brown v. Board of Education*: Law reform and the reconstructive paradox." *William and Mary Law Review* 36 (1995).

Diamond, Laura. "Collegiate ban proposed: Plans target students unable to prove legal U.S. residency." *Atlanta Journal-Constitution*, September 22, 2010, A1.

———. "470-plus students' residency unclear." *Atlanta Journal-Constitution*, August 11, 2010, B1.

DiIulio, John J. *Governing prisons*. New York: Free Press, 1987.

Dillon, Sam. "In schools across U.S., the melting pot overflows." *New York Times*, August 27, 2006, YT-1.

Dinan, Stephen. "McCain caters to GOP voters." *Washington Times*, October 31, 2007, A1.

Dodd, Chris. "Dodd to sponsor rare private bill preventing Haitian girl's deportation." Press release. July 16, 2004. Available at http://dodd.senate.gov/?q=node/3270/print&pr=press/Releases/04/0716.htm.

Dolan, Maura, and Larry Gordon. "In-state tuition benefit upheld." *Los Angeles Times*, November 16, 2010, A1. Available at http://www.latimes.com/news/local/la-me-illegal-students-20101116,0,2917015.story.

Dotinga, Randy, and Mary Know Merrill. "Schools crack down on students living in Mexico." *Santa Fe New Mexican*, May 27, 2008, C6.

Doty, Roxanne L. *The law into their own hands: Immigration and the politics of exceptionalism*. Tucson: University of Arizona Press, 2009.

Dougherty, Kevin J., H. Kenny Nienhusser, and Blanca E. Vega. *Undocumented immigrants and state higher education policy: The contrasting politics of in-state tuition eligibility in Texas and Arizona*. IHELG Monograph 09-11. Houston: Institute of Higher Education Law and Governance, University of Houston Law Center, 2009. Available at http://www.law.uh.edu/ihelg/monograph/09-11.pdf.

Dowty, Alan. *Closed borders: The contemporary assault on freedom of movement*. New Haven: Yale University Press, 1987.

Draper, Robert. "It's just a Texas-governor thing." *New York Times Magazine*, December 6, 2009, 30.

"Dreaming of reform." Editorial. *New York Times*, November 30, 2010, A30.

Eckstein, Megan. "College Board announces support for immigration bill." *Chronicle of Higher Education*, April 22, 2009. Available at http://chronicle.com/article/College-Board-Announces/47203.

———. "In-state tuition for undocumented students: Not quite yet." *Chronicle of Higher Education*, May 8, 2009, A19.

"Edward M. Kennedy." *New York Times*, September 3, 2009. Available at http://topics.nytimes.com/top/reference/timestopics/people/k/edward_m_kennedy/index.html?scp=1-spot&sq=edward%20kennedy&st=cse.

Egelko, Bob. "Fight over illegals' tuition reaches high court." *San Francisco Chronicle*, October 6, 2010, C1.

Engle, Karen. "The political economy of state and local immigration regulation: Comments on Olivas and Hollifield, Hunt & Tichenor." *SMU Law Review* 61 (2008).

Esbenshade, Jill. *Division and dislocation: Regulating immigration through local housing ordinances*. Washington, DC: American Immigration Law Foundation, 2007.

Fausset, Richard. "Young migrants protest uncertain fate." *Los Angeles Times*, April 10, 2011, A18.

Feder, Jody. *Unauthorized alien students, higher education, and in-state tuition rates: A legal analysis*. Report RS22500. Washington, DC: Congressional Research Service, U.S. Library of Congress, 2010.

Federal Judicial Center. "Biographical directory of federal judges: Pfaelzer, Mariana R." Available at http://www.fjc.gov/servlet/nGetInfo?jid=1876&cid=999&ctype=na&instate=na (accessed September 9, 2009).

Federation for American Immigration Reform (FAIR). "Breaking the piggy bank: How illegal immigration is sending schools into the red." June 2005. Available at http://www.fairus.org/site/News2?page=NewsArticle&id=17193&security=1601&news_iv_ctrl=1901.

———. "Birthright Citizenship." Updated August 2010. Available at http://www.fairus.org/site/News2?news_iv_ctrl=1010&cmd=articles&page=NewsArticle&security=1601&id=16535&start=3.

Feldman, Paul. "Texas case looms over Prop. 187's legal future: U.S. high court voided that state's '75 law on illegal immigrants, but panel has shifted to the right." *Los Angeles Times*, October 23, 1994, A1.

Fernandez, Manny. "In jury selection for hate crime, a struggle to find tolerance." *New York Times*, March 9, 2010, A20.

———. "Lawsuit filed by estate of immigrant killed on Long Island," *New York Times*, November 22, 2010, A27.

———. "L.I. teenagers hunted Latinos for 'sport,' prosecutor says." *New York Times*, March 19, 2010, A18.

———. "Racial slurs preceded L.I. attack, victim's friend testifies." *New York Times*, March 25, 2010, A24.

Ferry, Barbara. "'Out of the shadows,' immigrant women shed fears to lead push for rights in Santa Fe." *Santa Fe New Mexican*, June 12, 2006, A1.

Field, Kelly. "Deal is reached on immigration bill affecting students, says Senate leader." *Chronicle of Higher Education*, November 24, 2008. Available at http://chronicle.com/article/Deal-Is-Reached-on-Immigrat/42007.

———. "The Dream Act is dead, at least for now." *Chronicle of Higher Education*, September 22, 2010. Available at http://chronicle.com/article/The-Dream-Act-Is-Dead-at/124560/?sid=at&utm_source=at&utm_medium=en.

Finn, Michael G. *Stay rates of foreign doctorate recipients from U.S. universities, 2007*. Oak Ridge, TN: Oak Ridge Institute for Science and Education, 2010.

Fischer, Howard. "Sheriff: Schools should question students' citizen status." *Yuma (AZ) Sun*, April 28, 2009. Available at 2009 WLNR 7985977.

Fisher, Louis. *The Constitution and 9/11: Recurring threats to America's freedoms*. Lawrence: University Press of Kansas, 2008.

Flores, Stella M. "The first state Dream act: In-state resident tuition and immigration in Texas." *Educational Evaluation and Policy Analysis* 32 (December 2010).

———. "State Dream acts: The effect of in-state resident tuition policies and undocumented Latino students." *Review of Higher Education* 33 (2010).

Florida, Richard. "How the crash will reshape America." *Atlantic Monthly*, March 2009, 44.

Foley, Neil. *The white scourge: Mexicans, blacks, and poor whites in Texas cotton culture*. Berkeley: University of California Press, 1997.

Forebrand, Ronald. "Re: domicile matter." Virginia Attorney General memo. March 6, 2008. Available at www.law.uh.edu/ihelg.

"From the editors: Mayoral takeovers in education: A recipe for progress or peril?" *Harvard Education Review* 76 (Summer 2006).

Fry, Brian. *Nativism and immigration: Regulating the American dream*. El Paso, TX: LFB, 2006.

Fry, Rick, and Felisa Gonzales. *One-in-five and growing fast: A profile of Hispanic public school students*. Washington, DC: Pew Hispanic Center, 2008. Available at http://pewhispanic.org/files/reports/92.pdf.

Garamone, Jim. "DREAM Act would expand recruiting pool." American Forces Press Service, December 2, 2010. Available at http://www.defense.gov/news/newsarticle.aspx?id=61928.

Garcia Lisa D., and William G. Tierney. "Undocumented immigrants in higher education: A preliminary analysis." *Teachers College Record* 113, no. 12 (2011). Available at http://www.tcrecord.org/PrintContent.asp?ContentID=16204.

García, Mario T. *Mexican Americans: Leadership, ideology, and identity, 1930–1960*. New Haven: Yale University Press, 1989.

Garcia, Ruben J. "Critical race theory and Proposition 187: The racial politics of immigration law." *Chicano-Latino Law Review* 17 (1995).

García Hernández, César Cuauhtémoc. "La migra in the mirror: Immigration enforcement and racial profiling on the Texas border." *Notre Dame Journal of Law, Ethics and Public Policy* 23 (2009).

Gastelum, Juan E. "How immigration activists are fighting deportation policy with social media." Mashable.com, April 19, 2011. Available at http://mashable.com/2011/04/19/immigration-activism-social-media/.

"Georgia urged to end ban on undocumented students at top colleges." Fox News Latino, April 14, 2011. Available at http://latino.foxnews.com/latino/news/2011/04/14/georgia-urged-end-ban-undocumented-students-colleges.

Gildersleeve, Ryan Evely. *Fracturing opportunity: Mexican migrant students and college-going literacy*. New York: Peter Lang, 2010.

Gladstein, Hannah, Annie Lai, Jennifer Wagner, and Michael Wishnie. *Blurring the lines: A profile of state and local police enforcement of immigration law using the National Crime Information Center database, 2002–04*. Washington, DC: Migration Policy Institute, 2005.

Gómez, Laura E. "The birth of the 'Hispanic' generation: Attitudes of Mexican-American political elites toward the Hispanic label." *Latin American Perspectives* 75 (1992).

————. *Manifest destinies: The making of the Mexican American race.* New York: NYU Press, 2007.

————. "What's race got to do with it? Press coverage of the Latino electorate in the 2008 presidential primary season." *St. John's Journal of Legal Commentary* 24 (2009).

Gonzales, Roberto G. "On the wrong side of the tracks: Understanding the effects of school structure and social capital in the educational pursuits of undocumented immigrant students." *Peabody Journal of Education* 85 (2010).

————. *Young lives on hold: The college dreams of undocumented students.* New York: College Board, 2009. Available at http://professionals.collegeboard.com/profdownload/young-lives-on-hold-college-board.pdf.

Gonzalez, Cindy. "Fairbury next in immigration battle." *Omaha World-Herald,* September 1, 2010. Available at http://www.omaha.com/article/20100901/NEWS01/709019918#fairbury-next-in-immigration-battle.

Gonzalez, Daniel. "'Wilson Four' deportation case settled: Panel says students wrongly targeted." *Arizona Republic,* December 12, 2006, 10A.

Gonzalez, Gilbert G. *Chicano education in the era of segregation.* Philadelphia: Balch Institute Press, 1990.

Gonzalez, Jennifer. "North Carolina community colleges to resume enrolling illegal immigrants." *Chronicle of Higher Education,* September 18, 2009.

"A good session overall." Editorial. *Deseret Morning News,* March 2, 2007, A14.

Gordon, Larry. "Immigrants face Cal State fee hike." *Los Angeles Times,* September 9, 1992, A3.

Gordon, Larry, and Amina Khan. "Regents OK hike in UC fees." *Los Angeles Times,* November 20, 2009, A3.

Graglia, Lino A. "Birthright citizenship for children of illegal aliens: An irrational public policy." *Texas Review of Law and Politics* 14 (2009).

Greenfield, Gary A., and Don B. Kates, Jr. "Mexican Americans, racial discrimination, and the Civil Rights Act of 1866." *California Law Review* 63 (1975).

Greenhouse, Linda. "What would Justice Powell do? The 'Alien Children' case and the meaning of equal protection." *Constitutional Commentary* 25 (2008).

Griffith, Kelly. "E-2 kids hoping for a dream." *Orlando Sentinel,* September 10, 2006, J1.

Griswold, Daniel. *Comprehensive immigration reform: Finally getting it right.* Free Trade Bulletin No. 29. Washington, DC: Cato Institute, Center for Trade Policy Studies, 2007.

Griswold del Castillo, Richard, and Anthony Accardo, *César Chávez: The struggle for justice.* Norman, OK: Piñata Books, 2002.

Gutiérrez-Jones, Carl. *Rethinking the borderlands: Between Chicano culture and legal discourse.* Berkeley: University of California Press, 1995.

Hamilton, Reeve. "Undocumented students stump for the DREAM Act." *Texas Tribune,* November 11, 2010. Available at http://www.texastribune.org/immigration-in-texas/immigration/undocumented-students-stump-for-the-dream-act/.

Haney López, Ian F. "Race, ethnicity, erasure: The salience of race to LatCrit theory," *California Law Review* 85 (1998).

————. *White by law: The legal construction of race.* New York: NYU Press, 1996.

Hebel, Sara. "Arizona college officials worry that a new measure approved by voters will require them to shift hefty portions of their budgets so that they can play backup for the border patrol." *Chronicle of Higher Education,* November 24, 2006, A27.

————. "Candidates grapple with how to expand access to college." *Chronicle of Higher Education*, September 14, 2007, A17.

————. "States take diverging approaches on tuition rates for illegal immigrants." *Chronicle of Higher Education*, November 30, 2001, A22.

Hegstrom, Edward, and Elena Vega. "One nation, two worlds: Creating an American life." *Houston Chronicle*, December 6, 2005, A1.

Heise, Michael. "State constitutional litigation, educational finance, and legal impact: An empirical analysis." *University of Cincinnati Law Review* 63 (1995).

———— "The story of *San Antonio Independent School Dist. v. Rodriguez*: School finance, local control, and constitutional limits." In *Education Law Stories*, ed. Michael A. Olivas and Ronna Greff Schneider, 51–82. New York: Foundation, 2008.

Henkin, Louis. "The Constitution and United States sovereignty: A century of Chinese exclusion and its progeny." *Harvard Law Review* 100 (1987).

Herman, Eric. "Schools cry 'uncle.'" *Chicago Sun-Times*, February 25, 2006, A3.

Hernandez, Marie-Theresa. "The French Banlieue riots of 2005 and their impact on US immigration policy: A transatlantic study." *Atlantic Studies* 7 (2010).

Herszenhorn, David M. "Democrats use power of majority to pursue agenda." *New York Times*, September 17, 2010, A17.

————. "Move to end 'Don't Ask, Don't Tell' stalls in Senate." *New York Times*, September 22, 2010, A1.

————. "Passion and politics on immigration act." *New York Times*, September 22, 2010, A18.

————. "Reid to push to allow end of 'Don't Ask, Don't Tell.'" *New York Times*, November 18, 2010, A23. Available at http://www.nytimes.com/2010/11/18/us/politics/18gays.html?nl=todaysheadlines&emc=a24.

————. "Republicans threaten to bring Senate to halt over tax dispute." *New York Times*, December 2, 2010, A24.

Herszenhorn, David M., and Tamar Levin. "Student loan overhaul approved by Congress." *New York Times*, March 26, 2010, A16.

Herszenhorn, David M., and Robert Pear. "Democrats put lower priority on health bill." *New York Times*, January 27, 2010, A27.

Heyboer, Kelly. "Rutgers University students protest illegal immigrant tuition during president's fundraising speech." *Newark Star-Ledger*, September 25, 2010. Available at http://www.nj.com/news/index.ssf/2010/09/rutgers_students_question_ille.html.

Hockstader, Lee. "Immigration awaits its turn." *Washington Post*, September 13, 2009, A23.

Hood, Lucy. "Educating immigrant students." *Carnegie Reporter* 4 (2007). Available at http://carnegie.org/publications/carnegie-reporter/single/view/article/item/174/.

————. *Immigrant students, urban high schools: The challenge continues*. New York: Carnegie Corporation of New York, 2003.

Hopfensperger, Jean. "Immigration proposals clash: The governor and DFL lawmakers offered differing views on issues involving the state's immigrants." *Minneapolis Star-Tribune*, February 15, 2007, 5B.

Houston Independent School District. "Alternative and charter listings." Available at www.houstonisd.org/HISDConnectDS/v/index.jsp?vgnextchannel=bc697438901d8210VgnVCM10000028147fa6RCRD&vgnextfmt=alt10 (accessed September 20, 2009).

Hoy, Serena. "Remarks at the 6th annual Immigration Law and Policy Conference at Georgetown University Law Center." June 26, 2008. Webcast. Available at http://www.law.georgetown.edu/webcast/eventDetail.cfm?eventID=863.

Hsu, Spencer S. "Obama presses Congress to rework immigration laws." *Washington Post*, November 14, 2009, A16.

Hulse, Carl. "Democrats gain as Stevens loses his Senate race." *New York Times*, November 19, 2008, A1.

———. "Senate ends military ban on gays serving openly." *New York Times*, December 19, 2010, A1.

Hulse, Carl, and Adam Nagourney. "Obama's Afghanistan decision is straining ties with Democrats." *New York Times*, December 4, 2009, A20.

———. "Specter switches parties." *New York Times*, April 28, 2009, A1.

Hulse, Carl, and Sheryl Gay Stolberg. "His health bill stalled, Obama juggles an altered agenda." *New York Times*, January 29, 2010, A1.

Huntington, Clare. "The constitutional dimension of immigration federalism." *Vanderbilt Law Review* 61 (2008).

Huntington, Samuel P. *Who are we? The challenges to America's national identity*. New York: Simon and Schuster, 2004.

Hutchinson, Dennis J. "More substantive equal protection? A note on *Plyler v. Doe*." *Supreme Court Review*, 1982.

Illinois State Board of Education. "Immigrant students' rights." Available at http://www.isbe.state.il.us (accessed September 21, 2009).

Immigration Policy Center. *Breaking down the problems: What's wrong with our immigration system?* Washington, DC: Immigration Policy Center, 2009. Available at www.immigrationpolicy.org/sites/default/files/docs/Problem_Paper_FINAL_102109_0.pdf.

———. *E-Verify and Arizona: Early experiences for employers, employees, and the economy portend a rough road ahead*. Washington, DC: Immigration Policy Center, May 5, 2008. Available at www.immigrationpolicy.org/just-facts/e-verify-and-arizona-early-experiences-portend-rough-road-ahead.

———. *Anti-immigrant group issues deceptive report on DREAM Act*. Washington, DC: Immigration Policy Center, December 2010. Available at http://myemail.constantcontact.com/Anti-Immigrant-Group-Issues-Deceptive-Report-on-DREAM-Act.html?soid=1101677093769&aid=02IOb7XIIhEc.

———. *DHS progress report: The challenge of reform*. Washington, DC: Immigration Policy Center, March 2, 2010. Available at http://immigrationpolicy.org/special-reports/dhs-progress-report-challenge-reform.

———. "Dispelling DREAM Act myths." Washington, DC: Immigration Policy Center, November 23, 2010. Available at http://www.immigrationpolicy.org/just-facts/dispelling-dream-act-myths.

"In the child's best interest? The consequences of losing a lawful immigrant parent to deportation. International Human Rights Law Clinic, University of California, Berkeley, School of Law; Warren Institute on Race, Ethnicity and Diversity, University of California, Berkeley, School of Law; Immigration Law Clinic; University of California, Davis, School of Law. March 2010.

Jacobson, Robin Dale. *The new nativism: Proposition 187 and the debate over immigration*. Minneapolis: University of Minnesota Press, 2008.

Jeffries, John C., Jr. *Justice Lewis F. Powell, Jr.* New York: Scribner's, 1994.

Johnson, Alex M., Jr. "Bid whist, tonk, and *United States v. Fordice*: Why integrationism fails African-Americans again." *California Law Review* 81 (1993).

Johnson, Kevin R. "The Antiterrorism Act, the Immigration Reform Act and ideological regulation in the immigration laws: Important lessons for citizens and noncitizens." *St. Mary's Law Journal* 28 (1997).

———. "Civil rights and immigration: Challenges for the Latino community in the twenty-first century." *La Raza Law Journal* 8 (1995).

———. "An essay on immigration politics, popular democracy, and California's Proposition 187: The political relevance and legal irrelevance of race." *Washington Law Review* 70 (1995).

———. *The "huddled masses" myth: Immigration and civil rights.* Philadelphia: Temple University Press, 2004.

———. "Hurricane Katrina: Lessons about immigrants in the administrative state." *Houston Law Review* 45 (2008).

———. "It's the economy, stupid: The hijacking of the debate over immigration reform by monsters, ghosts, and goblins (or the war on drugs, war on terror, narcoterrorists, etc.)." *Chapman Law Review* 13 (2010).

———. *Opening the floodgates: Why America needs to rethink its borders and immigration laws.* New York: NYU Press, 2007.

———. "Public benefits and immigration: The intersection of immigration status, ethnicity, gender, and class." *UCLA Law Review* 42 (1995).

———. "September 11 and Mexican immigrants: Collateral damage comes home." *DePaul Law Review* 52 (2003).

Johnson, Kevin R., Raquel Aldana, Bill Ong Hing, Leticia Saucedo, and Enid F. Trucios-Haynes. "Federalism and alienage law." In *Understanding immigration law.* LexisNexis, 2009.

Johnson, Mark. "N.C. community college board votes to allow illegal immigrants." *Charlotte Observer*, March 19, 2010. Available at http://www.charlotteobserver.com/2010/03/19/1324052/nc-community-college-board-votes.html.

Jones, Maggie. "Coming out illegal." *New York Times Magazine*, October 24, 2010, MM36–39.

Jordan, Miriam. "Illegal at Princeton." *Wall Street Journal*, April 15, 2006, A1.

———. "Mortgage prospects dim for illegal immigrants." *Wall Street Journal*, October 22, 2008, A3.

———. "Princeton's 2006 salutatorian heads to Oxford, still an illegal immigrant." *Wall Street Journal*, September 14, 2006, B1.

———. "A route to citizenship in defense bill: Legislation offers illegal residents chance to become Americans through military service or college; Foes call it amnesty." *Wall Street Journal*, September 18, 2010, A5.

Kane, Paul, and Shailagh Murray. "Democrats confused about road forward." *Washington Post*, January 29, 2010, A1.

Kasarda, Ralph W. "Affirmative action gone haywire: Why state laws granting college tuition preferences to illegal aliens are preempted by federal law." *BYU Education and Law Journal* 2 (2009).

Kauffman, Albert H. "Judge William Wayne Justice: A life of human dignity and refractory mules." *St. Mary's Law Journal* 41 (2009).

Kaushal, Neeraj. "In-state tuition for the undocumented: Education effects on Mexican young adults." *Journal of Policy Analysis and Management* 27 (2008).

Kellar, William H. *Make haste slowly: Moderates, conservatives, and school desegregation in Houston.* College Station: Texas A&M University Press, 1999.

Kemerer, Frank R. *William Wayne Justice: A judicial biography.* Austin: University of Texas Press, 1991.

Khatcheressian, Laura. "FERPA and the Immigration and Naturalization Service: A guide for university counsel on federal rules for collecting, maintaining and releasing information about foreign students." *Journal of College and University Law* 29 (2003).

Kidder, William C. "The struggle for access from *Sweatt* to *Grutter*: A history of African American, Latino, and American Indian law school admissions, 1950–2000." *Harvard BlackLetter Law Journal* 19 (2003).

Kiefer, Michael. "Maricopa court upholds migrant smuggling law: Those caught can be charged in conspiracy." *Arizona Republic*, June 10, 2006, 1B.

Kim, Keun Dong. "Current developments in the legislative branch: Comprehensive immigration reform nixed." *Georgetown Immigration Law Journal* 21 (2007).

Kinzie, Susan. "The university of uncertainty: Va. children of illegal immigrants lack in-state status." *Washington Post*, March 14, 2008, B1.

———. "U-VA accepts residency claim." *Washington Post*, March 24, 2008, B5.

Kobach, Kris W. "The quintessential force multiplier: The inherent authority of local police to make immigration arrests." *Albany Law Review* 69 (2005).

———. "Immigration, amnesty, and the rule of law." *Hofstra Law Review* 36 (2008).

———. "Immigration nullification: In-state tuition and lawmakers who disregard the law." *New York University Journal of Legislation and Public Policy* 10 (2006–2007).

———. *The Senate immigration bill: A national security nightmare.* WebMemo #1513. Washington, DC: Heritage Foundation, 2007. Available at http://www.heritage.org/Research/Reports/2007/06/The-Senate-Immigration-Bill-A-National-Security-Nightmare.

———. *The Senate immigration bill rewards lawbreaking: Why the DREAM Act is a nightmare.* Backgrounder #1960. Washington, DC: Heritage Foundation, 2006. Available at www.heritage.org/Research/Reports/2006/08/The-Senate-Immigration-Bill-Rewards-Lawbreaking-Why-the-DREAM-Act-Is-a-Nightmare.

Koger, Gregory. "Making change: A six-month review." *Forum*, July 2009. Available at http://www.bepress.com/forum/vol7/iss3/art8.

Koh, Harold H. "Equality with a human face: Justice Blackmun and the equal protection of aliens." *Hamline Law Review* 8 (1985).

Konet, Dawn. *Unauthorized youths and higher education: The ongoing debate.* Washington, DC: Migration Policy Institute, 2007.

Korosec, Thomas. "Leasing rule sent to voters for OK: Councilman says Farmers Branch may set precedent on illegal residents." *Houston Chronicle*, January 23, 2007, B1.

Kovach, Gretel C. "Dallas suburb amends its ban on renting to illegal immigrants." *New York Times*, January 25, 2007, A22.

Krehbiel, Randy. "Hispanics decry House bill." *Tulsa World*, March 16, 2010, A9.

———. "Tulsa Hispanic leaders oppose school bill." *Tulsa World*, March 15, 2010. Available at http://www.tulsaworld.com/news/article.aspx?subjectid=19&articl eid=20100315_12_0_Abillp998569.

Krueger, Carl. *In-state tuition for undocumented immigrants*. Denver: Education Commission of the States, 2005.

Krutchik, Laurence M. Comment. "Down but not out: A comparison of previous attempts at immigration reform and the resulting implemented changes." *Nova Law Review* 32 (2008).

KTBC television station. "Email warns of illegal immigration crackdowns in classrooms." Texas Civil Rights Project Newsclip. April 4, 2006. Available at http://www.texascivil-rightsproject.org/newspub/clip_060426_email_warns.html.

Kurland, Phillip B., and Dennis J. Hutchinson. "The business of the Supreme Court, [October term] 1982." *University of Chicago Law Review* 50 (1983).

Kwong, Jessica. "Student freed as Feinstein steps in." *San Francisco Chronicle*, November 20, 2010, C1.

"Law lowers tuition for immigrants." *Albany Times Union*, August 10, 2002, B4.

Legomsky, Stephen H. "Fear and loathing in Congress and the courts: Immigration and judicial review." *Texas Law Review* 78 (2000).

———. "Immigration, federalism, and the welfare state." *UCLA Law Review* 42 (1995).

———. "Immigration law and the principle of plenary congressional power." *Supreme Court Review*, 1984.

Legomsky, Stephen H., and Cristina M. Rodriguez. *Immigration and refugee law and policy*. 5th ed. New York: Foundation, 2009.

Lelyveld, Joseph. "The border dividing Arizona." *New York Times Magazine*, October 15, 2006, 40.

Lewin, Tamar. "A crown jewel of education struggles with cuts in California." *New York Times*, November 20, 2009, A1.

Lewin, Tamar, and Rebecca Cathcart. "Students protest decision to raise tuition in California." *New York Times*, November 20, 2009, A25.

Lewis, Raphael. "In-state tuition not a draw for many immigrants." *Boston Globe*, November 9, 2005, A1.

Libman, Gary. "Losing out on a dream?" *Los Angeles Times*, January 23, 1992, E3.

Lindsay, Matthew J. "Immigration as invasion: Sovereignty, security, and the origins of the federal immigration power." *Harvard Civil Rights–Civil Liberties Law Review* 45 (2010).

Lipman, Francine J. "Bearing witness to economic injustices of undocumented immigrant families: A new class of 'undeserving poor.'" *Nevada Law Journal* 7 (2007).

———. "Saving Private Ryan's tax refund: Poverty relief for all working poor military families." *ABA Section of Taxation News Quarterly* 9 (Winter 2010).

———. "The taxation of undocumented immigrants: Separate, unequal, and without representation." *Harvard Latino Law Review* 9 (2006).

Lizza, Ryan. "Return of the nativist." *New Yorker*, December 17, 2007, 46.

Long, Jeff. "'Bully' contract leads to apology: District 26 denies Spanish speakers were targeted." *Chicago Tribune*, December 13, 2006, Metro-1.

López, María Pabón. "More than a license to drive: State restrictions on the use of driver's licenses." *Southern Illinois University Law Journal* 29 (2004).

————. "Reflections on educating Latino and Latina undocumented children: Beyond *Plyler v. Doe.*" *Seton Hall Law Review* 35 (2005).

López, María Pabón, and Gerardo R. López. *Persistent inequality: Contemporary realities in the education of undocumented Latina/o students.* New York: Routledge, 2010.

Lu, Meng. "Not part of the family: U.S. immigration policy and foreign students." *Thurgood Marshall Law Review* 34 (2009).

Ludwig, Melissa. "DREAM Act hunger strike spreads in Texas." *San Antonio Express-News*, November 24, 2010, B8. Available at http://www.mysanantonio.com/news/dream_act_hunger_strike_spreads_110273704.html?showFullArticle=y.

————. "15 DREAM Act demonstrators arrested." *San Antonio Express-News*, November 30, 2010, A1. Available at http://www.mysanantonio.com/news/police_respond_to_dream_act_rally_111008674.html?showFullArticle=y.

Luna, Guadalupe. "En el nombre de Dios todo-poderoso: The Treaty of Guadalupe Hidalgo and narrativos legales." *Southwestern Journal of Law and Trade in the Americas* 5 (1998).

————. "On the complexities of race: The Treaty of Guadalupe Hidalgo and *Dred Scott v. Sandford.*" *University of Miami Law Review* 53 (1999).

Luo, Michael. "McCain says immigration reform should be top priority." *The Caucus* (blog), *New York Times*, May 22, 2008. Available at http://thecaucus.blogs.nytimes.com/2008/05/22/mccain-says-immigration-reform-should-be-top-priority/.

————. "Romney's words testify to threat from Huckabee." *New York Times*, December 2, 2007, YT-29.

Mailman, Stanley, and Stephen Yale-Loehr. "College for undocumented immigrants after all?" *New York Law Journal*, June 25, 2001, 3.

Mangan, Katherine. "Illegal voices: 4 undocumented students describe uncertain futures." *Chronicle of Higher Education*, September 24, 2010, B17–19. Available at http://chronicle.com/article/Illegal-Voices-Undocumented/124441.

————. "Most colleges knowingly admit illegal immigrants as students, survey finds." *Chronicle of Higher Education*, March 17, 2009. Available at http://chronicle.com/news/index.php?id=6139&utm_source=pm&utm_medium=en.

Mann, Anastasia R. *Garden State dreams: In-state tuition for undocumented kids.* Trenton: New Jersey Policy Perspective, 2010. Available at http://www.njpp.org/assets/reports/budget-fiscal/2-rpt_tuition.pdf.

Marcum, Diana. "He's the Cal State Fresno student body president—and an illegal immigrant." *Los Angeles Times*, November 18, 2010. Available at http://www.latimes.com/news/local/la-me-1118-illegal-immigrant-presiden20101118,0,5635027.story.

————. "Standing up for a dream." *Los Angeles Times*, November 28, 2010, A1. Available at http://www.latimes.com/news/local/la-me-dream-act-20101128,0,5057601.story.

Marcus, Ruth. "Immigration's scrambled politics." *Washington Post*, April 4, 2006, A23.

Marklein, Mary Beth. "Illegal immigrants face threat of no college." *USA Today*, July 7, 2008, A1.

Márquez, Benjamin. *LULAC: The evolution of a Mexican American organization.* Austin: University of Texas Press, 1993.

Márquez, Benjamin, and John F. Witte. "Immigration reform: Strategies for legislative action." *Forum* 7 (2009). Available at http://www.bepress.com/cgi/viewcontent.cgi?article=1324&context=forum.

Martinez, George A. "The legal construction of race: Mexican-Americans and whiteness." *Harvard Latino Law Review* 2 (1997).

———. "Legal indeterminacy, judicial discretion, and the Mexican American litigation experience: 1930–1980." *U.C. Davis Law Review* 27 (1994).

Martínez, Sandra Baltazar. "Arizona teen pursues education in friendlier state." *Santa Fe New Mexican*, September 7, 2010. Available at http://www.santafenewmexican.com/PrintStory/Illegal-immigration—Arizona-teen-pursues-college-dream-in-frie.

Mastony, Colleen, and Diane Redo. "Barred teen pleased as lawsuit is dropped: Elmwood Park district reluctantly ends fight." *Chicago Tribune*, February 28, 2006, Metro-1.

———. "Elmwood Park schools give in: To keep state funds, district drops fight on immigrant student." *Chicago Tribune*, February 25, 2006, News-1.

Maynard, Rebecca A., and Daniel J. McGrath. "Family structure, fertility and child welfare." In *The social benefits of education*, ed. Jere R. Behrman and Nevzer Stacey. Ann Arbor: University of Michigan Press, 1997.

McCarty First, Joan. *New voices: Immigrant students in U.S. public schools.* Boston: National Coalition of Advocates for Students, 1988.

McCormick, Elizabeth. "The Oklahoma Taxpayer and Citizen Protection Act: Blowing off steam or setting wildfires?" *Georgetown Immigration Law Journal* 23 (2009).

McDonnell, Patrick J. "Davis won't appeal Prop. 187 ruling, ending court battles." *Los Angeles Times*, July 29, 1999, A1.

———. "Prop. 187 talks offered Davis few choices." *Los Angeles Times*, July 30, 1999, A3.

McKanders, Karla Mari. "The constitutionality of state and local laws targeting immigrants." *University of Arkansas at Little Rock Law Review* 31 (2009).

———. "Welcome to Hazleton! 'Illegal' immigrants beware: Local immigration ordinances and what the federal government must do about it." *Loyola University Chicago Law Journal* 39 (2007).

McKay, Dan. "Sanctuary policy change delayed." *Albuquerque Journal*, December 17, 2009, A1.

McKinley, James C., Jr. "Governor's race exposes Republican rift in Texas." *New York Times*, August 15, 2009, A11.

———. "A Texas senator, now a challenger lagging in polls." *New York Times*, February 21, 2010, A14.

McNutt, Michael. "Bill seeks non-U.S. students' details." *Oklahoman*, February 25, 2010, A3.

Melear, Kerry Brian. "The contractual relationship between student and institution: Discipline, academic, and consumer contexts." *Journal of College and University Law* 30 (2003).

———. "Undocumented immigrant access to public higher education: The Virginia response." *Education Law Reporter* 194 (2005).

Melendez, Mel. "Doors finally open for 4 Phoenix migrant youths a year after beating MIT in robotics competition." *Arizona Republic*, April 23, 2005, 1A

Menjívar, Cecilia. "Liminal legality: Salvadoran and Guatemalan immigrants' lives in the United States." *American Journal of Sociology* 111 (2006).

Meola, Olympia. "Colleges' admittance of illegals opposed: Bill would end practice at some Va. schools of allowing undocumented immigrants." *Richmond Times-Dispatch*, January 18, 2008, A1.

Mexican American Legal Defense and Education Fund (MALDEF). "Providing access to a quality education." Available at http://www.maldef.org/education/litigation/index.html (accessed March 15, 2010).

Miller, Amy. "APS safe for migrant students." *Albuquerque Journal*, June 2, 2006, A1.

———. "Migrants are safe at APS." *Albuquerque Journal*, June 15, 2006, C1.

Miller, Kristen, and Celina Moreno. Martinez v. Regents: *Mis-step or wave of the future?* IHELG Monograph 08-07. Houston: Institute of Higher Education Law and Governance, University of Houston Law Center, 2008. Available at http://www.law.uh.edu/ihelg/monograph/08-07.pdf.

Missouri Department of Elementary and Secondary Education. "Guidelines regarding the use of Social Security numbers and the attendance at school of undocumented students." Available at http://www.dese.mo.gov/schoollaw/freqaskques/undocumented-students.htm (accessed Apr. 24, 2011).

Moltz, David. "Big win for undocumented students." *Inside Higher Ed*, November 16, 2010. Available at http://www.insidehighered.com/news/2010/11/16/california.

Montejano, David. *Anglos and Mexicans in the making of Texas, 1836–1986*. Austin: University of Texas Press, 1987.

Montgomery, David. "No turning back: Rep. Luis Gutierrez is making immigration reform a personal cause." *Washington Post*, May 8, 2009, C1.

Montini, E. J. "Dream Act kids facing a political nightmare." *Arizona Republic*, November 24, 2010, B1. Available at http://www.azcentral.com/phpbin/clicktrack/email.php/9542002.

Montoya, Margaret E. "A brief history of Chicana/o school segregation: One rationale for affirmative action." *Berkeley La Raza Law Journal* 12 (2001).

Moon, Chris. "Immigrant tuition vote typifies fragile statehouse ties." *Topeka Capital-Journal*, February 17, 2006, A1.

Morgan, Richard. "Ole Miss student faces deportation for revealing illegal status: Family secret threatens daughter." *Memphis Commercial Appeal*, September 16, 2010. Available at http://www.commercialappeal.com/news/2010/sep/16/family-secret-threatens-daughter/.

Motomura, Hiroshi. "Immigration and alienage, federalism and Proposition 187." *Virginia Journal of International Law* 35 (1994).

———. "Immigration law after a century of plenary power: Phantom constitutional norms and statutory interpretation." *Yale Law Journal* 100 (1990).

———. "Immigration outside the law." *Columbia Law Review* 108 (2008).

Muller, Thomas. *Immigrants and the American city*. New York: NYU Press, 1993.

National Academies. *Policy implications of international graduate students and postdoctoral scholars in the United States*. Washington, DC: National Academies Press, 2005.

National Conference of State Legislatures. "Enacted Social Security numbers legislation—2010 session." Available at http://www.ncsl.org/default.aspx?tabid=20634 (accessed April 24, 2011).

———. "Immigration reform—official policy." Available at http://www.ncsl.org/default.aspx?tabid=18094 (accessed March 17, 2010).

———. "State laws related to immigrants and immigration." July 17, 2009. Available at http://www.ncsl.org/default.aspx?tabid=18030.

———. "2010 Immigration-Related Laws and Resolutions in the States (January 1–December 31, 2010)." January 5, 2011. Available at http://www.ncsl.org/default. aspx?tabid=21857 (accessed May 6, 2011).

National Education Association, Office of General Counsel. *Immigration status and the right to a free public education.* Washington, DC: National Education Association, 2008. Available at http://www.nea.org/assets/img/pubToday/0801/ImmigrationStatusand-Rights.pdf.

National Immigration Law Center. "Basic facts about in-state tuition for undocumented immigrant students." Los Angeles: National Immigration Law Center, 2006.

———. "DREAM Act." Available at http://www.nilc.org/immlawpolicy/DREAM/index. htm (accessed Apr. 24, 2011).

———. *DREAM Act: Basic information.* Los Angeles: National Immigration Law Center, 2005. Available at http://www.nilc.org/immlawpolicy/DREAM/dream_basic_info_0406.pdf.

National School Board Association and National Education Association. *Legal issues for school districts related to the education of undocumented children.* Washington, DC: National School Board Association, 2009.

Nelson, Libby. "Undocumented college students could become citizens faster under new House proposal." *Chronicle of Higher Education*, December 15, 2009. Available at http://chronicle.com/article/Undocumented-College-Students/49496.

Neuman, Gerald L. "Aliens as outlaws: Government services, Proposition 187, and the structure of equal protection doctrine." *UCLA Law Review* 42 (1995).

———. "Jurisdiction and the rule of law after the 1996 Immigration Act." *Harvard Law Review* 113 (2000).

———. "The lost century of American immigration law (1776–1875)." *Columbia Law Review* 93 (1993).

———. "*Wong Wing v. United States*: The Bill of Rights protects illegal aliens." In *Immigration Stories*, ed. David A. Martin and Peter Schuck. New York: Foundation, 2005.

Newton, Jim. "Brennan dishes on his colleagues." *Slate*, January 11, 2007.

Ngai, Mae M. *Impossible subjects: Illegal aliens and the making of modern America.* Princeton: Princeton University Press, 2004.

———. "The strange career of the illegal alien: Immigration restriction and deportation policy in the United States, 1924–1965." *Law and History Review* 21 (2003).

Nicholas, Peter. "Immigration plan offered to Obama." *Los Angeles Times*, March 12, 2010, AA1.

Nienhusser, H. Kenny, and Kevin J. Dougherty. *Implementation of college in-state tuition for undocumented immigrants in New York.* Albany: SUNY, New York Latino Research and Resources Network, spring 2010.

Nolan, Jim. "Va. Senate backs bill to restrict tuition benefits for illegal immigrants." *Richmond Times-Dispatch*, January 27, 2009, A4.

———. "What's happening at the legislature?" *Richmond Times-Dispatch*, January 28, 2009, A6.

Northwestern Journal of Law and Social Policy 3, no. 2 (2008). Special *Plyler v. Doe* issue. Available at http://www.law.northwestern.edu/journals/njlsp/v3/n2/.

Núñez, Claudia. "California border schools to ask students for papers." *New America Media*, August 27, 2010. Available at http://newamericamedia.org/2010/08/california-border-schools-to-ask-students-for-papers.php.

Núñez, D. Carolina. "Fractured membership: Deconstructing territoriality to secure rights and remedies for the undocumented worker." *Wisconsin Law Review,* 2010.

Oboler, Suzanne. *Ethnic labels, Latino lives.* Minneapolis: University of Minnesota Press, 1995.

———. "The politics of labeling: Latino/a cultural identities of self and others." *Latin American Perspectives* 75 (1992).

Olivas, Michael A. "The chronicles, my grandfather's stories, and immigration law: The slave traders chronicle as racial history." *St. Louis University Law Journal* 34 (1990).

———, ed. *"Colored men" and "hombres aqui": Hernandez v. Texas and the emergence of Mexican-American lawyering.* Houston: Arte Público, 2006.

———. "IIRIRA, the DREAM Act, and undocumented college student residency." *Journal of College and University Law* 30 (2004).

———. "Immigration-related state statutes and local ordinances: Preemption, prejudice, and the proper role for enforcement." *University of Chicago Legal Forum,* 2007.

———. "In memoriam: Joe Vail," *Bender's Immigration Bulletin* 13 (2008).

———, ed. *Latino college students.* New York: Teachers College Press, 1986.

———. "Lawmakers gone wild? College residency and the response to Professor Kobach." *SMU Law Review* 61 (2008).

———. "A legislative history of the Ohio Board of Regents." *Capital University Law Review* 19 (1990).

———. Letter to the Georgia Board of Regents. April 4, 2007. Available at http://www.law.uh.edu/ihelg/documents/MAOtoGeorgia17April2007.pdf.

———. "*Plyler v. Doe, Toll v. Moreno,* and postsecondary admissions: Undocumented adults and 'enduring disability.'" *Journal of Law and Education* 15 (1986).

———. "The political economy of the DREAM Act and the legislative process: A case study of comprehensive immigration reform." *Wayne Law Review* 55 (2010).

———. "The political economy of immigration, intellectual property, and racial harassment: Case studies of the implementation of legal change on campus." *Journal of Higher Education* 63 (1992).

———. "Preempting preemption: Foreign affairs, state rights, and alienage classifications." *Virginia Journal of International Law* 35 (1994).

———. "A rebuttal to FAIR." *University Business,* June 2002, 72.

———. "A reply to Chavez." *Reconstruction* 2 (1993).

———. "The story of *Plyler v. Doe,* the education of undocumented children, and the polity." In *Immigration Stories,* ed. David Martin and Peter Schuck. New York: Foundation, 2005.

———. "Storytelling out of school: Undocumented college residency, race, and reaction." *Hastings Constitutional Law Quarterly* 22 (1995).

———. "Torching Zozobra: The problem with Linda Chavez." *Reconstruction* 2 (1993).

———. "The 'trial of the century' that never was: Staff Sgt. Macario Garcia, the Congressional Medal of Honor, and the Oasis Café." *Indiana Law Journal* 83 (2008).

———. "Undocumented college students, taxation, and financial aid: A technical note." *Review of Higher Education* 32 (2009).

———. "What the 'war on terror' has meant for U.S. colleges and universities." In *Doctoral Education and the Faculty of the Future,* ed. Ronald G. Ehrenberg and Charlotte V. Kuh. Ithaca: Cornell University Press, 2009.

Olsen, Laurie. *Crossing the schoolhouse border: Immigrant students and the California public schools.* San Francisco: California Tomorrow, 1988.

Ontiveros, Maria L. "To help those most in need: Undocumented workers' rights and remedies under Title VII." *New York University Review of Law and Social Change* 20 (1993–1994).

Ontiveros, Maria L., and Joshua R. Drexler. "The Thirteenth Amendment and access to education for children of undocumented workers: A new look at *Plyler v. Doe.*" *University of San Francisco Law Review* 42 (2008).

Oosting, Jonathan. "U.S. immigration agents accused of 'stalking' parents dropping off kids at Detroit school." MLive.com, April 7, 2011. Available at http://www.mlive.com/news/detroit/index.ssf/2011/04/federal_immigration_agents_acc.html.

Orellana, Roxana. "DREAM Act supporter jailed for refusing to leave federal building." *Salt Lake Tribune*, December 1, 2010, A1.

Orozco, Cynthia E. *No Mexicans, women, or dogs allowed: The rise of the Mexican American civil rights movement.* Austin: University of Texas Press, 2009.

———. "Rodriguez v. San Antonio ISD." *Handbook of Texas Online.* Available at http://www.tshaonline.org/handbook/online/articles/jrrht (accessed August 30, 2009).

Pacific Legal Foundation. "PLF and American Civil Rights Foundation file two lawsuits against Los Angeles Unified School District for violating Prop. 209." Available at http://www.pacificlegal.org/page.aspx?pid=272 (accessed Apr. 24, 2011).

Palomo, Juan R. "Judge Seals calls Spanish comment 'senseless, dreadful.'" *Houston Post*, March 7, 1980, 3B.

Pantoja, Antonia. *The making of a Nuyorican: A memoir.* Houston: Arte Público, 2002.

Parker, Phil, and Mark Oswald. "Annual event not Shuster's idea, foundation says." *Albuquerque Journal*, August 27, 2009, A1.

Passel, Jeffrey S. *Unauthorized migrants: Numbers and characteristics; Background briefing prepared for Task Force on Immigration and America's Future.* Washington, DC: Pew Hispanic Center, 2005.

Passel, Jeffrey S., and D'Vera Cohn. *A portrait of unauthorized immigrants in the United States.* Washington, DC: Pew Hispanic Center, 2009.

Pear, Robert, and David M. Herszenhorn. "House approves health overhaul, sending landmark bill to Obama." *New York Times*, March 22, 2010, A1.

Pendergraph, Jim. Letter to Thomas J. Ziko. July 28, 2008. Available at http://www.nacua.org/documents/AdmissionUndocAlien072008.pdf.

Perea, Juan F. "A brief history of race and the U.S.-Mexican border: Tracing the trajectories of conquest." *UCLA Law Review* 51 (2003).

———. "*Buscando* America: Why integration and equal protection fail to protect Latinos." *Harvard Law Review* 117 (2004).

Perez Huber, Lindsay, Corina Benavides Lopez, Maria C. Malagon, Veronica Vélez, and Daniel G. Solórzano. "Getting beyond the 'symptom,' acknowledging the 'disease': Theorizing racist nativism." *Contemporary Justice Review* 11 (2008).

Perrefort, Dirk. "Filibuster blocks tuition bill: Proposal would have allowed illegal immigrants to pay in-state rates to Connecticut schools." *Danbury News-Times*, March 16, 2007, A1.

Pew Hispanic Center. "Statistical portrait of the foreign-born population in the United States, 2007." Washington DC: Pew Hispanic Center, March 2009. Available at http://pewhispanic.org/factsheets/factsheet.php?FactsheetID=45.

Pham, Huyen. "The constitutional right not to cooperate? Local sovereignty and the federal immigration power." *University of Cincinnati Law Review* 74 (2006).

Pizarro, Marcos. *Chicanas and Chicanos in school: Racial profiling, identity battles, and empowerment.* Austin: University of Texas Press, 2005.

Poulin, Jeffrey N. "Current developments in the legislative branch: The piecemeal approach falls short of achieving the DREAM of immigration reform." *Georgetown Immigration Law Journal* 22 (2008).

Preston, Julia. "Administration spares students in deportations." *New York Times*, August 9, 2010, A1.

———. "After false dawn, anxiety for students who are illegal immigrants." *New York Times*, February 9, 2011, A15.

———. "Bill for immigrant students fails test vote in Senate." *New York Times*, October 25, 2007, A1.

———. "Congress quarrels on covering immigrants." *New York Times*, November 4, 2009, A1.

———. "Democrats reach out to Hispanics on immigration bill." *New York Times*, September 17, 2010, A15.

———. "Illegal immigrant students publicly take up a cause." *New York Times*, December 11, 2009, A25.

———. "Illegal worker, troubled citizen and stolen name." *New York Times*, March 22, 2007, A1.

———. "In shadow of health care vote, immigrant advocates keep pushing for change." *New York Times*, March 21, 2010, A12.

———. "Latinos and Democrats press Obama to curb deportations." *New York Times*, April 21, 2011, A18.

———. "Measure on legal status for immigrant students blocked." *New York Times*, September 28, 2007, A1.

———. "Measure would offer legal status to illegal immigrant students." *New York Times*, September 20, 2007, A1.

———. "Obama links immigration overhaul in 2010 to G.O.P. backing." *New York Times*, March 12, 2010, A12.

———. "A professor fights illegal immigration one court at a time." *New York Times*, July 21, 2009, A10.

———. "Students spell out messages on their immigration frustration." *New York Times*, September 21, 2010, A14.

———. "To overhaul immigration, advocates alter tactics." *New York Times*, January 2, 2010, A11.

———. "2 senators offer immigration overhaul." *New York Times*, March 19, 2010, A11.

———. "U.S. military will offer path to citizenship." *New York Times*, February 15, 2009, A1.

———. "White House plan on immigration includes legal status." *New York Times*, November 14, 2009, A10.

Pruitt, Lisa R. "Latina/os, locality, and law in the rural South." *Harvard Latino Law Review* 12 (2009).

Rabin, Nina, Mary Carol Combs, and Norma Gonzalez. "Understanding *Plyler*'s legacy: Voices from border schools." *Journal of Law and Education* 37 (2008).

Radcliffe, Jennifer. "1982 ruling a catalyst in immigration debate." *Houston Chronicle*, May 21, 2006, B1.

Ramakrishnan, S. Karthick, and Tom (Tak) Wong. *Immigration policies go local: The varying responses of local governments to undocumented immigration*. Berkeley, CA: Warren Institute on Race, Ethnicity, and Diversity, 2007. Available at http://www.law.berkeley.edu/centers/ewi/Ramakrishnan&Wongpaperfinal.pdf.

Ramirez, Eddy. "The crash course in citizenship." *U.S. News and World Report*, August 18, 2008, 46.

Ramos, Henry A. J. *The American GI Forum: In pursuit of the dream, 1948–1983*. Houston: Arte Público, 1998.

Rangel Jorge C., and Carlos M. Alcala, "De jure segregation of Chicanos in Texas schools." *Harvard Civil Rights–Civil Liberties Law Review* 7 (1972).

Raymond, Virginia. "Snid, Alberta Zepeda." *Handbook of Texas Online*. Available at http://www.tshaonline.org/handbook/online/articles/fsn12 (accessed August 30, 2009).

Redden, Elizabeth. "DREAM Act vote on tap." *Inside Higher Ed*, October 24, 2007. Available at http://insidehighered.com/news/2007/10/24/dream.

———. "Data on the undocumented." *Inside Higher Ed*, March 17, 2009. Available at http://www.insidehighered.com/news/2009/03/17/undocumented.

———. "For the undocumented: To admit or not to admit." *Inside Higher Ed*, August 18, 2008. Available at http://www.insidehighered.com/news/2008/08/18/immigrants.

———. "A message to prospective undocumented students." *Inside Higher Ed*, October 16, 2008. Available at http://www.insidehighered.com/news/2008/10/16/vassar.

Reich, Gary, and Alvar Ayala Mendoza. "'Educating kids' versus 'coddling criminals': Framing the debate over in-state tuition for undocumented students in Kansas." *State Politics and Policy Quarterly* 8 (2008).

Reich, Peter L. "Environmental metaphor in the alien benefits debate." *UCLA Law Review* 42 (1995).

Reid, Harry. "Issues: immigration." Harry Reid's Senate website. Available at http://reid.senate.gov/issues/immigration.cfm (accessed Apr. 24, 2011).

———. "Reid remarks at NALEO National Conference." Press release. June 26, 2008. Available at http://reid.senate.gov/newsroom/pr_070308_NALEO.cfm.

———. "Remarks at the Netroots Nation Conference in Las Vegas." July 24, 2010. Available at http://www.youtube.com/watch?v=8eoQXsh24Ac.

Reid, Leslie Williams, Harold E. Weiss, Robert M. Adelman, and Charles Jaret. "The immigration crime relationship: Evidence across U.S. metro areas." *Social Science Research* 34 (2005).

Rein, Lisa. "[Maryland] House heats up over bill to give illegal immigrants in-state tuition." *Washington Post*, March 28, 2007, B2.

Republican Party Platform of 1996. *American Presidency Project*. Available at http://www.presidency.ucsb.edu/ws/index.php?pid=25848.

Reyes, Augustina H. "Does money make a difference for Hispanic students in urban schools?" *Education and Urban Society* 36 (2003).

———. "The right to an education for homeless students: The children of Katrina." In *Children, law, and disasters: What have we learned from the hurricanes of 2005?*, ed. Laura Oren, Ellen Marrus, and H. Davidson. Washington, DC, and Houston: American Bar Association and the Center for Children, Law and Policy, 2009.

Reyes, Luis O. "The ASPIRA consent decree: A thirtieth-anniversary retrospective of bilingual education in New York City." *Harvard Education Review* 76 (Fall 2006).

Ricard, Martin. "Students stage mock graduation to advocate for undocumented." *Washington Post*, June 24, 2009, B2.

Rich, Eric. "Immigration enforcement's shift in the workplace: Case of Md. restaurateurs reflects use of criminal investigations, rather than fines, against employers," *Washington Post*, April 16, 2006, C6.

Ricke, Jesse. "Student organization rallies for DREAM Act in Times Square." *Brooklyn Progressive Examiner*, November 29, 2010. Available at http://www.examiner.com/ progressive-in-new-york/student-organization-rallies-for-dream-act-times-square.

Rivera, Carla. "Budget cuts hit broad swath of Cal State." *Los Angeles Times*, November 29, 2009, A1.

Roberts, Michelle. "District gives pop quiz on residency." *Virginian-Pilot*, September 22, 2009, A3.

———. "Superintendent tells Mexican residents attending U.S. schools: Prove Texas residency or leave." *Chicago Tribune*, September 21, 2009. Available at http://abcnews. go.com/US/wirestory?id=8637664&page=3.

Robison, Clay. "Budget hits include judges' pay hike." *Houston Chronicle*, June 18, 2001, 1A.

Robison, Clay, and R. G. Ratcliffe. "Perry to stick by law giving tuition breaks to illegal immigrants: He also predicts legislation against repeat predators of children will be strengthened." *Houston Chronicle*, January 12, 2007, B4.

Rodriguez, Juan Carlos. "Family came to N.M. to escape immigration law." *Albuquerque Journal*, August 30, 2010, A1.

Rodriguez, Marc S. "A movement made of 'young Mexican Americans seeking change': Critical citizenship, migration and the Chicano movement in Texas and Wisconsin, 1960–1975." *Western Historical Quarterly* 34 (2003).

Rogin, Josh. "McCain and Graham lash out at Levin over defense bill." *The Cable* (blog), *Foreign Policy*, September 14, 2010. Available at http://thecable.foreignpolicy.com/ posts/2010/09/14/mccain_and_graham_lash_out_at_levin_over_defense_bill.

Romero, Mary. "'Go after the women': Mothers against Illegal Aliens' campaign against Mexican immigrant women and their children." *Indiana Law Journal* 83 (2008).

Romero, Victor C. "Noncitizen students and immigration policy post-9/11." *Georgetown Immigration Law Journal* 17 (2003).

———. "Postsecondary school education benefits for undocumented immigrants: Promises and pitfalls." *North Carolina Journal of International Law and Commercial Regulation* 27 (2002).

Romo, Ricardo. "Southern California and the origins of Latino civil rights activism." *Western Legal History* 3 (1990).

Roos, Peter D. *Postsecondary Plyler.* Monograph 91-7. Houston: Institute of Higher Education Law and Governance, University of Houston Law Center, 1991. Available at http:// www.law.uh.edu/ihelg/monograph/91-7.pdf.

Ross, Timberly. "Nebraska judge tosses illegal immigrant tuition suit." CNSNews. com, December 17, 2010. Available at http://www.cnsnews.com/news/article/ nebraska-judge-tosses-illegal-immigrant.

Rossi, Rosalind. "Schools slammed for barring child." *Chicago Sun-Times*, February 24, 2006, A8.

Rothstein, Mark A. *Health insurance reforms: Unintended consequences.* Hastings Center Bioethics Forum, forthcoming 2010. Available at http://ssrn.com/abstract=1551397.

Rubin, Daniel. "More courage from a dreamer on immigration." *Philadelphia Inquirer,* April 11, 2011, B1.

Ruelas, Richard. "Dream Act students risk deportation to win support." *Arizona Republic,* November 16, 2010, D1. Available at http://www.azcentral.com/php-bin/clicktrack/email.php/9541290.

———. "The hard way home." *Arizona Republic,* August 31, 2010, D1. Available at http://www.azcentral.com/php-bin/clicktrack/email.php/9541294.

Ruiz, Vicki L. "'We always tell our children they are Americans': *Mendez v. Westminster* and the California road to *Brown v. Board of Education.*" *College Board Review* 200 (Fall 2003).

Ruiz-de-Velasco, Jorge, Michael E. Fix, and Beatriz Chu Clewell. *Overlooked and underserved: Immigrant students in U.S. secondary schools.* Washington, DC: Urban Institute, 2000. Available at http://www.urban.org/publications/310022.html.

Rumbaut, Rubén G., and Walter A. Ewing. *The myth of immigrant criminality and the paradox of assimilation: Incarceration rates among native and foreign-born men.* Washington, DC: Immigration Policy Center, 2007.

Sacchetti, Maria. "Illegal immigrant students tell of lost opportunities." *Boston Globe,* November 26, 2010. Available at http://www.boston.com/news/local/massachusetts/articles/2010/11/26/illegal_immigrant_students_tell_of_lost_opportunities/?page=full.

———. "Lynn's immigrants and police share a gulf." *Boston Globe,* September 25, 2009, Metro-1.

Sack, Kevin. "The breaking point: Hospital falters as refuge for illegal immigrants." *New York Times,* November 21, 2009, A1.

Salinas, Guadalupe. "Mexican-Americans and the desegregation of schools in the Southwest." *Houston Law Review* 8 (1971).

Salsbury, Jessica. "Evading 'residence': Higher education, undocumented students, and the states." *American University Law Review* 53 (2003).

Sánchez, George J. *Becoming Mexican American: Ethnicity, culture and identity in Chicano Los Angeles, 1900–1945.* New York: Oxford University Press, 1993.

Sandoval, Stephanie. "Funding intact for youth group." *Dallas Morning News,* September 21, 2006, 1B.

———. "Restraining order issued against rental ordinance." *Dallas Morning News,* September 13, 2008, B1.

San Miguel, Guadalupe, Jr. *Brown, not white: School integration and the Chicano movement in Houston.* College Station: Texas A&M University Press, 2001.

———. *"Let all of them take heed": Mexican Americans and the campaign for educational equality in Texas, 1910–1981.* Austin: University of Texas Press, 1987.

Santiago-Santiago, Isaura. "*Aspira v. Board of Education* revisited." *American Journal of Education* 95 (1986).

Santos, Fernanda. "Demand for English lessons outstrips supply." *New York Times,* February 27, 2007, A1.

Saucedo, Leticia M. "National origin, immigrants, and the workplace: The employment cases in Latinos and the law and the advocates' perspective." *Harvard Latino Law Review* 12 (2009).

————. "Three theories of discrimination in the brown collar workplace." *University of Chicago Legal Forum*, 2009.

Savage, Charlie. "Senate confirms Sotomayor for the Supreme Court." *New York Times*, August 7, 2009, A1.

Schrag, Peter. *The unwanted: Immigration and nativism in America.* Washington, DC: Immigration Policy Center, September 13, 2010.

Schrag, Philip G. *A well-founded fear: The congressional battle to save political asylum in America.* New York: Routledge, 2000.

Schuck, Peter H. "The message of Proposition 187." *Pacific Law Journal* 26 (1995).

————. "The transformation of immigration law." *Columbia Law Review* 84 (1984).

Schuck, Peter H., and Rogers M. Smith. *Citizenship without consent: Illegal aliens in the American polity.* New Haven: Yale University Press, 1985.

Schumer, Charles E. "Schumer announces principles for comprehensive immigration reform bill in works in Senate." Press release. June 24, 2009. Available at http://schumer.senate.gov/new_website/record_print.cfm?id=314990 and http://www.law.georgetown.edu/webcast/eventDetail.cfm?eventID=866 (GULC webcast).

Schumer, Charles E., and Lindsey O. Graham. "The right way to mend immigration." *Washington Post*, March 19, 2010, A23. Available at http://www.washingtonpost.com/wp-dyn/content/article/2010/03/17/AR2010031703115.html?referrer=emailarticle.

Seelye, Katharine Q. "Specter feels squeeze from new friends and old." *New York Times*, January 27, 2010, A12.

Semple, Kirk. "Immigration agency's tactic spurs alarm." *New York Times*, September 18, 2010, A15.

"Senate Democrats renew DREAM Act push." *Inside Higher Ed*, September 15, 2010. Available at http://www.insidehighered.com/news/2010/09/15/qt#238171.

"Senate leader will press for passage of 'Dream Act' this year." *The Ticker* (blog), *Chronicle of Higher Education*, September 14, 2010. Available at http://chronicle.com/blogPost/Senate-Leader-Will-Press-fo/26922/.

Shabazz, Amilcar. *Advancing democracy: African Americans and the struggle for access and equity in higher education in Texas.* Chapel Hill: University of North Carolina Press, 2004.

Shachar, Ayelet. *The birthright lottery: Citizenship and global inequality.* Cambridge: Harvard University Press, 2009.

Sheehy, Daniel. *Fighting immigration anarchy.* Bloomington, IN: Rooftop, 2009.

Sheridan, Clare "'Another white race': Mexican Americans and the paradox of whiteness in jury selection." *Law and History Review* 21 (2003).

Sherry, Allison. "Tuition tussle takes shape." *Denver Post*, August 15, 2007, A1.

Sieff, Kevin. "No way out: Will the border patrol use hurricane evacuations to snag undocumented immigrants?" *Texas Observer*, August 7, 2009. Available at http://www.texasobserver.org/features/no-way-out.

Siegal, Allan M., and William G. Connolly. *The New York Times manual of style and usage.* New York: Three Rivers, 1999.

Simon, Julian L. *The economic consequences of immigration.* Ann Arbor: University of Michigan Press, 1999.

Simon, Rita J. *Public opinion and the immigrant: Print media coverage, 1880–1980.* Lexington, MA: Lexington Books, 1985.

Sinclair, Barbara. *Party wars: Polarization and the politics of national policy making.* Norman: University of Oklahoma Press, 2006.

———. "Question: What's wrong with Congress? Answer: It's a democratic legislature." *Boston University Law Review* 89 (2009).

Singer, Paula N., and Linda Dodd-Major. "Identification numbers and U.S. government compliance initiatives." *Tax Notes* 104 (September 20, 2004).

Smith, Cheryl. "Immigrants tell country to 'listen up.'" *Austin Chronicle,* May 4, 2007. Available at http://www.austinchronicle.com/gyrobase/Issue/story?oid=oid:471800.

Smith, Rogers M. "The second founding: Birthright citizenship and the Fourteenth Amendment in 1868 and 2008." *University of Pennsylvania Journal of Constitutional Law* 11 (2009).

Smithson, J. Austin. Comment. "Educate the exile: Creating a double standard in education for *Plyler* students who want to sit for the bar exam." *Scholar: St. Mary's Law Review on Minority Issues* 11 (2008).

Snyder, Mike. "HISD's ESL enrollment belies census numbers on immigrants." *Houston Chronicle,* April 5, 2007, B1.

Solis, Dianne. "Judge rejects rental ban." *Dallas Morning News,* March 25, 2010, B1.

Sorkin, Andrew Ross. *Too big to fail: The inside story of how Wall Street and Washington fought to save the financial system from crisis—and themselves.* New York: Viking, 2009.

Spalding, Matthew. *Getting reform right: The White House's immigration initiative.* WebMemo #1585. Washington, DC: Heritage Foundation, 2007. Available at http://www.heritage.org/Research/Reports/2007/08/Getting-Reform-Right-The-White-Houses-Immigration-Initiative.

Spencer, Jason. "HISD board names [Abelardo] Saavedra as only finalist: He would be the first Hispanic to lead city schools." *Houston Chronicle,* November 14, 2004, A1.

Spencer, Mark. "Immigrant tuition endorsed." *Hartford Courant,* February 14, 2007, B10.

Spener, David. *Clandestine crossings: Migrants and coyotes on the Texas-Mexico border.* Ithaca: Cornell University Press, 2009.

Spiro, Peter J. *Beyond citizenship: American identity after globalization.* New York: Oxford University Press, 2008.

———. "The states and immigration in an era of demi-sovereignties." *Virginia Journal of International Law* 35 (1994).

Staff of Joint Commission on Taxation. "Present law and background relating to individual taxpayer identification numbers." March 5, 2004.

Stanton, John. "Reid may push DREAM Act in lieu of immigration reform." *Roll Call,* July 21, 2010. Available at http://www.rollcall.com/news/48542-1.html.

Stein, Dan. "Why illegal immigrants should not receive in-state tuition subsidies." *University Business,* April 2002, 64.

Steinhauer, Jennifer. "Finances push Beverly Hills schools to rescind welcome to neighbors." *New York Times,* December 21, 2009, A16.

Stock, Margaret D. "The DREAM Act: Tapping an overlooked pool of home-grown talent to meet military enlistment needs." *Engage* 6 (2005). Available at http://hq.democracyinaction.org/dia/organizations/NILC/images/Stock_on_DREAM_Act.pdf.

Stock, Margaret D., and Kristan K. Exner. "Immigration issues relating to military service: Practical problems and solutions." In *Immigration and nationality law handbook, 2009–10,* ed. Rizwan Hassan. Washington, DC: American Immigration Lawyers Association, 2009.

Stoddard, Martha. "In-state tuition repeal unlikely." *Omaha World-Herald*, February 2, 2010. Available at http://www.omaha.com/article/20100202/NEWS01/702029941.

Stripling, Jack. "Georgia bars admission of illegal immigrants." *Inside Higher Ed*, October 14, 2010. Available at http://www.insidehighered.com/news/2010/10/14/georgia.

"Strong illegal immigration bill biggest legislative achievement." *Charleston (SC) Post and Courier*, June 7, 2008, A10.

Sulzberger, A. G. "Growing anti-immigrant sentiments in an unlikely state." *New York Times*, October 3, 2010, A16.

Supreme Court of the United States. "Biographies of current Justices of the Supreme Court: Elena Kagan." Available at http://www.supremecourt.gov/about/biographies. aspx (accessed Apr. 24, 2011).

Swarns, Rachel L. "In Georgia, newest immigrants unsettle an old sense of place." *New York Times*, August 4, 2006, A1.

Swedlund, Eric. "In-state tuition safeguard a concern: AZ schools to verify that illegal entrants pay top rate." *Arizona Daily Star*, March 9, 2007, A1, A4.

Terry, Laurel S. "The Bologna process and its implications for U.S. legal education." *Journal of Legal Education* 57 (2007).

"Texas group sues to block in-state tuition for undocumented students." *The Ticker* (blog), *Chronicle of Higher Education*, December 15, 2009. Available at http://chronicle.com/blogPost/ Texas-Group-Sues-to-Block/9223/?sid=pm&utm_source=pm&utm_medium=en.

Texas Comptroller of Public Accounts. *Undocumented immigrants in Texas: A financial analysis of the impact to the state budget and economy*. December 2006. Available at http://www.cpa.state.tx.us/specialrpt/undocumented/undocumented.pdf.

Thompson, Amy. *A child alone and without papers*. Austin, TX: Center for Public Policy Priorities, 2008. Available at http://www.cppp.org/repatriation.

Thompson, Doug. "Panel rejects immigrant tuition bill." *Morning News of Northwest Arkansas* (Little Rock), March 23, 2009.

Thronson, David B. "Entering the mainstream: Making children matter in immigration law." *Fordham Urban Law Journal* 38 (2010).

Tichenor, Daniel J. *Dividing lines: The politics of immigration control in America*. Princeton: Princeton University Press, 2002.

———. "Navigating an American minefield: The politics of illegal immigration." *Forum*, July 2009. Available at http://www.bepress.com/forum/vol7/iss3/art1.

Timmons, Susan E., and Margaret D. Stock. "Immigration issues faced by U.S. service-members: Challenges and solutions." *Clearinghouse Review: Journal of Poverty Law and Policy* 43 (September–October 2009).

Tobar, Hector. "Law grad's legal quandary." *Los Angeles Times*, November 26, 2010, A2. Available at http://www.latimes.com/news/local/la-me-tobar-20101126,0,1358739.column.

Tresaugue, Matthew, and R. G. Radcliffe. "Illegal immigrants may see tuition hike: Legislation would end Texas' pioneering law granting in-state rate, financial aid." *Houston Chronicle*, January 11, 2007, B1.

Triche, Alicia. "Local enforcement and federal preemption." *Bender's Immigration Bulletin* 11 (2006).

Tushnet, Mark V. "Justice Lewis F. Powell and the jurisprudence of centrism." *Michigan Law Review* 93 (1995).

————. *Making civil rights law: Thurgood Marshall and the Supreme Court, 1936–1961.* New York: Oxford University Press, 1994.

————. *The NAACP's legal strategy against segregated education, 1925–1950.* Chapel Hill: University of North Carolina Press, 1987.

University System of Georgia. "Regents adopt new policies on undocumented students." Press release. October 13, 2010. Available at http://www.usg.edu/news/release/regents_adopt_new_policies_on_undocumented_students/.

Unmuth, Katherine Leal. "Number of illegal immigrants getting in-state tuition for Texas colleges rises." *Dallas Morning News,* March 15, 2010. Available at http://www.dallasnews.com/sharedcontent/dws/dn/latestnews/stories/0315dnmetimmigcount.3d35b14.html.

————. "25 years ago, Tyler case opened schools to illegal migrants." *Dallas Morning News,* June 11, 2007, A1.

U.S. Congress. *Amending the Illegal Immigration Reform Act of 1996.* S. Rep. 108-224. 108th Cong., 2d sess. (2004).

————. *American Dream Act of 2006.* H.R. 5131. 109th Cong., 2d sess. (April 6, 2006).

————. *American Dream Act.* H.R. 1275. 110th Cong., 1st sess. (March 1, 2007).

————. *Comprehensive Immigration Reform Act of 2006.* S. 2611. 109th Cong., 2d sess. (April 6, 2006).

————. *Comprehensive Immigration Reform Act of 2007.* S. 1348. 110th Cong., 1st sess. (May 9, 2007).

————. *DREAM Act of 2001.* S. 1291. 107th Cong., 1st sess. (August 1, 2001).

————. *DREAM Act of 2003.* S. 1545. 108th Cong., 1st sess. (July 21, 2003).

————. *DREAM Act of 2005.* S. 2075. 109th Cong., 1st sess. (November 18, 2005).

————. *DREAM Act of 2007.* S. 774. 110th Cong., 1st sess. (March 6, 2007).

————. *DREAM Act of 2007.* S. 2205. 110th Cong., 1st sess. (October 18, 2007).

————. *Education Access for Rightful Noncitizens (EARN) Act.* H.R. 1221. 110th Cong., 1st sess. (February 28, 2007).

————. *Security through Regularized Immigration and a Vibrant Economy (STRIVE) Act of 2007.* H.R. 1645. 110th Cong., 1st sess. (March 22, 2007).

————. *Student Adjustment Act of 2001.* H.R. 1918. 107th Cong., 1st sess. (May 21, 2001).

————. *Student Adjustment Act of 2003.* H.R. 1684. 108th Cong., 1st sess. (April 9, 2003).

U.S. Congress, House Committee on Judiciary, Subcommittee on Immigration, Citizenship, Refugees, Border Security and International Law. *The future of undocumented immigrant students: Hearing on comprehensive immigration reform.* 110th Cong., 1st sess. (May 18, 2007).

————. *Hearing on H.R. 1645, the "Security through Regularized Immigration and a Vibrant Economy Act of 2007 (STRIVE Act)."* 110th Cong., 1st sess. (September 6, 2007). Available at http://judiciary.house.gov/hearings/September2007/hear_090607_2.html (taped remarks); http://judiciary.house.gov/hearings/printers/110th/37603.PDF (report).

U.S. Department of Education. "Eligibility for Title IV program assistance for victims of human trafficking." Student Aid on the Web (DCL ID: GEN-06-09). May 2006. Available at http://ifap.ed.gov/dpcletters/GEN0609.html.

————. "FAQs—new process benefits victims of human trafficking seeking college aid." Student Aid on the Web. May 11, 2006. Available at http://studentaid.ed.gov/PORTALS-WebApp/students/english/TraffickingFaqs.jsp.

U.S. Department of Education, National Center for Education Statistics. *Digest of education statistics.* 2008. Available at http://nces.ed.gov/fastFacts/display.asp?id=98.

U.S. Department of Homeland Security, Office of Inspector General. *The performance of 287(g) agreements.* September 2010. Available at http://www.dhs.gov/xoig/assets/mgmtrpts/OIG_10-124_Sep10.pdf.

U.S. Department of State. "Biography: Vilma Martinez." Available at http://www.state.gov/r/pa/ei/biog/129351.htm (accessed March 15, 2010).

Valencia, Richard R. *Chicano students and the courts: The Mexican American struggle for educational equality.* New York: NYU Press, 2008.

Valenzuela, Angela. *Subtractive schooling: U.S.-Mexican youth and the politics of caring.* Albany: SUNY Press, 1999.

Vedantam, Shankar. "Senate to look at Dream Act for illegal immigrants." *Washington Post*, September 21, 2010, A2.

———. "Undocumented youths chasing a dream." *Washington Post*, November 28, 2010, C1.

Vélez, Veronica, Lindsay Perez Huber, Corina Benavides Lopez, Ariana de la Luz, and Daniel G. Solórzano. "Battling for human rights and social justice: A Latina/o critical race analysis of Latina/o student youth activism in the wake of 2006 anti-immigrant sentiment." *Social Justice* 7 (2008).

Walfish, Daniel. Note. "Student visas and the illogic of the intent requirement." *Georgetown Immigration Law Journal* 17 (2003).

Walker, Anders. "Diversity's strange career: Recovering the racial pluralism of Lewis F. Powell, Jr." *Santa Clara Law Review* 50 (2010).

Walker, Tim. "Caught in the crossfire: Schools in Oklahoma grapple with new laws targeting illegal immigration." *NEA Today*, January 2008. Available at http://www.nea.org/home/7855.htm.

Walton, Don. "It's all about 'rule of law': Kansas law prof. argues Nebraska tuition statute violates federal law." *Lincoln Journal-Star*, February 22, 2010, B1.

Warikoo, Niraj. "Immigration agents improperly targeted Detroit school parents, feds admit." *Detroit Free Press*, April 7, 2011. Available at http://www.freep.com/article/20110407/NEWS01/110407041/Immigration-agents-improperly-targeted-Detroit-school-parents-feds-admit.

Wasem, Ruth Ellen. *Immigration reform: Brief synthesis of issue.* Report RS2257. Washington, DC: Congressional Research Service, U.S. Library of Congress, 2007.

Watanabe, Teresa. "Illegal immigrant youths in a benefits twilight zone: State policies toward such children vary, reflecting sympathy for their situation and disapproval of their parents' behavior." *Los Angeles Times*, January 25, 2007, B1.

Wells, Miriam J. "The grassroots reconfiguration of U.S. immigration policy." *International Migration Review* 38 (2004).

White House. "Statement of Administration Policy on DREAM Act." Available at http://dreamact.info/forum/archive/index.php?t-6594.html (archived copy of White House statement opposing DREAM Act, October 24, 2007, http://www.whitehouse.gov/omb/legislative/sap/110-1/s2205sap-s.pdf).

Wilson, Steven H. "Brown over 'other white': Mexican Americans' legal arguments and litigation strategy in school desegregation lawsuits." *Law and History Review* 21 (2003).

Winerip, Michael. "Dreaming of having an American life in full." *New York Times*, February 21, 2011, A10.

Wingett, Yvonne. "Arizona's colleges struggle to enforce new tuition statute." *Arizona Republic*, January 3, 2007, A1.

Wishnie, Michael. "Laboratories of bigotry? Devolution of the immigration power, equal protection and federalism." *New York University Law Review* 76 (2001).

Wong, Carolyn. *Lobbying for inclusion: Rights politics and the making of immigration policy.* Stanford: Stanford University Press, 2006.

Wong, Raam. "ICE picks up dad at school: District, city officials upset with timing, location of arrest." *Albuquerque Journal*, March 29, 2007, A1.

Wong, Scott. "Democratic Senator Reid moves forward with Dream Act." *Politico*, November 30, 2010. Available at http://www.politico.com/news/stories/1110/45761.html#ixzz16qY5uwVG.

"A worthy immigration bill: The Dream Act rewards military service and student achievement." *Wall Street Journal*, November 27, 2010, A16. Available at http://online.wsj.com/article/SB10001424052748703572404575635202343271966.html?KEYWORDS=a+worthy+immigration+bill.

Wu, Frank H. *Yellow: Race in America beyond black and white.* New York: Basic Books, 2002.

Yates, Laura S. "*Plyler v. Doe* and the rights of undocumented immigrants to higher education: Should undocumented students be eligible for in-state college tuition rates?" *Washington University Law Quarterly* 82 (2004).

Young, JoAnne. "Senators hear arguments on repealing Nebraska Dream Act." *Lincoln Journal Star*, February 2, 2010, A1.

Zakaria, Fareed. *The post-American world.* New York: Norton, 2008.

Zehr, Mary Ann. "Case touched many parts of community." *Education Week*, June 6, 2007, 13.

———. "Undocumented students get a break in California." *Education Week*, November 17, 2010. Available at http://blogs.edweek.org/edweek/learning-thelanguage/2010/11/undocumented_students_get_a_br.html.

———. "With immigrants, districts balance safety, legalities." *Education Week*, September 12, 2007, 1–15.

———. "Working immigrants get new school options." *Education Week*, September 22, 2004, 5.

Zohar, Gadi. "Habitual residence: An alternative to the common law concept of domicile?" *Whittier Journal of Child and Family Advocacy* 9 (2009).

Zolberg, Aristide R. *A nation by design: Immigration policy in the fashioning of America.* Cambridge: Harvard University Press, 2006.

Index

About the Author

MICHAEL A. OLIVAS is the William B. Bates Distinguished Chair in Law at the University of Houston Law Center and Director of the Institute for Higher Education Law and Governance at the University of Houston. His books include *"Colored Men" and "Hombres Aqui"*: Hernandez v. Texas *and the Emergence of Mexican-American Lawyering*; *The Law and Higher Education: Cases and Materials on Colleges in Court*, 3rd ed.; and (with Ronna Greff Schneider) *Education Law Stories*.